# Down to the Last Pitch

# Also by Tim Wendel

# Down to the Last Pitch

## HOW THE 1991 MINNESOTA TWINS AND THE ATLANTA BRAVES GAVE US THE BEST WORLD SERIES OF ALL TIME

## TIM WENDEL

**Da Capo**

A MEMBER OF THE PERSEUS BOOKS GROUP

Editorial production by Lori Hobkirk at the Book Factory.
Designed by Anita Koury.
Set in 10.6 point Chronicle by The Perseus Books Group.

First Da Capo Press edition 2014

Cataloging-in-Publication data for this book is available from the Library of Congress.

ISBN: 978-0-306-82276-6 (hardcover)
ISBN: 978-0-306-82277-3 (e-book)

Published by Da Capo Press
A Member of the Perseus Books Group
www.dacapopress.com

Da Capo Press books are available at special discounts for bulk purchases in the U.S.
by corporations, institutions, and other organizations.
For more information, please contact the Special Markets Department at the
Perseus Books Group, 2300 Chestnut Street, Suite 200, Philadelphia, PA 19103,
or call (800) 810-4145, ext. 5000, or
e-mail special.markets@perseusbooks.com.


10   9   8   7   6   5   4   3   2   1

*For Jacqueline, Sarah, and Chris*

*In memory of Bill Glavin, John Douglas, and Eric Wendel,
and to the backyard ballgames of yesteryear on Canal Road
and the West Bluff*

# CONTENTS

# PREFACE

In 1991 Verlyn Klinkenborg came out with a book entitled *The Last Fine Time*. It was the story of his father-in-law, Eddie Wenzek, who once operated a family-owned tavern on the east side of Buffalo, New York. I grew up in Lockport, New York, only forty minutes away, and Buffalo was once the big city for me. It's where I saw my first baseball game, taken by my grandfather, along with my younger brother, Chris, to War Memorial Stadium, aka "The Rockpile." Although many of the scenes from *The Natural* were filmed here, The Rockpile would never be mistaken for any of the sports palaces of today. As my uncle Brock Yates once wrote, the ballpark "looks as if whatever war it was a memorial to had been fought within its confines."

No matter how many rough edges may be involved, I believe that every era, every life, for that matter, has a "last fine time." It can be a brief moment or two when everything comes together in a remarkable way, and even when the world again barrels ahead, intent on reinventing itself once again, we can hold tight to such memories.

When I look back at baseball, which I have written about for several decades, the 1991 season remains for me one of the last fine times. That season was the beginning of *Baseball Weekly*, a new publishing venture at *USA Today*. I was fortunate to be on the original staff there, and in 1991 I covered my first World Series, and doing so gave me an inside look at the sea changes that were changing the game forever—soaring team payrolls, an approaching labor storm, the rise of retro-style ballparks and the corporate groupthink in which too many believed that everything could be fixed by firing this guy and hiring somebody else.

The '91 season marked the first time that a cellar dweller went from last to first place when the Atlanta Braves and Minnesota Twins rose from the ashes to play each other in the World Series. And what a showdown it was. Experts rank it among the top World Series ever played, and many consider it the best ever.

We always enjoy a story with a beginning, middle, and an end. Perhaps such elements become even more precious in the age of Facebook and Twitter, when so much comes at us so quickly and sometimes with misguided intent. A tale that happened out there, somewhere in the not-so-distant past, can be reassuring to us. So let's start somewhere near the beginning then—only a few blocks from the banks of the Mississippi River. Even though the late October winds funneled down the wide avenues of downtown Minneapolis early in the day, inside the Hubert H. Humphrey Metrodome conditions remain comfortably warm and ear-splittingly loud.

# Game One

As the hometown Twins took the field, the sellout crowd broke into another sustained roar. Clamorous and downright chaotic, the rising earsplitting din could have been a beast reawakening after a long sleep.

As shortstop Greg Gagne jogged out to his position, he decided the fans were as loud as they had been in 1987, the last time the Twins played in the World Series. They just had to be. The fans were ready to raise a ruckus and wake up the echoes of yesteryear. The best home-field advantage in sports had been brought back to life again, with the promise of another wild ride in the offing. Now, would the hometown team be able to do its part?

As Gagne took his position for the top of the first inning, he thought about how much the Twins' lineup had changed in recent years. Sure, such Minnesota favorites as Kent Hrbek and Kirby Puckett were still among the regulars, but besides those two stars, only Gagne, Randy Bush, Al Newman, Dan Gladden, and Gene Larkin remained from the last World Series team, and Larkin had somehow stayed on the postseason roster despite a bad knee, leaving him barely able to run. Here in the infield of hard-bounce Astroturf, with only dirt cutouts

1

around the bases, Gagne was flanked by a pair of relative newcomers on this night. Scott Leius had taken the place of Twins favorite Gary Gaetti at third base. Gaetti, a.k.a. "The Rat," now played in California. To Gagne's left stood another rookie, Chuck Knoblauch. Even though the sparkplug of a kid had led first-year American League players in hits, doubles, and RBIs, the hands-down favorite to win rookie-of-the-year honors, no one knew how he would react when things became fickle and unpredictable, as they surely would with so much at stake. After all, this was the World Series, with everybody watching, and like any good story, nobody dared predict the ending or who would be the hero or the goat.

One last time Gagne glanced at the fresh faces to either side of him, everyone now ready for the first pitch, and he could only smile at how baseball worked—so cutthroat one minute, in need of team unity the next.

"What people forget is that both of them—Chuck Knoblauch and Scott Leius—were originally shortstops," he said years later. "They came into the organization playing my position, looking to take my job. . . . But the thing with baseball, once things are decided, you pick yourself up and do your best. I mean, what choice do you have? Either of those guys, Knobby or Leius, wanted my job back in the spring. But it didn't matter. Now we had to come together and try to beat a really, really good Braves team."

Behind the plate Twins catcher Brian Harper caught the last of Jack Morris's warm-up pitches, heartened that Black Jack's split-finger fastball, his signature pitch, had plenty of bite on this night. After throwing down to second base, Harper glanced around the infield one last time before settling into his crouch. Years later the Twins' catcher and shortstop would realize that they were thinking nearly the same thing at this point, on the eve of it all: the Twins' infield, ready to go amid the noise, alternated between veterans and kids—Hrbek to Knoblauch, Gagne to Leius—all the way around the horn. Although Harper had almost as many years in the majors as Hrbek or Puckett, he hadn't exactly made a mark for himself, at least not on this big a stage. After bouncing between five ball clubs—California, Pittsburgh, St. Louis, Detroit, and Oakland—he hadn't caught more than a hundred games in a season until after he arrived in the Twin Cities in 1988. Now he was back in the World Series, after almost being an improbable postseason hero once with the Cardinals.

The Atlanta Braves liked to run the bases, push the envelope, and Harper's arm wasn't the strongest in the league. He couldn't argue with that. So as the Braves' Lonnie Smith stepped in and the crowd ramped it up a few more decibels, Harper took a deep breath and told himself be like Hrbek, Gagne, and Puckett out there in centerfield. Nothing against the newcomers—they had plenty of talent, for sure. Still, Harper couldn't help thinking that experienced hands would ultimately carry the day in this unlikely matchup.

Nobody in uniform for either team knew they were about to take the first step into a series for the ages, one that many would soon regard as among the best in baseball history, perhaps the best of all time. Such postseason classics can be counted on a hand or two and include the 1975 matchup between the Cincinnati Reds and the Boston Red Sox, when Carlton Fisk homered in the twelfth inning of Game Six. Back in 1972, the start of Oakland's dynasty run, that Series served up six one-run games. In 1968 a taut seven-game series between the Detroit Tigers and St. Louis Cardinals helped a grieving nation carry on after the tragic assassinations of Dr. Martin Luther King and Bobby Kennedy. Of course, there was Bill Mazeroski's walk-off home run in 1960 that carried Pittsburgh past the New York Yankees. And in 1955 the Brooklyn Dodgers finally broke through against the Yankees' juggernaut. All of them were memorable times for sure, but none would have five games determined in the home team's last at-bat. That would be the case in 1991—a Series that would see four games decided on the last pitch.

To truly appreciate what unfolded in 1991, we need to go deep into each ballgame, letting these contents play out in the actions and words of those who were on the field. "Every pitch, every strike, every ball every inning—everything mattered in every game," said Terry Pendleton, who played third base for Atlanta in this epic showdown.

"My father told me—and I think he was right—he said that each game is like you're reading a book," Twins manager Tom Kelly later said. "You've got chapter one or Game One, and then Two, and it's getting better and better and better and better and better."

Yet, as we do so, we need to keep in mind that almost everything of merit often cuts both ways. Braves general manager John Schuerholz called the 1991 series "great for our industry." Maybe. Maybe not.

In having two teams go from last place to the Fall Classic, it underscored that any team could—dare we say *should*—be able to reach such heights. In the profound changes of the early 1990s—the end of the Cold War and the beginning of the War on Terror, the shift in national leadership from the "Greatest Generation" to the baby boomers, the rapid transition from family-owned companies to corporate multinationals—everything became much more demanding. Everybody seemingly became more impatient for results and success. Nobody really talked about rebuilding anymore, about being in it for the long haul. Instead the buzz word became *retool*, which often was explained as an almost magical phenomenon that didn't require methodical and careful reconstruction or perhaps even due diligence. You could almost hear owners throughout sports, strongly mirroring what was going in the private sector, saying to themselves that if the Twins and the Braves could reach the World Series, then why not us? Telling their general managers and front-office personnel to fix it or else they would be sent packing too.

The notable firsts began early and often in this 1991 championship. The Braves' Lonnie Smith was the designated hitter for Game One, and in batting leadoff for the visiting Braves, his appearance marked only the third time in the last sixty-one World Series games that the DH had taken the first swings in a contest. Amazingly, in all three cases Smith was the guy. He was also the designated hitter, batting leadoff, in Game Four of the 1980 Series and in Game Five of the 1982 series. Also, on this night in Minneapolis Smith became the first player in baseball history to appear in the World Series with four different teams—the Kansas City Royals, Philadelphia Phillies, St. Louis Cardinals, and now the Atlanta Braves. Perhaps these were nothing more than footnotes for anybody else, but Smith's exploits at the plate and certainly on the basepaths would loom large in this Fall Classic.

Smith began the game by lining out to Twins left fielder Dan Gladden. From there Morris kept the Braves off the scoreboard early on, with Atlanta starter Charlie Leibrandt matching him. Some had found Leibrandt a curious choice to start Game One over twenty-game winner Tom Glavine. Yet Braves manager Bobby Cox often depended on Leibrandt, who had a decade at the major-league level, between Cincinnati and Kansas City before coming to Atlanta in 1990. The left-hander had posted a 15–13 record during the regular season and was regarded as the elder statesman on a pitching staff of young guns that also included Steve Avery and John Smoltz.

In the bottom of third inning the Twins broke through for the Series' first run. Gladden, who had tracked down three fly balls in the first three innings of the game, walked and then stole second base. Rookie Chuck Knoblauch promptly drove him in with an opposite-field flare to right field. Gladden crossed home plate, and Knoblauch was tagged out trying to stretch his single into a double.

The Twins had decided months before that they could live with such rookie mistakes, though. Drafted in the first round out of Texas A&M in 1989, Knoblauch had risen quickly through the minor leagues, sticking with the big-league ballclub coming out of spring training. His father, Ray, had been a minor-league pitcher, and his uncle, Ed, was an outfielder in the Texas League. Originally a shortstop whose boyhood hero had been Ozzie Smith, Knoblauch switched to second base at Double-A Orlando, realizing it was the fast track to the majors. In winning the regular job during the spring, he filled a hole in the Twins' lineup that had seen the likes of Steve Lombardozzi, Tom Herr, Chip Hale, Fred Manrique and Wally Backman in recent years.

Off field, the twenty-three-year-old often acted like the rookie he was, telling reporters how big a fan he was of the soap opera *Days of Our Lives* and how breakfast most mornings was a heaping bowl of Frosted Flakes. But on the field Knoblauch regularly came through, and that's all anybody in the Twin Cities cared about at the time.

"Chuck's development is a major reason why we're here," Twins general manager Andy MacPhail said. "What I first liked about him is that he knows the game."

Twins hitting coach Terry Crowley added, "What Chuck has done this season is one of the most difficult things to do in baseball. He's stepped in and made a good team that much better."

"I don't think of him as a rookie anymore," Kent Hrbek said. "He's done too good a job to still be called a rookie."

Throughout baseball, teams were increasingly on the lookout for somebody like Knoblauch, a kid who could move into the regular lineup without a lot of fanfare or hand-holding. For opportunity awaited with the ballclubs that could quickly flesh out their rosters and prove that they could compete. Since the 1969 season Major League Baseball no longer crowned one regular-season champion in the American and National Leagues, respectively, and then had them go directly to the World Series. Instead, baseball now sported divisional winners, a total of four teams in the postseason, with the promise of more divisional champions and even wild-card berths on the horizon.

As the 1991 season began, the Atlanta Braves had plenty of young stars of their own. The pitching staff not only sported Glavine, who would go on to win the Cy Young Award, but also left-hander Steve Avery and right-hander John Smoltz as well. In the everyday lineup fan favorite Dale Murphy had been traded to Philadelphia the year before to make room for David Justice. Perhaps this was a painful move for Braves followers, but it certainly paid off. Despite such potential, the Braves spun their wheels throughout the first half of the season. It wasn't until after the All-Star break that they took off, winning fifty-five of eight-three games, including twenty-one of their last twenty-nine, as they surged past the Los Angeles Dodgers.

"It was a glamour team against a Cinderella team," team president Stan Kasten said of the National League stretch drive. "This was a race people will talk about for years to come."

The Braves clinched the Western Division title on the next-to-last day of the 1991 season, finishing with ninety-four victories. That total was an Atlanta team record and twenty-nine more victories than they recorded the year before.

The Twins also got off to slow start in 1991 before putting together a fifteen-game winning streak that lifted them into first place in June. Minnesota had a promising young hurler of its own in right-hander Scott Erickson, who won twenty games, including twelve in a row this season. Perhaps the decisive series of the regular season occurred in mid-August when the Oakland Athletics, the reigning American League champions, arrived in the Twin Cities for four games. Although Minnesota had been in a slump, after dropping three of four to the California Angels, the Twins turned the tables on the Athletics, winning three games behind Morris and bullpen victories by relievers Carl Willis and Rick Aguilera.

Perhaps the telling moment that the worst-to-first underdogs could take the AL West came after the third victory. In the bowels of the Metrodome several of the A's hurried from the visiting clubhouse, eager to avoid questions from the media. One of them appeared to be José Canseco, who was considered to be among the best players in the game at the time after hitting forty-two home runs and stealing forty bases in 1988. Of course, this was long before evidence of steroids and performance-enhancing drugs became so overwhelming.

Canseco opened the clubhouse door and saw a half-dozen or so members of the press. Glaring at them, he swung the door shut, and the loud thud echoed down the hallway. With that, Canseco strode off. Yet after a few long strides he stopped and looked back with a thin smile. "Just kidding," he said.

The Twins weren't kidding around in 1991 as they finished with ninety-five victories, one more than the Braves over in the National League, eight games ahead of the Chicago White Sox, and eleven games up on Canseco's Athletics when the regular season ended.

"I just never felt like we were a last-place team," Brian Harper said when comparing the Twins' 1990 and 1991 editions. "It was unbelievable how [in 1990] when we hit we didn't pitch, and when we pitched well we didn't hit. Last year was the weirdest year I've ever seen."

But it wouldn't hold a candle to what was about to happen in the 1991 postseason.

———

Round ball. Round bat.

Ted Williams once said that having them greet each other so the impact is square and solid remains the most difficult feat to accomplish in sports, and any slugger who has come before or after him will echo those words.

What do we make of those moments when ball and bat do meet just so? When the ball flies off the bat as though it had a mind of its own and for an instant the only role it knows in life is to soar over the outfield fence like a flock of geese heading for the horizon? What registers in the batter's box? What does one remember?

"It's the feel," said Frank Robinson, who hit 586 home runs during his career. "You don't feel anything down the bat handle. I'm not trying to make a joke. That's how it is.

"When you've really hit the ball there are no vibrations. You could be swinging through air. That's how perfect it is."

Besides the feel in the hands, there is the sweet smack to a well-hit ball. Robinson cautioned that each ballpark has different acoustics and dimensions, so the sound can sometimes fool you. But every slugger worth his salt knows the crisp reverberation that a home run ball often makes. At first Robinson described it as "a gun shot," but then he searched for better words. A gun shot, in this day and age, seemed too callous for something so magical.

Robinson and I once discussed such things during batting practice at a major-league game. As the home team continued to hit, Robinson paused, simply listening, waiting for that sound again. Even though the clamor built for another game, Robinson was able to tune such diversions out. When the next batter stepped into the cage the rhythmic rat-tat-tat of bat-hitting-ball began again. It could have been a carpenter driving nails or a woodsman splitting wood, except there was a particular fullness or certainty to this particular sound.

"There it is," Robinson said, and moments later a deep fly sailed past the outfield fence. "It's like you're out in the woods and you step on branch. A dry branch. It's that snap that goes just so. But you have to be careful. The sound comes and goes depending upon the ballpark, the crowd that day. You can't wait for the sound to tell you every time the ball is going out."

Together we turned back to the batting cage, and here it came again. For a brief second that sound, that snap of a ball well hit, broke through the mounting anticipation of another game, no matter how loud the commotion may have been. Another well-hit ball soared into the sky and landed in the stands beyond the fence.

"Nothing else offers the kind of excitement that a home run does," Robinson said. "Not even a perfect game. Because a home run is instant—it's so surprising."

And so it was again, this time in Game One of the 1991 World Series. In the bottom of the fifth inning Kent Hrbek roped a 2–0 pitch from Charlie Leibrandt to right field for a stand-up double. Scott Leius followed with a soft single into left, with Hrbek holding at third base. Leibrandt may have trailed only 1–0 at this point, but he wasn't fooling many of the Twins' hitters.

Then came that sound again. Despite the crowd of more than fifty-five thousand at the Metrodome, pretty much all of them now on their feet, cheering and waving those infernal white Homer Hankies, that sound of a dry branch breaking in the woods, an echo of every long fly that's ever happened in this game, was about to occur again.

Gagne, the number-nine hitter in the Minnesota hitter, came to the plate. If anything, the Twins' shortstop wanted to do better this time around, his second appearance in the World Series. Back in 1987, when the Twins defeated the Cardinals, the last time the Metrodome was really transformed into the "Thunderdome" for an extended period, Gagne had hit a paltry .200.

Now, four years later, Leibrandt got him to swing wildly at an off-speed offering in the dirt. But when the second pitch sailed toward the inside half of the plate, Gagne was ready. With an almost effortless swing, he caught it square and solid, and the ball began to soar toward the left-field fence, landing eight rows or so into the bleachers. With that, Minnesota took a 4–0 lead.

Decades later, watching footage of the game, you can still hear that sound Robinson talked about. For an instant it was there again. The surprise. The snap. The siren call that Robinson and almost any other slugger who has ever picked up a bat through the years knows by heart. For this is what any slugger dreams about, what they worry won't ever return when they're buried in a slump.

"I told myself to be ready for the fastball," Gagne said. "Actually, I was looking to go the other way. I wanted to hit the ball in the hole [between the first and second basemen], but I got a hold of it, and out it went."

Twins manager Tom Kelly and others on the Minnesota bench were stunned that Leibrandt threw Gagne a low fastball on the inner half of the plate. "That's what Gags can hit out of the park, and somehow that's what he got," Kelly said.

Years later, in describing this particular home run, Gagne still sounded surprised with himself and what had actually transpired. "It reminds me how unpredictable baseball will always be," he said. "In my previous at-bat, Leibrandt had made me look foolish. He struck me out, and every pitch had been a changeup. I wasn't close to any of them.

"Back in the dugout I talked with Kelly, and he told me to just sit on the change. Just be ready for that one pitch. I'll be honest with you—that made me kind of uncomfortable. Everybody has a different approach at the plate, and somebody like Dan Gladden, well, he could go up there looking off-speed and be confident that he could also get around on the hard stuff. I wasn't so sure of myself. . . . But my last at-bat had been so lousy, I decided to try it Danny's way.

"So I'm up there now, looking for Leibrandt's changeup, and he had a good one too. I just wanted to drive it the other way. Then he threw me a fastball, and it caught too much of the inner half of the plate."

When Gagne saw the fastball from Leibrandt, he simply reacted to it. "If I'd thought at all about it, I would have missed it. It would have been by me," he said. "I saw fastball and just swung, and as soon as I hit it I knew it was gone."

The homer was Gagne's fourth in postseason play and the first ever given up in the playoffs by Leibrandt, who was soon lifted from the game and replaced by reliever Jim Clancy.

The Twins squandered a chance to break the game wide open later in the same inning when Gladden was thrown out at the plate. With one out and Gladden on third base, Brian Harper hit a liner down the left-field line. Believing it would drop for a hit, Gladden first broke for the plate and then had to scramble back to the bag when Braves outfielder Brian Hunter caught it. He compounded his mistake by then trying to tag up and score, coming in with spikes somewhat high on Atlanta catcher Greg Olson. Even though the ball arrived well ahead of Gladden, the resulting collision sent Olson flying backward, rocking him on to his head and flipping him completely over. It became the cover shot on *Sports Illustrated*. "I never saw Danny do that before," Kelly later told team announcer Ted Robinson. "You learn from day one that if the ball goes in the air to the outfield, you go back to the base."

It wouldn't be the last bang-bang play with major contact at the plate in this Series. Despite the hard slide, Olson refused to criticize Gladden afterward. Instead, the catcher stuck up for Leibrandt, insisting that outside of the mistake to Gagne, Atlanta's starting pitcher had done a good job. "He's got the best changeup on the team," Olson said. "He struck out Kirby Puckett twice, and anytime you can do that you've got to be doing something right."

———

Legend has it that the Curley brothers, Tom and John, were pretty bummed when they heard that the *Sporting News* was dropping baseball box scores. The bad news came in late 1990, and we were years away from such results being computerized and available 24/7 on the Internet.

So when the Curley brothers heard about the "Bible of Baseball" dropping full boxes, their first reaction was, *how were they going to keep their fantasy league going?* But the baseball-loving brothers held a far different station in life from most seamheads. As top executives for the Gannett Corporation, they soon realized that if the *Sporting News* wasn't going to publish baseball box scores anymore, they very well could.

In short order they told Paul White, then baseball editor for *USA Today*, to pull together a prototype of what a baseball-only, tabloid-style publication could look like, with a week's worth of box scores filling up the back end. The frenzied process continued into the new year, and soon several of the top advertisers in the United States— Budweiser, General Motors and Miller—showed major interest. A staff of twenty was proposed, and after some dickering, eighteen of us came on board, the new tenants on the twenty-first floor of the second of the company's skyscrapers along the Potomac River.

Start-ups invariably mean long hours and making up things on the fly. Still, I love them, and I've been a part of several during my journalism career (*Sports Bulletin, Sports Inc.*, and *The National*). Most start-ups fail, and perhaps that's why I'll always have a soft spot for *Baseball Weekly*. It still exists in kind of an altered state out there in the marketplace.

———

What made the "Worst to First" World Series so unlikely, so improbable, was that the Twins and Braves arguably defeated better ballclubs on paper—the Toronto Blue Jays and the Pittsburgh Pirates—in the league championship series. The Blue Jays and Pirates were considered to be among the best teams in baseball, with their rosters studded with such stars as Joe Carter, Roberto Alomar, Bobby Bonilla, and Barry Bonds. Both teams would lose in gut-wrenching fashion in this year's postseason. Only one team, the Blue Jays, would soon rebound from such heartbreak.

In 1991 Toronto's chances took a major hit in Game Three when Joe Carter, their all-star right fielder, crashed into the outfield wall and injured his ankle. Until this point Toronto seemed to have things well in hand. But with Carter hobbled, coupled with curious decisions by Blue Jays manager Cito Gaston, the Twins soon won out and advanced to the World Series.

The League Championship Series began in 1969 as a five-game series and expanded to a seven-game format in 1985. Back in 1991 that seemed to favor the Blue Jays, who had a deeper pitching staff than Minnesota did. Yet Gaston chose knuckleballer Tom Candiotti to pitch the first game in Minneapolis over young fireballer Juan Guzmán and consistent left-hander Jimmy Key. The Twins scored two runs in the first and second innings off Candiotti and held on for a 5–4 victory.

In Game Two of the ALCS the Blue Jays did what other teams could only dream of: they defeated the Twins in the Metrodome. With Guzmán in command, Toronto stopped Minnesota from winning its eighth consecutive game at home, which would have tied a postseason record.

After gaining a split on the road, Toronto returned home and once again appeared to have the pitching advantage. Twins right-hander Scott Erickson may have gone 20–8 during the regular season and been nicknamed "The Prince of Darkness" for using a black glove and wearing dark socks on the days he pitched, but due to a sore elbow, his aura of invincibility had been broken weeks ago. In Game Three Erickson's scowl was still there, yet his pitches lacked velocity. Twins manager Tom Kelly later admitted that he had been worried when Erickson threw thirty-one pitches in the first inning as the Blue Jays took a 2–0 lead. "Damn right I was worried," he said. "[You're] trying to get through a best-of-seven series with just three starters like we are, then you'd be worried too."

As Erickson labored, Toronto starter Jimmy Key tied an American League postseason record by retiring the first eleven batters he faced. In the top of the fifth, though, Carter climbed the fence in right, trying to corral Shane Mack's hard liner. In doing so, Carter strained ligaments in his right ankle, and Mack's drive went for a triple. He would later score on Kent Hrbek's groundout.

"Sure, you wonder what could have been," Carter said years later. "You wish you could always play at your best, be healthy. Unfortunately that's not the nature of the game. It's something you file away and look to have go your way the next time you find yourself in that position."

Meanwhile Kelly successfully deployed his bullpen, setting down several Toronto threats. The game went into extra innings, and this would soon be a trend for this postseason, when the Twins caught lightning in a bottle. Mike Pagliarulo homered off rookie reliever Mike Timlin, and then Rick Aguilera pitched a scoreless inning to cement the Minnesota victory.

Kelly said Pagliarulo's home run "surprised everyone in the stadium, including me."

After hitting just .254 for San Diego, Pagliarulo signed with the Twins before the 1991 season. "I wasn't begging for a job," he later insisted. "There were a couple of teams still interested. But I needed to find a situation that was right for me. That's why I signed with the Twins."

In doing so, he got together with Twins hitting coach Terry Crowley, who tweaked Pagliarulo's swing, searching for more power. "A lot of people thought he was washed up," Kirby Puckett said. "But we knew he could play."

The next two games would be in Toronto, and Puckett cautioned that his Twins "weren't exactly in the driver's seat." Still, the Blue Jays were heading for the ditch thanks to the extra-inning loss and Carter's injury. The Toronto slugger stayed in the lineup as the designated hitter and tried to stay active by playing ping-pong in the Blue Jays' clubhouse. But it was no good. With Toronto already holding a 1–0 lead, Carter struck out with two men on in the third inning.

The Twins took Game Four, 9–3, and then clinched the AL pennant by scoring six runs in the last four innings to win 8–5 the following evening.

As Gladden drifted back to catch a fly ball on the warning track for the final out, CBS Sports' Dick Stockton told viewers, "And the Minnesota Twins have gone from the cellar to the penthouse in the American League."

Once again the Blue Jays had come close to reaching the World Series, only to fade in the ALCS. Three times (1985, 1989, and now 1991) in the previous six years Toronto had been one step away from reaching its first World Series and fell agonizingly short.

Despite such disappointment, Blue Jays general manager Pat Gillick decided to retain Gaston as his manager. "We had a very patient ownership group in Toronto, which allowed us to build that team the way it should be," Gillick explained decades later. "It was like we were climbing a mountain. We went through a lot of trials and tribulations. We made the playoffs in ninety-one, and we didn't get there. All those bumps along the road just make you appreciate when you do win a World Series."

Thanks in large part to Gillick's patience, the Blue Jays finally did reach baseball's summit the season after losing to the Twins. It began a run for the Blue Jays that would see them win two consecutive World Series titles, the first team to do so since the New York Yankees in 1977 and 1978.

Gillick was once asked what makes a general manager successful. "Respect," he replied. "Not respect for myself but respect for the employees who are in those positions. Many times we hire people to do jobs, and we don't let them do their jobs."

To be an effective leader Gillick believed that "you have to be a good listener. And you can't be a good listener when you're talking."

Gillick maintained that his employees "knew that I listened to them. They went back and said, 'I made a contribution. He listened to me. He took in what I had to say. He may not have done exactly what I told him to do, but I know he listened to me.'"

Gillick would eventually be selected to the National Baseball Hall of Fame in Cooperstown, New York, a member of the class of 2011, along with former Twins pitcher Bert Blyleven and former Blue Jay Roberto Alomar.

Back in 1991, though, Gillick seemed a long way away from the victory champagne. This time around it was Andy MacPhail's eyes that were smarting, his hair matted down from a dousing of the bubbly after the Twins took the American League pennant. In the victorious Twins' clubhouse, he was the general manager explaining how he had rebuilt his ballclub into a pennant winner when a massive right hand broke through the throng surrounding him.

"Thanks for that phone call," said Twins designated hitter Chili Davis, who signed with Minnesota during the previous offseason. Davis, like Mike Pagliarulo, had proven to be a key addition for Minnesota.

"Thanks for coming here," replied MacPhail. "Thanks for leaving home."

Davis smiled and said, "It was the best phone call I've ever made."

In becoming the first team to win three games on the road in a league championship series, the Twins had plenty of heroes to go around, many of whom MacPhail had brought aboard. Besides Pagliarulo and Davis, there were pitchers Kevin Tapani, David West, and Rick Aguilera. Those young arms had come to the Twin Cities in a controversial trade with the New York Mets when MacPhail sent staff ace Frank Viola packing. Tapani, West, and Aguilera had pitched in the deciding game against Toronto.

"I said it last year when it wasn't a popular thing to say, but I'll say it again: everybody got what they thought they were going to get in that trade," MacPhail said. "The Mets got a twenty-game winner. They were a big market team—they could afford him. We needed numbers. We needed a little bit of relief from payroll. We got the young pitchers we thought we were getting, and they got the big-stud left-hander that they thought they were getting."

———

In the bottom of the sixth inning of World Series Game One, the Twins' Kent Hrbek lofted a high foul ball down the left-field line. Braves third baseman Terry Pendleton drifted over toward the temporary box seats where the game's VIPs were often seated, but he couldn't snag it. Instead the ball came straight down, striking Anne Vincent, the commissioner's daughter, on the back of the head. She would be taken to the Metrodome's first-aid room, but she refused treatment. Sporting a good-sized lump, she soon returned to her seat.

"She was more embarrassed than anything," said Fay Vincent, her father and baseball's commissioner.

Anne Vincent was still rubbing the back of her head when Hrbek laced a 3–1 offering from Braves reliever Jim Clancy into the upper deck in right field. The solo shot gave the Twins a four-run lead. After going only 3-for-21 (.143) in the ALCS against Toronto, Hrbek already had a double and home run in the 1991 World Series.

A local hero in the Twin Cities, he grew up near the old Metropolitan Stadium in Bloomington and in 1982 was the runner-up to Cal Ripken for American League Rookie of the Year. A big guy, outspoken and even goofy, Hrbek was a favorite with fans and media alike. ESPN's Tim Kurkjian once called Hrbek "the most human baseball player ever."

"The only person who tells me what to do now is my wife," Hrbek once said. "TK [manager Tom Kelly] can't tell me to bunt. The coaches can't tell me what to do. The only person I take orders from is my wife. She told me to cut the lawn today. So I cut the lawn."

If Herbie was smiling and circling the bases, then life was good in Twins Land. But one wouldn't know it from by looking at Kelly. The Twins' manager either had a scowl or thin smile as he watched the Series begin to unfold. Sure, he slapped hands with Hrbek, even stealing another glance down to the commissioner's box to see how Anne Vincent was doing. But Kelly was already scheming how best to shut down the Braves over the next three innings, the quickest way to securing nine outs and the victory of this World Series game.

In 1991 Tom Kelly and Andy MacPhail may have been the oddest couple in baseball. MacPhail's father, Lee, once presided as president of the American League, and his grandfather, Larry, was general manager with the Brooklyn Dodgers and New York Yankees. In comparison, Kelly came from the other side of the tracks. The oldest son of a minor-league pitcher, Kelly was born in Graceville, Minnesota, and this gave him as much claim to being a local hero as Hrbek. In reality Kelly spent much of his childhood in New Jersey, where his father pursued semi-pro baseball.

"We'd always wondered what Tom would be doing if he wasn't in baseball," his younger brother, Joe, once said. "Thankfully, none of us ever had to find out."

"If I wasn't managing baseball, what would I be doing?" Tom Kelly answered. "Probably be [working] on a farm."

Undoubtedly on a farm with race horses. Until a few months before the 1991 World Series began he and his brother had owned several harness horses and ran them at Freehold, the Yonkers and the Meadowlands raceways. "We were small-time," Joe Kelly said. "It was a hobby for us. We sure didn't get rich from it."

Together the brothers mucked stalls and walked their horses over a few winters. "It gave me an understanding of horses," Kelly later told the *New York Times*, "and I think you can often understand people when you understand horses. I learned patience. I learned that you can't be too hard on horses. I learned the saying in racing: 'If you send out a good horse, you'll get a good horse back. Send out a lame horse, and you'll get a lame horse back.'

"So I like to rest my players as often as I can. You want to keep them healthy. And that's why I try to use the entire roster of players. And attitude is important with horses and players. I like to rest a player on the up note. If he goes 0-for-four and I rest him, he's bothered about his bad day. But if he goes two-for-three and I rest him, he's a happier player."

Although there were lessons to be learned at the horse track, nothing overshadowed the ball diamond for Tom Kelly. He played in the minors for thirteen seasons, and in 1975 he reached the Twins for forty-nine games, where he batted .181 and hit his only major-league home run off the Tigers' Vern Ruhle. In 1987, his first time managing in postseason play, Kelly was sometimes abrasive and ill at ease with the influx of media. But he huddled with media consultants before the 1991 postseason and then insisted he was actually enjoying his team's return to the World Series.

Certainly his players enjoyed playing for him. Hrbek told a story about when the Twins once trailed the Angels, 3–0.

"You ain't doing diddly, TK," said Hrbek, who had been given the day off and wasn't at his usual post in the field.

"Think you can do better, Herbie?" Kelly replied.

"Can't do worse."

So Kelly sat alone at the end of the bench, and nobody did much of anything as the Twins rallied to tie the game.

"That's it, Skip," Hrbek finally said. "I'm exhausted from thinking so much. You have it back."

The bench broke up as Kelly once again officially took the helm.

———

Heading into the top of the eighth inning, Kelly and the Twins appeared to be in control. They held a 5–1 lead, with their best pitcher, Jack Morris, on the mound. Despite such success, Kelly debated with himself whether to lift his staff ace. The Twins' bullpen was well rested after having five days off before the start of the World Series, and the Minnesota manager noticed that Morris didn't exactly have his best stuff in Game One. The right-hander with the bushy mustache, which gave him the air of an ornery aging gunslinger, had gotten by more on grit and guile this evening. Still, he had thrown only eighty-nine pitches to this point, so Kelly decided to let him start the eighth inning against the top of the Atlanta order, his fourth time through the lineup.

From the get-go, Kelly realized that leaving Morris in the game was a mistake, perhaps even a game-changer. He watched his starting pitcher walk Lonnie Smith and then Jeff Treadway to start the inning. That put two men on with none out, leaving the Twins' bullpen in a bit of a bind. Kelly, like many managers, liked to give his relievers a clean slate when possible—nobody on base to start an inning. In his autobiography, *Season of Dreams*, Kelly said that his father, a minor-league pitcher, instilled another important lesson in him: "When you see the ball hit hard, it's time to make a change. If you've seen some warning signs and you wait too long, then you're not doing your job."

Although Morris hadn't exactly shot up red flares of distress—he had sent down the Braves in order in the seventh—by this inning he was out of sorts, slipping several times in his delivery to the mound.

"Jack was such a competitor that he rarely wanted to come out of games," catcher Brian Harper said. "He was from the old school, where starting pitchers were determined to finish what they started. He was a throwback to guys like Don Drysdale, Sandy Koufax, and Nolan Ryan. But he had also pitched a lot of innings that year and the seasons before. He was a workhorse, no doubt about it, but TK knew that sometimes those are the guys you have to really keep an eye on."

Later Morris said he had "just run out of gas" in Game One. So much so that when Kelly came out to the mound, Morris simply handed him the ball without any protest. Atlanta had two men on with the heart of their order—Terry Pendleton, David Justice, and Ron Gant—due up. The first Twins' reliever would be left-hander Mark Guthrie to face the switch-hitting Pendleton.

As things shifted in their favor, many in the Braves' dugout began to manipulate their hats, going to their "rally caps." This had become the team's MO during the great run in the second half of the season, catching the Dodgers and then upsetting the Pittsburgh Pirates in the National League Championship Series. Although rally caps, an appeal to the baseball gods, seemingly have been around forever, they didn't really take off at the big-league level until 1977 with the Texas Rangers. Those on the bench turned their ballcaps inside out or backward to inspire a rally, usually in the later innings. During the 1986 season the Boston Red Sox, Houston Astros, and New York Mets joined in, with the Mets continuing the practice all the way to a World Series title.

Certainly no ballclub ever had as many rally formations for their team lids than the 1991 Braves. There was the "Bonnet," where the back of the cap was tucked in and the bill pointing upward, and the "Spout," in which cap wasn't turned completely inside out and the bill of the cap stuck out like a spout of a watering can or jug.

"We didn't invent the rally caps, but we sure had a lot of fun with them," said Mark Grant, who traveled with the team and was in uniform on the Braves' bench despite missing the season with a torn labrum in his pitching shoulder. "We started to develop different types of rally caps for different times of the game. Pretty much everybody got into it because not only was it fun, but the rally caps thing seemed to be working for us."

Atlanta's favorite saw the bill turned sidewise, sitting atop the head like a dorsal fin on a large fish. This rendition, credited to pitcher Steve Avery, was simply called the "Shark" and was deployed "when we've got a rally in progress and we want to go for the kill," the left-hander explained. Now, in Game One, many players on the Atlanta bench, urged on by Grant and Avery, turned their cap around in this fashion, a smile creeping across their faces. They had rallied many times in the late innings this season, so why not do it again? This time in the belly of the beast—the feared Metrodome.

Only a few days ago the Braves had shut out the favored Pirates in back-to-back games behind young pitchers Avery and John Smoltz to reach the Fall Classic. "I was doing deep-breathing exercises," Braves general manager John Schuerholz remembered. "I was trying prayerful concentration, anything I thought could work."

Against Pittsburgh, Braves pitchers had stopped Barry Bonds, one of the game's best hitters. "We noticed that Barry had a tendency to swing for the fences once the playoffs rolled around," explained Atlanta pitching coach Leo Mazzone. "He was such a great hitter during the regular season, but we felt the bigger the game, the more he tried to pull the ball and jack it out of the park. We felt we could get him out down and away, that we could pitch him so that he could do everything but pull it."

Bonds hit only .148 in the 1991 NLCS versus Atlanta and didn't drive in a run.

Behind Avery, the Braves won Game Six of the NLCS, 1–0, and a night later they took Game Seven, 4–0, with Smoltz in command. As Mazzone pointed out decades later, "[We] had a twenty-one-year-old, a twenty-three-year-old, and a twenty-five-year-old, Steve Avery, John Smoltz and Tom Glavine, plus Pete Smith and Charlie Leibrandt, a guy a lot of people thought was washed up. They got us to the seventh game of the World Series."

Avery pitched a playoff record sixteen and a third scoreless innings in the NLCS, prompting Pirates outfielder Andy Van Slyke to say, "If he's going to keep pitching like that, I'm going to come up with a disease every time we see him. It's going to be some kind of stomach disorder, Avery-itis. No, make that Poison Avery."

Certainly some kind of malady hit hard in the Steel City after the 1991 NCLS. Thanks to the game's economics, the escalating gap between the rich and poor teams, the small-market Pirates weren't able to hang on to their stars for much longer. Bonds would sign with the San Francisco Giants after the 1992 season, while Bobby Bonilla would soon join the New York Mets and Van Slyke would finish his career in Baltimore and Philadelphia.

"Back in '91 we knew we were right up against the team with the best pitching in baseball," Van Slyke said. "In looking back on it I think if [the Braves] had gone on that winning streak of theirs earlier in the season, it could have been a different story for us in the NLCS. The reason I say that is they were just on such a great winning streak, we just knew it was going to be tough for us.

"It's like when you're on a run and you get into your third or fourth mile, the endorphins are released in your body and you feel like you could go for another ten miles after that. You could see that those Braves were on an endorphin run when we faced them in the postseason. The way they won—how they won—set them up for the postseason.

"I think it's similar to how you see teams that get the wild card these days coming down the stretch. They're still on this great run, and they aren't feeling any pressure. They think that they can't lose. And when you think you can't lose, you often end up being a better player than you probably are."

Of course, the Pirates returned to the playoffs in 1992, only to lose another Game Seven to Atlanta again, as Sid Bream this time rumbled around third base for the winning run. After that, a curse seemed to settle upon western Pennsylvania. Despite management's best intentions and the construction of a beautiful downtown ballpark, the ballclub wouldn't finish above .500 for more than two decades and wouldn't return to postseason play until 2013. Yet such angst and agony was well down the road on this night, the first game of the 1991 World Series. There were most pressing decisions at hand.

When Jack Morris had been on the mound for Minnesota, the Braves' Pendleton batted from the left side, going 0-for-3. Despite such success, Tom Kelly liked to turn switch hitters around late in a game, make them hit from the other side. The Twins' manager felt it played with the batters' mind. In addition, Pendleton had hit only four of his career-high twenty-two home runs during the regular season from the right side. All in all Kelly liked his odds with a left-hander, even a journeyman like Mark Guthrie, on the mound.

For a moment it appeared such mind games wouldn't add up to much, as Pendleton smoked Guthrie's second pitch to the right-field side of second base. Yet somehow Chuck Knoblauch backhanded the ball on one hop and then threw to Gagne to start a double play. Time and again in the Series the Twins' middle infielders looked like they had been together for years rather than being thrown together for this season. They could turn a double play with the best of them and, by the end of this Series, would turn a DP for the ages, a pantomime of style and grace, done entirely without a ball.

Tonight it was good enough for a crucial, real-life twin killing. With first base now open, Guthrie pitched carefully to David Justice, eventually walking him, the third free pass of the inning. That put runners on first and third with two out. Twins closer Rick Aguilera was brought in to face Gant, who singled to bring home Smith. It was Gant's third hit in the game. Once again the Braves were threatening, with the tying run now coming to the plate. But Aguilera made sure there would be no late-inning heroics from Sid Bream on this evening, as he induced the Braves' first baseman to fly out to Puckett in center field on his first pitch.

From there Aguilera would set down the Braves in order in the ninth, and Minnesota took the opening game of the 1991 World Series, 5–2.

Afterward Kelly walked to the commissioner's box and gave the lineup card to umpire Steve Palermo. Partially paralyzed in a shooting incident, Palermo had gone to the mound on crutches and thrown out the first pitch. Kelly had seen Palermo in the Twins' dugout before the game but wasn't sure what to say, so he decided to give him the lineup card instead. To Kelly, that seemed more appropriate than any attempt at chit-chat. After all, things were about to get serious in a hurry.

———

**FINAL SCORE: TWINS 5, BRAVES 2**

|       | 1 | 2 | 3 | 4 | 5 | 6 | 7 | 8 | 9 | R | H | E |
|-------|---|---|---|---|---|---|---|---|---|---|---|---|
| **ATL** | 0 | 0 | 0 | 0 | 0 | 1 | 0 | 1 | 0 | 2 | 6 | 1 |
| **MIN** | 0 | 0 | 1 | 0 | 3 | 1 | 0 | 0 | X | 5 | 9 | 1 |

**ATTENDANCE: 55,108**     **LENGTH OF GAME: 3 HOURS**

# Game Two

SUNDAY, OCTOBER 20, 1991
AT HUBERT H. HUMPHREY METRODOME
MINNEAPOLIS, MINNESOTA

The Metrodome opened for business in April 1982, becoming the third domed facility in baseball, after the Astrodome in Houston and Seattle's Kingdome. Over the years it would host the World Series, NCAA's Final Four, the Super Bowl, and such rock headliners as Paul McCartney and the Rolling Stones. In essence the Metrodome, which was eventually rechristened Mall of America Field, stood as the multipurpose venue that cities were once so eager to embrace. But when you talk to the ballplayers about the Teflon-topped, multipurpose stadium that was slated to be replaced after the 2013 football season, what they remember is the earsplitting noise and that infernal, mesmerizing roof.

Sellout crowds jammed the Dome in the autumn of 1991, with the off-white lid holding all the commotion inside, making it as loud as a jet plane taking off. One of the loudest noise levels ever recorded at a sports stadium occurred here during the 1987 World Series. St. Louis Cardinals pitcher Joe Magrane wore earplugs, and infielders for both teams had to use hand signals to communicate with each other, with bullpen coaches putting a foot atop the phone receiver. Often it was too loud inside the Metrodome to hear the next call for a reliever, so coaches learned to go with the vibration instead.

"They ought to nuke this place," St. Louis manager Whitey Herzog said after his ballclub lost four in a row there in the postseason.

Opposing pitcher Dan Quisenberry echoed this theme of annihilation, adding, "I don't think there are any good uses for nuclear weapons, but then, this may be one."

Besides the high-decibel noise, the stadium's off-white, daze inducing roof also drove the ballplayers to distraction. As ESPN's Jim Caple once wrote, the space-age lid was "so thin that you can tell when the sun goes behind a cloud during a day game. You can also hear the rain pelting on the roof during a thunderstorm."

Sounds kind of poetic, almost tranquil, doesn't it? But good luck getting a bead on a ball hit in the air in the old Metrodome, especially with the stands filled and everyone yelling their heads off. "Everybody that plays here has a problem with the roof," said Chuck Knoblauch, who lost track of a fly ball in the American League Championship Series despite having a season's experience in the place. "Line drives seem to get lost in the lights. Even a simple pop-up gets lost for a split second."

Catcher Brian Harper added, "In outdoor ballparks you can take your eye off the ball and then pick it up again when you're an outfielder or base runner. You cannot do that in the Metrodome because the ball and roof are so close to being the same color. We knew that on the Twins. We knew that you never took your eye off the ball."

Never take your eye off the ball. To their regret, the Braves would be reminded of this adage throughout the series, once at the most inopportune time.

In Game Two of the 1991 series where the game took place did make headlines again. After the Braves went down in order in the top of the first inning, Twins leadoff hitter Dan Gladden lofted Tom Glavine's first pitch to short right field. Mark Lemke, who had taken Jeff Treadway's spot at second base, ran out headlong in pursuit.

"Lemke has much better range," Atlanta manager Bobby Cox told the media when explaining the lineup switch.

Between the roar of the crowd and the tint of the roof, however, Lemke looked like a man chasing his hat in the wind. At the same time Lemke was running out, Braves right fielder David Justice was running in, ready to position himself to make a play on the ball. The two of them bumped together, and the ball fell to the artificial turf, putting Gladden on second base.

A bit rattled, Glavine walked Knoblauch, and the Twins were in business. Not even Kirby Puckett hitting into a double play could stem the tide as Chili Davis followed by homering to left-center field. The blow staked Minnesota to a 2–0 lead, and the home run was the first World Series hit of Davis's career.

The Twins' slugger initially thought he had hit a Glavine fastball. But later, after studying the replay, he decided it must have been a changeup. "Sometimes a guy guesses right, you know?" Davis said.

A switch-hitter, Davis was in his eleventh big-league season in 1991 and had come to Minnesota after breaking in with the San Francisco Giants and then spending three seasons with the California Angels. Bothered by a lower-back strain, he was held to 113 games in 1990, hitting only twelve home runs. After the Angels let him go in free agency, the Twins became his only real suitor. Through it all general manager Andy MacPhail believed Davis would be a good fit in the Minnesota order. A switch-hitter, David could balance the Minnesota lineup, helping to protect Kent Hrbek against right-handed pitching.

Such negotiations underscored the growing divide between the richer and poorer teams in baseball, even back in 1991. The top team payrolls that season belonged to the Los Angeles Dodgers, Boston Red Sox, New York Mets, and, ironically, the Oakland Athletics. They were all at $33 million, give or take a few million. The Twins' payroll stood at more than $22 million, roughly the middle of the pack financially. As a result, MacPhail couldn't bid that high for such top free agents as Terry Pendleton, Rob Deer, or Darryl Strawberry, especially after signing Steve Bedrosian, Carl Willis, and Jack Morris to bolster the pitching staff.

Healthy for the 1991 season, Davis led the team in home runs (twenty-nine) and runs batted in (ninety-three). He insisted that he wasn't on a mission or trying to prove anybody wrong after most teams ignored him during free agency. Still, Davis told his agent, Tom Reich, that "they'll be sorry that they let me get away. I'm not hurt. I'm not lazy. I'm not stupid."

Kelly agreed that Davis's arrival initially took pressure off Hrbek and Puckett. Then, as he continued his comeback season, Davis's performance forced everyone to eventually step up their game too. "They didn't want to be embarrassed by the new guy," Kelly told the (St. Paul) *Star-Tribune*. "He helped everybody."

But of what help would Davis be when the series shifted to Atlanta for Games Three, Four, and Five? The team's designated hitter, Davis wouldn't have a regular spot in the batting order and would probably be relegated to a pinch-hitting role. Hrbek and others feared that could severely slow the Twins' attack. Through it all Davis tried to stay upbeat. "I think the guys won about 75 percent of the games I didn't start," he said.

———

As long as there are umpires, there will be a degree of human error in the game. The national pastime, unlike the National Football League, wouldn't fully embrace instant replay until the 2014 season. Well-trained human beings, not machines, are always considered the best option, but it can lead to intriguing twists and turns, even with the game's top officials between the lines.

Of course, baseball has had plenty of umpiring controversies over the years. For example, Jim Joyce's blown call in 2010 cost the Tigers' Armando Galarraga a perfect game. Yet when it comes to postseason miscues, Don Denkinger still tops the list. He became a household name to angry St. Louis fans after he called Jorge Orta safe at first base in the ninth inning of Game Six in the 1985 World Series. Replays showed that Orta was clearly out, and the Cardinals could have closed the game out and been crowned world champions.

"A bad call—it's synonymous with my name," Denkinger told the Associated Press after Jim Joyce's blown call with Galarraga. "Any time there's a bad call they call me."

He also told ESPN, "Had I got that play right, or they had instant replay and got it corrected, they would remember the '85 World Series, but they wouldn't have remembered my name."

Six years later after the 1985 controversy, the Braves came into the World Series ready to take advantage on the basepaths. Several of the Twins' pitchers had high leg kicks, which led to good jumps, and Twins catcher Brian Harper had an average arm at best. "My back and my arm were killing me by the end of that season," Harper later admitted. "And they liked to run. It wasn't the most comfortable of situations for me."

With two out in the top of the third inning and Lonnie Smith on first base, Gant slapped Kevin Tapani's 1–1 fastball into left field. Dan Gladden's throw to third base was off line, and the ball dribbled past the bag toward home plate. Tapani backed up the play, and once he saw Gant take a wide turn around first base, he fired the ball across the diamond to Hrbek.

In the Twins' dugout manager Tom Kelly wasn't thrilled with Tapani's decision. "I was angry because I don't like seeing the ball thrown all over the field," he later wrote. "If Tap makes a bad throw, we have a circus with people running all over the place. We try to stay away from circuses."

Yet what ensued proved to be much more than an errant throw and could have played in the main ring at Bozo's Big Top. Gant beat Tapani's throw and returned to first base safely, standing up. Hrbek slapped the tag on Gant anyway, and the two of them became entangled, looking like a pair of awkward dancers at the far edge of the dance floor. Together they stumbled into foul territory, with Hrbek still holding the glove with the ball on Gant's leg. When Gant came off the bag, first baseman umpire Drew Coble called the Braves' base runner out.

The Atlanta dugout erupted in protest, with manager Bobby Cox running onto the field to join Gant and first-base coach Pat Corrales in confronting Coble.

"I was clearly on the base," Gant later said, pointing out that Hrbek was "double my size."

In the official tale of the tape Gant stood six-foot, 170 pounds, with Hrbek four inches taller and easily weighing more than 200 pounds.

"The officiating has got to be better than that," Gant added. "If he hadn't pulled me off, I would have stayed on the base."

Of course, Hrbek had a different interpretation of the pivotal play. "He came into the base and pushed into me. I kind of fell back and he fell over me with his foot coming off the base. If I had pushed him, I'd have pushed him back on the base."

The Twins' first baseman added that he played the moment like "a charge" in basketball.

Coble had umpired in the American League since 1979, and this was his first World Series appearance. His take on the play? "[Gant] lunged into the bag. His momentum was carrying toward the first-base dugout. When he did that, he began to switch feet. He tried to pick up one foot and bring the other down. . . . [In] my judgment, his momentum carried him over the top of Hrbek."

Ironically, Don Denkinger himself was on the field that night, umpiring down the right-field line. A bit of cruel irony that Braves third baseman Terry Pendleton, who was on the Cardinals in the 1985 World Series, couldn't help but notice.

At one point, after Game Two, Denkinger took it upon himself to answer questions from the pool reporter directed at Coble. "There is a judgment call by this umpire," Denkinger declared. "There is no appeal to the plate umpire in this case."

The explanations, on the field and after the game, didn't sit very well with the Braves and certainly not their manager. "You don't like to cry about umpire's call," Bobby Cox said. "[But] you can't move a guy off an occupied base. I don't care if it's just a little nudge. You can't do it. I don't think [Coble] meant to call the play wrong, but in our minds it was wrong. It was as simple as that."

The Twins' Dan Gladden disagreed: "The only thing controversial about that play," he said years later, "was that Ron Gant forgot to slide."

Watching from the Minnesota dugout, catcher Brian Harper also noted who the men in blue were this evening. He had been on the 1985 Cardinals along with Pendleton. Until Denkinger's blown call, Harper was in line to be the hero, as his pinch-hit single had driven in the go-ahead run for St. Louis. In fact, Harper was rehearsing his answers for the press with teammate Andy Van Slyke, another member of that Cardinals team, when Denkinger called Orta safe.

"Andy was asking me the usual questions," Harper said. "How does it feel to win the World Series? That kind of stuff until Orta was ruled safe. Then it all went out the window. I was soon forgotten when it came to being the World Series hero."

In this World Series game things settled down without anybody being ejected. That had been Cox's main goal when he left the dugout—to make sure Gant didn't get tossed. Although the Braves' manager would be ejected a record 158 times during his twenty-nine-year major league career, he was downright civil this time. "Umpires don't like to be embarrassed," Cox later explained. "[Coble] probably thought he made the right call."

The play wasn't soon forgotten, though, not in the days or even years to come. Two decades later the Twins offered a Hrbek/Gant bobblehead of the play to the first ten thousand fans through the turnstiles. Even so the Atlanta ballclub remained a bit touchy about what had happened. "[We] begrudgingly gave our approval because although it wasn't a great moment in Braves history, it was for the Twins," a Braves' spokesperson told the (St. Paul) *Star Tribune*.

Twenty-two years later, when the Twins visited Atlanta for interleague play, Gladden brought along his Hrbek jersey and the two-headed bobblehead for announcing the game on Twins radio. After the Braves swept that two-game series he decided the whole incident "was still cursed, at least from my point of view. Winning in Atlanta, at least for teams from Minnesota, rarely seems to work out."

———

Seeing a chance to tie the game go by the boards would annoy many starting pitchers. Yet Braves starter Tom Glavine was unlike most pitchers. Almost from the time he made the big-league team for good in 1988 Glavine reminded pitching coach Leo Mazzone of Whitey Ford, the staff ace of the New York Yankees dynasty teams in the 1950s and 1960s. Both were left-handed control specialists, used to changing speeds and hitting spots, who kept their composure when the game was on the line. "Tommy is a stoic figure on the mound, like Whitey," Mazzone said. "And Tommy represents our Braves pitchers the same way Whitey represented those great Yankees teams."

In the bottom of the second inning, with the Metrodome faithful cheering for an early knockout, Glavine walked Ken Hrbek but then got Scott Leius to ground into a double play. In the bottom of the third he retired the Twins in order, striking out Dan Gladden and Kirby Puckett.

Earlier in his career Glavine would show all of his pitches—fastball, curveball, slider, and changeup. But after going 10–12 in 1990 the left-hander had decided to throw his two-seam circle changeup more. In doing so, he reached the twenty-victory plateau for the first time in this season—an amazing turn of events for a pitch he literally picked up one day.

The story goes that Glavine came to his signature pitch during spring training of 1989. With a fastball that would never be compared with Nolan Ryan's heater, Glavine knew he needed another offering to keep hitters off balance. Scouts often talk about range when it comes to pitching—that's why they will settle like crows behind home plate at games, monitoring every pitch with their own individual radar guns. What they often track is the difference in speed between a fastball and whatever kind of breaking ball the pitcher is throwing. A range of only a few miles per hour between different pitches won't get the job done. Batters will soon adjust and start hitting rockets to the far corners of the ballpark.

"They can dial up on that heater," Billy Ripken said. "But Ryan had that nasty hook to go along with the fastball. Randy Johnson had that nasty slider."

Glavine experimented with a split-fingered fastball and other breaking pitches, but he couldn't get any of them to work for him on a consistent basis. One day, in 1989, he was shagging balls during BP when he picked one up and adjusted his grip. His middle and ring fingers extended along the ball's seams, and he placed the tip of his index finger on top of the thumbnail. It was a more exaggerated grip than the four-seam changeup, and as Glavine threw it back into the infield, he realized he was on to something. The grip wasn't much different from other breaking pitches, "but it made all the difference to me," he said.

So much so that Glavine soon threw his changeup as much as forty times in a game and was never reluctant to deliver it on pivotal counts—3-and-2 or 3-and-1. That's how much he believed in what he had found. As Braves general manager John Schuerholz later pointed out, Glavine put together an impressive career "with his style of changeup after changeup after changeup. Come and hit this pitch if you think you can. If you do, I'll make it even more difficult for you to hit it the next time. As a painter of corners, he was an absolute Michelangelo."

In Game Two Glavine soon made believers out of the Twins, retiring fifteen batters in a row at one point. With him in control, Atlanta battled back to tie the game at 2–2 in the fifth inning.

Glavine, like many great athletes of yesteryear, learned early on to do what works and not to think too much about the where and why. When he was growing up every sport still had a season, giving players valuable time to reflect when that equipment from the last season was stowed away in the closet. Glavine's father, Fred, remembered when a scout wanted to see his son pitch again after Tom had appeared in a late-summer tryout camp before his senior year. The young pitcher told the scout he would have to wait until spring rolled around. Hockey season was on the horizon, and Glavine was so adept at his second sport that he would be offered a scholarship to play hockey at the University of Lowell and later be drafted in the fourth round by the Los Angeles Kings of the National Hockey League.

For Glavine there were few if any similarities between baseball and hockey. Still, he played them both through high school, believing that the routine gave him time to heal and stay mentally fresh. Of course, today's youth sports stars rarely are allowed such opportunities. Once a kid begins to excel at a particular sport, coaches and parents urge him to specialize—play his supposed sport year-round. But in doing so, so much can be lost.

Hall of Fame quarterback Joe Montana, for example, pitched no-hitters in Little League and excelled so much at high school basketball that he was offered a college basketball scholarship.

Mark McGwire quit baseball temporarily during his sophomore year in high school to play golf. If he hadn't been caught up in the steroids controversy, he would be playing in more pro-ams and may have caught on with the senior PGA Tour. He was almost as good with a golf club in his hands as he was with a baseball bat. The Braves' Deion Sanders was such a well-rounded athlete as a kid that he became the first athlete to play in both a World Series and a Super Bowl. "Parents need to make the major decisions that affect their kids' lives,"

Sanders said. "But when it comes to play, they shouldn't discourage a broad approach. When a child wants to color, do you tell him to use just one black crayon?"

Due to the huge influence of travel teams and the tantalizing hope of a college sports scholarship, the days when kids marked the seasons by a particular sport—football in fall, basketball and hockey in winter, and track, lacrosse, and baseball in spring—are just about gone forever. One wonders what would have happened to Glavine, Montana, or Sanders if they were young sports stars in this day and age.

Summer hockey, fall baseball, indoor winter soccer, elite year-round teams that travel far from their neighborhoods—these are all part of a new kid-centric culture in which specialization supposedly breeds success. But does it?

Sports psychologist Rick Wolff, author of *Coaching Kids for Dummies*, cautioned that "excelling in sports has become as much a part of the American dream for parents as getting their kids into the best school and living in the best neighborhoods."

Sanders added that parents "are using their kids as a lottery ticket. Before all this money came along, moms and dads didn't go crazy at games. They didn't curse their kids and get on them to play better. It was just fun. Now, there's a Yellow Brick Road, and parents think it's their ticket."

Years ago, when Joe Montana was as All-Pro quarterback for the San Francisco 49ers, he rallied his team for a last-minute victory at Candlestick Park. When reporters asked Montana about one of the pivotal plays, when he evaded a blitzing defender coming from his blind side, he smiled that Cheshire Cat grin of his and said, "Didn't you guys recognize that move?"

Puzzled looks all around. Nobody knew what he was talking about.

"It's an old basketball move," Montana explained. "Spin away from your man, remember? You guys forget I was a pretty good basketball player too. They offered me a college scholarship in that too."

Perhaps only a pitcher like Tom Glavine would really understand.

———

It takes two to have a pitching duel, and Kevin Tapani soon proved to be Glavine's equal in Game Two of the Series. He was nicked for a single run in the second inning and another in the fifth, when Minnesota native son Greg Olson doubled, went to third on Mark Lemke's groundout, and then scored on Rafael Belliard's sacrifice fly. After that, though, Tapani shut down the Braves' offense.

While Glavine dominated as the game went into the later innings, Tapani continued to match him on the scoreboard, zero for zero. Lying in the weeds, going about his job without a lot of fanfare had always been Tapani's way. Raised in Escanaba, Michigan, in the Upper Peninsula, Tapani played baseball in a land where the winters were so long that the high school season really didn't happen. There was only time left for American Legion ball, later in the short summers, for Tapani to show his stuff. "Everyone dreams about playing in the majors," he once told the *Sporting News*, "but I never thought I'd get a chance. Almost no one else from there had ever done it, so I didn't think about it. Baseball was just for fun."

Somehow Tapani received a scholarship offer to play at Central Michigan after turning heads at a tryout camp the Los Angeles Dodgers held. In 1986 Oakland drafted him in the second round, and he signed with the Athletics. After pitching at four levels of the A's system (Medford, Modesto, Huntsville, and Tacoma), Tapani became part of a three-team, eight-player deal that saw reliever Jesse Orosco go from the Mets to the Dodgers and starting pitcher Bob Welch move from Los Angeles to Oakland. For the next two seasons Tapani rose through the Mets' minor-league system. At the trading deadline in 1989 he came to Minnesota along with David West and Rick Aguilera in the deal that sent Frank Viola to the New York Mets. After another brief stint in the minors, Tapani was called up for good and finished fifth in the American League Rookie of the Year balloting, behind winner Sandy Alomar of the Cleveland Indians. In 1991 he finished seventh in the Cy Young balloting, behind Roger Clemens and teammates Scott Erickson and Jack Morris, who finished second and fourth, respectively.

Tapani, unlike many young pitchers, didn't suffer any delusions of grandeur. He knew his personal limitations, and according to Twins pitching coach Dick Such, he stayed within himself and didn't try to overpower hitters when he got behind in the count. At his best, as he was on this evening in late October 1991, Tapani attacked hitters with a methodical, measured approach. In that way he was a lot like Glavine. Neither pitcher was overpowering. At their best, though, they could make even major-league hitters look downright foolish.

"I've got to control their bat speed and keep them from getting good swings," Tapani once explained. "I know my pitches are hittable."

At his best Tapani was a poor man's Catfish Hunter. He could be roughed up some, even give up the occasional long ball, but he would invariably work through the tough patches and do what was needed to win.

"He almost always could command his fastball, which goes a long way toward winning in the big leagues," said Twins catcher Brian Harper. "And he had a real plus-major league changeup too.

"Tap could throw his change to right-handers and left-handers, and most importantly, he wasn't afraid to throw it at any time. Some pitchers try to spot that pitch, only throw it when they think they may have a big chance at success. But Tap had real confidence in that pitch. He would throw it any time, to anybody."

Such was the case, Harper remembered, in the top of the eighth inning. Belliard surprised the Twins by laying down a bunt up the third-base line on a 1–2 count. Lonnie Smith then sacrificed Belliard to second base, and the Braves now had the go-ahead run in scoring position. Terry Pendleton followed with a slow dribble to the right side. Kent Hrbek fielded it and threw on to first base, with Tapani covering. But in a bang-bang play, first-base umpire Drew Coble ruled a sliding Pendleton safe. (Replay showed it was the correct call.) That put men on first and third with only one out. Next up was up Gant, who was 4-for-7 to this point in the series.

With the count, 2–1, Tapani spotted a fastball on the outside corner. Gant, who was trying to pull the ball, popped up the offering behind home plate, and Harper barely tracked it down against the padded blue wall. Now there were two down.

"But who's up next?" Harper recalled years later. "David Justice— the absolutely last guy we wanted to face in that kind of situation."

Tapani and Harper huddled on the mound, with the catcher asking the right-hander what pitch he had the most confident in. Tapani told him that he wanted to use the fastball to set up the changeup. After Justice worked the count to 3–2, Tapani decided to roll the dice. Until this point in the at-bat, Tapani had been changing speeds and working the Braves' slugger consistently low and away. Now Tapani went away one last time. Yet this time the pitch was up, almost at shoulder level.

Justice pulled slightly off the ball, barely hitting it off the end of the bat. It became a fly ball to Dan Gladden in left field, and Minnesota and Tapani had wriggled free again, leaving another goose egg on the scoreboard.

"In looking back on things I don't know how I got out of that," Tapani recalled. "I just battled my way through it. Thankfully, Harp was thinking right along there with me. I mean, Gant and Justice? You cannot be predictable as a pitcher with hitters like that coming up. They will hit it out of the park if they can guess what's coming. I was thinking this and then that, always mixing it up, and my catcher was with me every step of the way."

In his understated way Tapani regularly did the right thing at the right time. One of my favorite stories about him occurred a decade later, in the frightening aftermath of 9/11. He was coming to the end of his baseball career by then, pitching for the Chicago Cubs. When the planes struck the World Trade Center in New York and the Pentagon in Washington, Tapani began to receive worried phone calls from the Twin Cities, where he still made his home. After receiving permission from management, Tapani drove the seven hours north to talk with his kids, who were then ages ten, six, and four.

The night he arrived the family all bunked down in the parents' bedroom, a big slumber party that reassured everyone. After a few days at home, with the kids back to their old selves, Tapani returned to playing baseball.

———

In 1991 the sport was on the verge of several sweeping changes. Some of them, notably in ballpark construction, would be for the better. Yet on many other fronts—labor unrest, a precipitous rise in performance-enhancing drugs, the lack of patience in what became our "fix it now" culture—baseball was headed for the cliff. That's why this season, specifically this Series, will always be remembered fondly among baseball pundits and aficionados.

"In a lot of ways it will always be this sweet spot in time," said Steve Hirdt of the Elias Sports Bureau, who worked with CBS Sports for the 1991 Series. "Not only did this one Series have everything you ever wanted in terms of pressure games and great performances, you also look back on it fondly because of what was to come, the challenges the game would soon face."

The previous spring the baseball owners had locked the players out of training camps for thirty-two days. Salary arbitration became the focal point of the dispute, with more problematic issues—a pay-for-performance system and a salary cap—also discussed. Ownership now saw a salary cap as a way, perhaps the only way, ballclubs in such smaller markets as Milwaukee, Kansas City, and Minnesota could compete. The players union, led by Donald Fehr, viewed such measures as a way for ownership to balance their books on the backs of the players.

Twenty-five years earlier Marvin Miller had taken charge of the Major League Baseball Players Association and transformed the organization into arguably the strongest union in the land. A former official with the United Steelworkers Union, Miller was adept, often acerbic in his dealings with baseball ownership, and the MLBPA grew in power while unions nationwide lost much of their clout.

"There's no question he did an outstanding job for the players," said Lee MacPhail, former American League president and Andy MacPhail's father. "Certainly, when he took over, the players weren't getting their fair share of the returns. If I had any criticism of Marvin at all, I didn't think he has any great feel for the game itself. His concerns have been strictly getting as much as he can for the players."

By 1990 Miller had stepped aside, replaced by Fehr, who proved to be just as capable when it came to hard-nosed negotiations. The owners were often represented by their six-member Player Relations Council, which included Chairman Bud Selig of the Milwaukee Brewers, Jerry Reinsdorf of the Chicago White Sox, Fred Wilpon of the New York Mets, John McMullen of the Houston Astros, Fred Kuhlmann of the St. Louis Cardinals and Carl Pohlad of the Minnesota Twins.

"The owners wanted nothing more than to turn back the clock," agent Tom Reich said. "To go back to that time before Marvin. Of course, Don Fehr had no intent of ever letting that happen."

In the end the lockout of 1990 concluded after three weeks. Instead of playing thirty spring training games, most clubs played fifteen. Although there was some grumbling about lost gate revenue for Cactus and Grapefruit games, overall losses were minimal. The season began on time, and soon most players and owners forgot about the shutdown. Yet the lockout had drawn Tom Glavine into union affairs. He explained that he "hated the feeling of waiting for someone to call." So the left-hander moved closer to the flame of labor relations and what would soon be an epic showdown between the players and owners. Although most players avoid labor issues at all costs, Glavine became the Braves' player representative, succeeding Dale Murphy. By 1994, when deep-seated labor acrimony and distrust on both sides caused the World Series to be canceled, he was the union's National League representative. He and David Cone became the public face for the MLBPA on television and in the papers.

"Fans were ticked off seeing my face on TV all the time," Glavine told *USA Today*'s Erik Brady. "I was associated with the problem. It was a kill-the-messenger thing. The thing about it is I was just trying to do my job."

Whether he was on the mound or at the negotiating table, Glavine didn't shy away from confrontation. Even though his best weapon was a changeup, a pitch of real deception, he threw it with a poker face and with as much resolve as any fireballer that brings the high heat: Here it is. Try to hit it. Just try.

———

In the bottom of the eighth inning, with the score still tied at two apiece, third baseman Scott Leius led off for the Minnesota Twins. Raised in Yonkers, New York, Leius had grown up a diehard Yankee fan, and his favorite player was Mike Pagliarulo. "I was a big fan of Mike's," Leius said. "I watched how he played defense. He was one of the best ever, in my opinion."

In one of the ironic twists that baseball often offers, Leius ended up platooning at third base with his boyhood hero during the 1991 season. Coming out of spring training, Twins manager Tom Kelly struggled to find a roster spot for Leius, a shortstop at heart. Soon the only choice was the team giving him a crash course at third base.

With only a handful of games left in spring training, Kelly decided to try a platoon system, with Leius and Pagliarulo at the hot corner. The left-handed Pagliarulo would hit against right-handers, and Leius would go against left-handers and back up Greg Gagne at shortstop. The only wrinkle was that Leius had never played third base in his life, at any level, even going back to Little League. "When I was a kid I was a center fielder, pitcher, and shortstop," Leius said. "I can't recall *ever* playing third base before that spring training."

Despite that, he joined Kelly at a back field in spring training, with coaches Terry Crowley and Dick Such taking turns snagging his throws from third base. Things went well enough that first afternoon, but it wasn't until the following morning, when Leius was riding the bus up to Dunedin, Florida, for a spring game against the Toronto Blue Jays, when he realized how far things had gone in a hurry. Greg Gagne, the regular shortstop, wasn't on this road trip, and when Leius saw the line card, the number five, for third base, instead of the number six, for shortstop, was penciled next to his name.

"At first I thought, 'Five. What in the hell is five?'" he recalled. "Then I saw that Al Newman was playing shortstop. That's how I learned that I was getting my first start at third base. I didn't know if I was really ready or not."

Despite the uncertainty, Leius remained determined to make the big-league ballclub. "I saw an opportunity and I went for it. I wasn't complaining. They were giving me a chance to make the team, a real good team, and I wanted to hold up my end of the deal to show that they were right, that I could do this."

Chuck Knoblauch, who was Leius's roommate, said the two of them "were both happy to make the team at first, but we wanted to do more than that. Both us wanted to prove that we could help the team."

Leius and Pagliarulo combined to hit eleven home runs and drive in fifty-six runs at third base during the regular season, and both won accolades for their defense.

Now, in the late innings of Game Two, Leius wasn't sure how to approach his at-bat against Tom Glavine. He spoke with Crowley, asking him what he should do, but the hitting coach refused to give him specific instructions, a refusal Leius later appreciated. "That's what made Terry a great coach," Leius recalled. "He never told you what to do. I was a hitting coach later in my career, and I learned you have to let guys figure it out for themselves. Be there, but they're the ones up there, against the pitcher.

"His advice was great: 'Know what you want to hit and get after it. If it happens to be the first pitch, so be it.' I mean I was just looking to get on base. Everybody knew I wasn't your prototypical home-run hitter."

Stepping in against Glavine, Leius decided that the Braves' left-hander would probably work him like Tapani had done in the top half of the eighth to the Atlanta hitters: some hard stuff away and get him to chase the change. Leius told himself to be ready. The main goal was to simply get on—a walk, hit . . . anything.

"Glavine had all his pitches going, so I had to find a pitch I could do something with. Not necessarily hit a home run, but see if I could hit the ball hard," Leius remembered. "When you're facing a guy like that, who's been so dominant in a ballgame, you don't want to fall too far behind. If that happens, the chances are he's going to get you.

"So I was lucky. He put a fastball out over the plate, pretty much where I was looking for it, and I was fortunate enough to put good wood on it."

The Twins' rookie drove Glavine's first pitch just over the Plexi-glas atop the left-field fence at the Metrodome. The drive settled a few rows into the stands, and the game had turned again. Moments after nearly taking the lead against Tapani, the Braves now trailed, 3–2.

Although Leius was a relative unknown to most fans, his improbable home run didn't surprise his teammates. "Like I say, 'Every night it's somebody different'," Kirby Puckett explained. "All season long different people have been stepping forward. Scott's done it before, and we knew he'd do it again sometime soon."

Staff ace Jack Morris said Leius's homer was another example of matters going the Twins' way in 1991: "This is the kind of team that we were," he said. "It was the kind of thing that wins championships."

After his dramatic hit, back in the Twins' dugout, Leius had to be prodded to take the first curtain call of his professional career. "I didn't know what to do," he remembered. "Puck said, 'You better go out there.' I just wanted to think about going back out to play defense, finish things off and take Game Two."

After giving up a single to Greg Gagne on the pitch after Leius's home run, Glavine soon settled down. Even though Gagne went to second on a balk, the Braves' starter got Knoblauch and Puckett to then ground out. So heading into the top of the ninth inning the Braves somehow found themselves trailing by a run.

With one swing of the bat, from an improbable source at that, the Twins were now in position to go two games up in the series. Closer Rick Aguilera came in from the bullpen to start the top of the ninth inning. Before the game Minnesota manager Tom Kelly had reassured the media that Aguilera would be ready if needed, even though he had closed out Game One the night before.

Although relief pitchers had been deployed in baseball for some time, their role became more specialized in the seasons leading up to the 1991 series. New York Giants manager John McGraw occasionally went with right-hander Claude Elliott to shut down the opposition as far back as 1905. In the 1950s knuckleballer Hoyt Wilhelm began putting up impressive numbers in relief, peaking with twenty-seven saves for the Chicago White Sox in 1964. Thanks in large part to manager Earl Weaver, Steve Dalkowski appeared destined to be the game's first bona fide closer, at least as we envision him today—a hard-throwing guy who could strike out the side with the game on the line.

In 1962, at Class A Elmira, Weaver simplified things for the bespectacled fireballer, telling Dalkowski to only throw his fastball and slider and to only throw as hard as he could when Weaver whistled from the dugout. (That signal came only when there were two strikes on the batter.) In the second half of that season Dalkowski, who rarely exhibited much control up to this point in his career, walked only eleven batters in fifty-two innings. The following spring, in Grapefruit League action, he struck out eleven batters in seven and two-thirds innings. Just like that the myopic left-hander with the thick

Coke-bottle glasses was slated to head north with the parent club as the Baltimore Orioles' short-relief specialist.

Baseball, though, often proves to be the cruelest of sports. On the same day Dalkowski was measured for his big-league uniform, he pitched against the New York Yankees in a spring training game. Things began smoothly enough. As his teammates marveled, Dalkowski struck out Roger Maris on three pitches. But when Dalkowski threw a slider to New York's Phil Linz, he felt something pop in his elbow. Despite the pain, he tried to stay on the mound. Yet a pitch to the next batter, the Yankees' Bobby Richardson, flew to the screen, and Dalkowski had to come out of the game. Ironically, if Dalkowski had been injured a decade or so later, after Tommy John successfully underwent ligament replacement surgery at the hand of Dr. Frank Jobe, his career probably could have been saved. As it was, however, the Orioles broke camp and headed north for the start of the regular season without Dalkowski. Instead, he started the season in Rochester and couldn't win a game. From there he was sent back to Elmira, where Weaver was still managing at the time. But not even the skipper who would one day be inducted into the Hall of Fame could save the career of one of his favorite players ever. Dalkowski threw forty-one innings, winning just two games. His legendary fastball was gone.

As Dalkowski soon disappeared from baseball, relievers such as Rollie Fingers, Bruce Sutter, Lee Smith and Rich "Goose" Gossage began to dominate in the late innings. Called firemen or stoppers, they often pitched two innings or more and filled in as the ballclub required. A season after saving a league-high twenty-six games for the White Sox in 1974, for example, Gossage started twenty-nine games and threw 224 innings.

Saves didn't become an official statistic until 1969, and those who performed this duty became known as closers because they finished or closed out the game from whatever point they went in. Specialized late-inning relief work and how closers could be deployed was relatively new to the game in 1991. This phase was redefined beginning in 1987 by Oakland Athletics manager Tony La Russa and pitching coach Dave Duncan, and its beneficiary was a very reluctant Dennis Eckersley.

In the late 1980s the Athletics were a pennant contender. Their attack was keyed by Rickey Henderson, José Canseco, Dave Henderson, and newcomer Mark McGwire. The top of the rotation had Dave Stewart and Curt Young, and that was where Eckersley figured he would be. After all, he had won at least twelve games in seven of his first eight seasons in the majors. He had pitched a no-hitter for Cleveland in 1977 and reached the twenty-victory plateau the following season. First and foremost, Eckersley saw himself as a starting pitcher.

That changed when Jay Howell, the A's primary reliever, developed arm problems. Howell had arrived in Oakland as part of the three-way trade that landed Kevin Tapani in New York. In a separate deal with the Chicago Cubs, Eckersley came home to the Bay Area. He was battling alcoholism at the time and wasn't looking for any major changes in his professional life. Yet La Russa and Duncan told Eckersley that he would be in the bullpen and pitch no more than an inning at a time. In other words, the entire relief corps, mixing and matching left-handed and right-handed pitchers depending who was at bat for the opposing team (something La Russa loved to do), a conga line of hurlers, would lead up to Eckersley, who would nail down the final outs.

"Eck always throws strikes," Duncan explained to *Sports Illustrated*, "and he has the heart of a giant. His natural response is to challenge a crisis head-on. That's what makes him such a great reliever. And it's not tough on his arm if he's used right. Think of it this way: Aren't you less likely to break down running two miles every day than 10 miles every fifth day?"

Despite Duncan's logic, the move upset Eckersley. I was covering the A's at the time, and the right-hander spoke about how disappointed he was. In his first season as a closer Eckersley saved sixteen games. "I sure wasn't happy about it," he said. "I thought it was a demotion, and I hoped it would only be a part-time assignment. When I first came up, the bullpen was pretty much where they put the guys who couldn't start."

But anyone could see that Eckersley was truly suited to his new role. Even when he lost a game he was able to turn the page better than any player I've ever covered. Along the way he came up with different nicknames for pitches like "cheese," "hair" and "cookie." He's often credited with coming up with the term "walk-off," as in a walk-off home run. Or a similar term he coined, "bridge job," meaning the losing pitcher wanted to jump off the nearest bridge after giving up the winning hit. I remember when Eckersley first mentioned bridge job one night after a rough outing, how he was tempted to jump off the Bay Bridge on the way home. That's when several of us in the media horde, hanging on his every word, offered to drive him home. That's how good a quote he was.

The 1987 season proved to be just the beginning for Eckersley in his new role as a closer. The following season he saved forty-five games, one fewer than Dave Righetti's major-league record at the time, and he saved all four games of the American League Championship Series against Boston before the Dodgers' Kirk Gibson hit a game-winning home run off Eckersley in the opener of the 1988 World Series. Talk about a bridge job.

The reluctant closer would go on to save 390 games and, in 1990, put together a season for the ages when he struck out seventy-three and walked only four batters in seventy-three and a third innings while compiling a 0.61 ERA. By the time 1991 rolled around, every team was looking to trade for or develop their own version of Dennis Eckersley.

In 1987 the same season Eckersley arrived in Oakland, Minnesota landed Jeff Reardon in a trade with Montreal. A fine closer in his own right, Reardon saved 162 games between 1979 and 1986. After helping the Twins win the 1987 championship, Reardon eventually signed with Boston, so the Twins were again looking for a new closer.

Before the 1990 season manager Tom Kelly called right-hander Rick Aguilera at home and told him he would be replacing Reardon as the team's closer. After hanging up, Aguilera wondered whether he had the necessary makeup to do the high-pressure job. After coming over in the Frank Viola trade, Aguilera had pitched in only eleven games for Minnesota, all as a starter. Yet with a quality split-finger fastball that he mixed with an above-average fastball and effective slider, Aguilera soon proved up to task, giving Minnesota its own version of the one-inning, shutdown closer. He saved thirty-two games in 1990 and forty-two the following season, when the Twins returned to the World Series against the Braves.

An all-league shortstop and third baseman in high school in southern California, Aguilera tried his hand at pitching only after his American Legion team ran out of hurlers. His versatility sometimes worked against him when he was with the Mets, as the team wasn't sure whether he should start or come out of the bullpen. Even after Aguilera stabilized the Twins' bullpen, Kelly still wondered what would have been if he had kept the promising right-hander in the rotation. "I called Aggie and said, 'You've got to be our stopper'," he remembered. "He said, 'Whatever you want.' But I hated to do that. It just broke my heart to move him out of the rotation after he'd finally gotten the knack of changing speeds."

Despite the second-guessing, Aguilera settled into his new role arguably as well as Eckersley had in Oakland. "It's easy to say you like something when things are going well for you," Aguilera told the (New York) *Daily News* in 1990 soon after the move was announced. "But I'm used like Jeff Reardon was, only in save situations."

On this night, in the first real nail-biter of the 1991 World Series, Aguilera knew he had to be at his best. He began by striking out Atlanta's Sid Bream. But when Brian Hunter singled sharply to center field, the Twins' closer briefly appeared more tired than his manager had let on in his pregame press conference. That's when Aguilera found something extra, striking out Braves catcher Greg Olson and then doing the same to Tommy Gregg, who was pinch-hitting for Mark Lemke.

"Off the field Aggie's a shy, almost unassuming guy," catcher Brian Harper later explained. "But put him on the mound, game on the line, and he becomes so locked in, all serious and sure of himself. There was no better closer in the game at that time."

In closing things out, Aguilera became the first reliever to save Games One and Two of the Fall Classic since Goose Gossage had accomplished the feat in 1981. With the 3–2 victory, the Twins appeared to have a firm hold on the World Series as the Fall Classic prepared to shift to Atlanta and the Deep South for the first time in baseball history.

Despite the heart-breaking loss, Braves manager Bobby Cox believed his team simply needed some home cooking. "If they're going to win it," he said after the Twins' Game Two victory, "they'll have to come back here to do it."

————

**FINAL SCORE: TWINS 3, BRAVES 2**

|     | 1 | 2 | 3 | 4 | 5 | 6 | 7 | 8 | 9 | R | H | E |
|-----|---|---|---|---|---|---|---|---|---|---|---|---|
| ATL | 0 | 1 | 0 | 0 | 1 | 0 | 0 | 0 | 0 | 2 | 8 | 1 |
| MIN | 2 | 0 | 0 | 0 | 0 | 0 | 0 | 1 | X | 3 | 4 | 1 |

ATTENDANCE: **55,145**     LENGTH OF GAME: **2 HOURS, 37 MINUTES**

# Game Three

TUESDAY, OCTOBER 22, 1991
AT ATLANTA-FULTON COUNTY STADIUM
ATLANTA, GEORGIA

The Braves had trailed throughout the 1991 season and rallied to win. So as the series shifted to Atlanta, the first time the South had ever hosted the Fall Classic, the attitude was, "Why not do it again?"

After all, the Braves had been nine and a half games behind the Los Angeles Dodgers in the National League West at the All-Star Break and somehow battled back to clinch the division. Atlanta began that run by winning nine of eleven contests after the All-Star Game at Toronto's SkyDome, quickly making a race of it. Coming down the stretch of the regular season, with the Braves and Dodgers never separated by more than two and a half games, Atlanta went on an eight-game winning streak. In going a remarkable 55–28 in the second half, Atlanta won ninety-four games and broke the two-million mark in attendance. To the disbelief of many fans in "Hotlanta," the team grew up to be champions right before their eyes.

On September 11 the Braves' young pitching staff combined to no-hit the San Diego Padres, with Kent Mercker, Mark Wohlers, and Alejandro Peña doing the job. As the season went on, the starting rotation soon became recognized as one of the best in the game. Left-hander

Tom Glavine led the way for much of the regular season, with John Smoltz coming on in the second half and Steve Avery starring in the postseason showdown against the Pittsburgh Pirates when the Braves again rallied, this time after trailing three games to two. In a series in which the teams combined for five shutouts, Atlanta blanked the Pirates in the final two games.

"That series, that season—we did the job," said reliever Mike Stanton. "We made the pitches we needed to make."

After the Braves eliminated the Pittsburgh Pirates to capture the National League pennant, David Justice said, "No one picked us to be in this position that we're in, and that's what makes it so sweet. Because coming into spring training, everyone picked us to basically be second to last, just ahead of Houston. But we knew what kind of team we had, and we knew it would depend how well we played together throughout the year and how much confidence we gained with each victory. We did it all."

In Game Three the Braves spotted the Twins another early lead; this time 1–0 in the first inning. Atlanta's adventures in the outfield continued as Twins leadoff hitter Dan Gladden lofted Avery's third pitch to right-center field. Justice and Ron Gant converged on what should have been an easy out, only to have the ball fall between them for a triple. Gladden came around home on Chuck Knoblauch's sacrifice fly. Justice had made his second fielding miscue of the series, ironically both coming on balls hit by Gladden.

Before the game Twins manager Tom Kelly told the media that the ballclub that usually wins the big games is the one that makes the routine plays, not the exceptional ones. As Game Three unfolded, he was about to be proven correct once again.

After the first-inning hiccup Avery settled down, delivering the kind of pitches that had made him the Most Valuable Player in the NLCS against Pittsburgh. He had the best fastball of any pitcher on either team, and his off-speed stuff was nearly as good as Kevin Tapani's or Tom Glavine's. Born in Trenton, Michigan, just south of Detroit, Avery turned down a scholarship to Stanford to sign professionally with the Braves. From 1985 through 1988 the Braves took a pitcher with their first-round pick in the amateur draft as they built up their staff. Bobby Cox declared the left-hander "a can't-miss guy" from the first time he saw Avery pitch for John F. Kennedy High School in 1988. That spring Atlanta made him their first-round selection, and Avery followed Tommy Greene, Kent Mercker, and Derek Lilliquist into the Braves' minor leagues. From the beginning, though, Avery exhibited a maturity and command of his pitches that belied his age and even those drafted in the years before him. "His concentration level is so great and his stuff is so great," Cox once told Rob Rains, my colleague at *Baseball Weekly*. "He's got three pitches, a fastball, curve, and changeup, and all are above-average."

Cox expected Avery to reach the majors in 1993. He beat those expectations by three years, and even though he struggled with a 3–11 record with Atlanta in 1990, many saw that he was in the majors to stay. Avery said he made it to the big leagues so quickly in large part because of the advice of his father, Ken, who once pitched in the Tigers' organization. For Detroit fans the 1991 postseason had to be painful to watch. Not only did Avery have strong Tigers ties, but right-hander John Smoltz now rounded out the Braves' rotation. He also grew up a Tigers fan and came to Atlanta in a deal that sent veteran hurler Doyle Alexander to Detroit. Tigers manager Sparky Anderson called the 1987 trade the worst of his tenure in the Motor City.

Smoltz's moment in this 1991 World Series would come soon enough, but tonight many expected Avery to take charge. Only twenty-one, Avery twice shut down the Pittsburgh Pirates in the NLCS. In sixteen overall innings he had struck out seventeen and allowed just nine hits in a pair of 1–0 shutouts. His performance already drew comparison with such postseason phenoms as Babe Ruth (thirteen consecutive shutout innings in 1916) and Jim Palmer (a World Series shutout at the age of twenty). "Makes you wonder why we even showed up," Kelly grumbled before the game after being reminded one too many times about Avery's impressive record so far in the postseason.

Once Avery retired the Twins in order in the top of the second inning, the Braves promptly tied it at 1–1. With two outs, catcher Greg Olson walked and Mark Lemke singled. After that, shortstop Rafael Belliard came through with a hit to left field to bring Olson around.

Although Avery was expected to get stronger as the game went on, building off his success earlier in the postseason, the Twins were unsure what to expect from their starting pitcher, Scott Erickson. During the regular season the right-hander became the first pitcher since Bob Grim in 1954 to win twenty games in his first calendar year in the major leagues. (In Erickson's case this was June 1990 to June 1991.) The young hurler had also taken Johnny Cash's "Man in Black" motif to another level by wearing black spikes, with any white covered with shoe polish as well as black stirrups pulled down low so no white sock was showing, and using a black glove instead of the customary brown one. Erickson denied he was superstitious ("It's just a style I prefer," he said).

"It's not his stirrups, shoes, or glove," said catcher Junior Ortiz. "It's his arm. I haven't seen a pitcher with his kind of nasty movement, and I've caught Dwight Gooden, Doug Drabek, and Tom Seaver."

Teammate Kevin Tapani came to call Erickson's starts "another day of death" for the opposing teams. Nicknamed "Rockhead" when he first made the team because he didn't say much of anything to anybody, Erickson soon demonstrated a wry sense of humor and a flair for the practical jokes. He once froze Ron Gardenhire's underwear and framed a teammate to take the blame. "He's like a snake in the grass," the third-base coach grumbled.

Intensely private away from the clubhouse, Erickson often stayed up until three in the morning after his starts, watching movies. *Rocky*, *Predator*, and *First Blood* were favorites, and he claimed to have seen *Top Gun* at least one hundred times. When more than one thousand fans turned up at a Twin Cities appearance for his autograph, he mumbled that they needed to get a life. Still, Erickson was proud of winning twenty games by the age of twenty-three. He would have started the All-Star Game for the American League if he hadn't been sidelined with a sore arm. Instead, teammate Jack Morris got the honors. "When I look at what else I have to worry about, there really isn't anything," the young hurler said.

Erickson regularly pitched to backup catcher Junior Ortiz, who was as easygoing as the pitcher was intense and cryptic. Always good for grins and giggles, Ortiz once brought his young son, who was named after him, into the Twins' clubhouse and introduced him as "Junior Junior." Even though Ortiz played only about one game a week, he did hit over .400 for a stretch in 1990, prompting the nickname "Ted Ortiz" in honor of Ted Williams, the last man to hit better than .400 in the major leagues.

By the postseason, though, Erickson's struggles weren't a laughing matter. Despite having Ortiz behind the plate, his arsenal of pitches was markedly slower. Since a stint on the disabled list in late June, he had struggled—something the Braves were well aware of.

In the bottom of the fourth inning Justice gained a measure of redemption for his earlier fielding error as he homered to right field. Erickson barely got out of the inning without any further damage, leaving Sid Bream stranded at third base. An inning later Erickson got into trouble again. With one out, Lonnie Smith hit a home run to left field. Terry Pendleton followed by working a walk, advancing to second base on an Erickson wild pitch. When Knoblauch made an error on Justice's hot grounder, the day was over for baseball's Man in Black. His line for the day would be four and two-thirds innings, three earned runs, and two home runs given up.

———

The ballclubs in Atlanta and the Twin Cities had come from somewhere else. The Senators vacated Washington in 1961, becoming the

Minnesota Twins, and the Braves' pair of moves bookended baseball's first major wave of franchise relocation.

The Braves initially shifted from Boston to Milwaukee in 1953 and saw more than 2.2 million people go through the turnstiles in 1957 when they culminated a memorable season by upsetting the New York Yankees in the World Series. In the season following the Braves' relocation to Milwaukee, the Athletics left Philadelphia for Kansas City, and in 1958, there was the radical realignment that rocked the baseball world, as the Brooklyn Dodgers and New York Giants headed to Los Angeles and San Francisco, respectively. After the American League Angels set up shop in southern California in 1961 and a National League franchise began in Houston a season later, the map of baseball was forever altered.

"When Walter O'Malley moved his Brooklyn Dodgers to Los Angeles in 1958, it marked the era of disloyal teams and changed the sports world forever," wrote economist Andrew Zimbalist, author of *Baseball and Billions*. "Despite O'Malley's perfidy in the eyes of Brooklyn, for many, family ownership is associated with stability in sports."

One can argue the pros and cons of family ownership, and Zimbalist himself maintained that corporate decision-makers are "more likely to be professional and proficient; less likely to be eccentric and errant. But no matter who was now in charge, ballclubs became more prone to leave town after the exodus by the Dodgers and Giants to the West Coast."

By the early 1960s the Milwaukee Braves themselves were struggling on the field, and their attendance in Wisconsin dropped below 1 million patrons annually. In 1965 ownership announced it was moving the ballclub again, this time to Atlanta. After several rounds in the courts, where arguments about baseball antitrust exemption and what, if anything, local ownership owed its fan base were debated, the Braves (with the help of Bowie Kuhn, who was a National League attorney at the time) got necessary approval to flee town and headed south in a hurry.

As Major League Baseball had gone west in a big way with the Dodgers and Giants, in doing so the national pastime had kind of forgotten about the Deep South and what a rich regional market that could be. In particular, many stellar ballplayers hailed from the "Peach State." In 2010 the Magnolia Chapter of the Society of American Baseball Research selected its all-time, Georgia-born all-star team, which included Jackie Robinson at second base, Josh Gibson behind the plate, and Fred "Dixie" Walker and Ty Cobb in the outfield. From 1901 to 1965 the Atlanta Crackers won fourteen championships at the minor-league level, more than any other team in organized baseball except for the Yankees. Eddie Mathews, Luke Appling, Tim McCarver, Paul Richards, Chuck Tanner, and announcer Ernie Harwell were among those who spent time in Atlanta before moving on to the major leagues.

When the Crackers went on the road their home field, Ponce de Leon Park, became home to the Black Crackers. When the park hosted Negro League teams, including two appearances by Satchel Paige in 1940, seating was open for Black Crackers games and segregated when the White Crackers returned home. According to historian Leslie Heaphy, black fans were relegated to bleacher seats in left field.

In April 1949 the Brooklyn Dodgers came to town for a three-game exhibition series with the Crackers. Of course, the Dodgers had such African American athletes as Roy Campanella and Jackie Robinson on the roster, and even though the Ku Klux Klan urged Atlanta residents to boycott the games, local fans packed the stands to overflowing, with hundreds more atop the three tiers of billboards between the outfield fence and the railroad tracks. The highlight of the final game was "Robinson's steal of home on the front end of a double steal in the second inning," Norman L. Macht later wrote. "There were no fights, no riots, or disturbances of any kind at any of the games."

At the local level professional baseball received impressive support, with the Coca-Cola Company, the Georgia Power Company, and the city of Atlanta owning the White Crackers at various points.

Even the Reverend Billy Graham proved to be a real fan of baseball in the South; in fact, the preacher once dreamed of playing first base for the Philadelphia Athletics and helped link fundamental Christianity and the national pastime together in the modern era. As a teenager Graham played on his high school baseball team in Charlotte, North Carolina, and met Babe Ruth when the Yankees came through town on a barnstorming tour.

"I'll never forget meeting him," Graham once told me. "He put his hand on my shoulder.

"It was my goal in life to be a baseball player. I went on to play semi-pro—paid five dollars a game, two dollars if we lost. The problem with me is that I couldn't hit very well."

At the age of five Graham had also heard Billy Sunday preach. Once an outfielder with the Chicago White Stockings, Sunday was the first baseball player to use his notoriety on the ball diamond to draw crowds in the name of his religious beliefs. Known for his blazing speed but weak bat, Sunday played in the majors from 1883 to 1890. He eventually quit the game at the age of twenty-eight. Drunk, sitting on a street corner, he was overcome with emotion when he heard the singing of a Salvation Army gospel group, wrote Mike Sowell in his book *July 2, 1903*. Sunday decided to be a preacher and soon became a household name, reportedly once converting 98,264 people during a ten-day revival meeting in New York.

Still, only after World War II did religion became an integral element in clubhouses and locker rooms of professional sports. Some ballplayers simply couldn't justify playing on Sunday. Lee Pfund, whose son Randy would one day coach the Los Angeles Lakers, pitched for the Brooklyn Dodgers in 1945. Added to his contract, in Branch Rickey's handwriting, was a clause citing that Pfund didn't have to pitch on Sundays.

Baseball and girls were Graham's major pursuits until he experienced a religious conversion in his senior year in high school and decided to become an evangelistic preacher. When Graham began his ministry, he turned to sports celebrities to draw a crowd. American mile runner Gil Dodds, the 1943 Sullivan Award winner, often ran while Graham spoke—once doing lap after lap for a crowd of sixty-five thousand at Chicago's Soldier Field. After his run Dodds would come up to the pulpit and say a few words about how sports and religion were a perfect match for anyone.

In the 1940s many of the top sports stars were amateurs like Dodds. But as professional sports took center stage in the 1950s, Graham began adding new faces to his regular group of amateur sportsmen— former gangsters and movie stars, according to Wheaton College (Illinois) professor James Mathiesen. Graham went to college at Florida Bible Institute, outside of Tampa. He attended spring training games and eventually "became acquainted with several players, then the owners with many of the clubs," he recalled. Bobby Richardson first attended one of Graham's Crusades for Christ in the late 1950s. The New York Yankees' second baseman would later speak at Graham rallies, including events in Hawaii and Japan. "He's from North Carolina, and I'm from South Carolina. So there's a common background," Richardson explained. "We immediately hit it off."

Their sons would later room together at Wheaton College, and Richardson attended Graham-sponsored seminars. Richardson and announcer Red Barber, who was from Columbus, Mississippi, organized the New York Yankees' chapel services. At first such gatherings were held away from the ballpark, often in a hotel banquet room. But when Mickey Mantle once left a Yankee service in Minneapolis early to beat the traffic and half of the congregation followed him, it was decided that the chapel service should be held at the ballpark.

In 1973, when *Detroit News* sportswriter Watson Spoelstra founded the Baseball Chapel, only a few teams regularly held chapel. When Commissioner Bowie Kuhn gave Sunday meetings at the ballpark his blessing, their popularity soared. Today, all major-league teams have chapel meetings, and many offer weekly Bible studies for players and their wives.

"I think baseball is good as our national pastime," Graham said. "We look to baseball as our game. It's a wonderful clean sport."

In the Old Testament the prophet Ezekiel envisioned that a river of new life, bringing with it hope and faith, would someday run through then-barren Israel. Some would claim that such a river, at least of dogma and good intentions, has flowed through the national pastime in particular and the sports world in general for several generations now. Yet anybody who has discussed religion at the family dinner table knows how divisive the subject can be. Baseball clubhouses are no different. Walk too much with the Lord, and a ballplayer can sometimes forget to walk with the bases loaded, Baltimore Orioles manager Earl Weaver once said. When he managed in southern California Dick Williams lamented that his Angels pitchers didn't throw inside enough. He blamed the distressing trend on too many of them being too clean living. After contending in 1978, several San Francisco Giants players—Gary Lavelle, Mike Ivie, Bob Knepper—went public about being born-again Christians, with Lavelle even warning that the Bay Area was the center of devil worship. They dropped well below .500 the next season, going 71–91, and faith became a lightning rod for team dissension and public criticism. If the Giants were a ballclub overwhelmed by religious fervor, the 1991 Minnesota Twins were arguably a squad that survived such a spiritual revival and the resulting controversy.

In winning it all in 1987, the Twins earned the reputation as a team that worked hard—real hard. "Whether we're at home or on the road, we always have guys hitting extra," Kirby Puckett once explained. "I'm one of those guys. I believe that there's always something that you can do better. . . . I'm always working on it, man."

For many of those seasons Gary Gaetti, the Twins' fiery third baseman, was right alongside Puckett and the others when it came to extra batting practice, clubhouse antics, and off-the-field partying. Puckett went as far as to call Gaetti the soul of the 1987 championship team. He was nicknamed the "Rat" because if a fastball is sometimes called cheese by ballplayers, as in high cheese, no pitcher could throw it past this Rat.

"He was a completely different breed," Puckett added. "Here was a guy who had such an impact, on me especially. He was the kind of guy that if you were beating the Twins, he couldn't take it. Gary Gaetti was just [liable] to scream at you when he was hitting. The next pitch he'd hit five hundred feet for a home run and be screaming at you as he went around the bases. . . . That's what I remember most about Gary."

Everything changed in Twins Land when Gaetti became born again after the 1987 World Series triumph. The guy who was always eager for extra BP, to confront an opposing pitcher, began to arrive later at the ballpark and spend more time at his locker reading the Bible, Puckett remembered. For Kent Hrbek the transformation was especially difficult. He and Gaetti had been roommates since Class A ball in Elizabethton, Tennessee. For years they had played ball, hunted, fished, and hit the bars together. Soon after the 1988 season began, Hrbek asked for a separate room when Gaetti began to talk to him about Jesus Christ. "That's where I drew the line," Hrbek said. "That's the only time we had any flak between us. He was into it deep the first year, and that's what everybody I talked to told me how it would be.

"I was quoted in the paper as saying it was like a death in the family. It was like I'd lost Gary Gaetti someplace. It was like he was a different person. A lot of people took offense to that, saying it can't be that bad. But it was. I'd lost somebody I'd like to chum with and hang out with, stay up to three o'clock in the morning and rant and rave all over the place and have a good time."

Hrbek was reminded how much things had changed when he watched the 1989 All-Star Game on television. A few seasons earlier he made the team, and Gaetti had watched from home. When Hrbek was introduced he held up a batting glove with Gaetti's number eight written on it. In 1988 Gaetti retuned the favor with HI REX, a reference to Hrbek's nickname T. Rex. By the 1989 All-Star Game, though, Gaetti had left his old buddy far behind. Before that All-Star

Game he distributed leaflets that included his picture and testimony. When it came time for the pregame introductions, his batting glove read, JESUS IS LORD. Back home in Minnesota Hrbek turned off the television.

By 1991 Gaetti was no longer on the Twins' roster, prompting the platoon of convenience at that position with Scott Leius and Mike Pagliarulo. General manager Andy MacPhail said Gaetti's newfound faith had "zero bearing" on the ballclub declining to re-sign him. "Gary Gaetti left us because he was offered $11.7 million over four years," MacPhail said, "two of it guaranteed. It had nothing to do with one's religion."

Sports analyst Greg Cylkowski, who was based in St. Paul, Minnesota, and had advised several Twins players during this period, said the ballclub's decision not to re-sign Gaetti was by design. MacPhail countered that the ballclub had not only offered Gaetti that four-year deal with $7.1 million guaranteed, but the unique contract also gave him the option to declare himself a free agent after the 1991, 1992, or 1993 seasons. In the end Gaetti headed to the West Coast, but the proposed deal with the novel option plan caught the eye of pitcher Jack Morris. When he signed with the Twins before the 1991 season he received a three-year deal and bargained a similar option, which could make him a free agent after his first and second years in the Twin Cities. Few at the time gave this wrinkle much thought. Morris was thirty-six years old and coming off a 15–18 year with Detroit. In addition, he was returning home, having been raised in St. Paul. Still, the Gaetti option would allow Morris to leave after one season with the Twins if he wanted.

———

Faith can rock a world. Combine it with vision, and everything can be turned upside down.

An independent operation for much of their history, the Crackers became the Class AA affiliate for the Braves in 1950. After the Southern

Association disbanded, Atlanta moved to the International League, becoming the top affiliate for the St. Louis Cardinals and then the Minnesota Twins, of all teams, for another season.

As the only professional franchise in town, the Braves drew well at first and won the National League West Division in 1969. Yet within three seasons, they fell twenty-five games back in the standings, and despite having home run king Hank Aaron in the lineup, attendance dropped like a stone. That development soon opened the door for one of baseball's real innovators—Ted Turner.

During the 1960s Turner brought his family's billboard company back from financial ruin. A decade later he turned to television, buying an independent UHF station in Atlanta (WJRJ) and making its fare movies and reruns of old TV series. Desperate for more programming, Turner turned to baseball. In 1974 he paid $600,000 for a five-year pact that allowed him to broadcast sixty games annually. At first Turner sent his signal to cable television operators only in the Southeast. Despite being heavily leveraged, he decided to take it up a notch by leasing a channel on a communications satellite. That made his station, soon to be redubbed WTBS, available on cable systems nationwide, and the Braves were on their way to becoming "America's Team" in the realm of baseball.

"When I look at heroes and people I worship, he has to be one of them I admire most," Hank Aaron said. "You're looking at a genius, someone who is two or three steps ahead of everyone else. Back when he was starting CNN, he'd walk through the stadium, and people thought he was crazy. Well, I'd like to be crazy like that."

Turner said the keys to his success were simple. "Early to bed, early to rise, work like hell and advertise," he once said.

As Turner's gambles began to pay off in a big way, Braves ownership continued to suffer at the gate, and they finally decided to sell. A group in Toronto was interested in buying the ballclub, but Major League Baseball wasn't eager to move the Braves for the third time in nearly a quarter century. A local buyer was preferable, so much so that Turner's offer to pay $1 million down and $9 million sometime in the future was accepted. At thirty-seven, with his only other sports experience being as the winning skipper in the 1977 America's Cup, Turner had a major-league franchise to call his own.

Although he continued to build his sports and media empire, purchasing the Atlanta Hawks of the National Basketball League and founding the all-news cable channel CNN, Turner sure had a sweet tooth for his Braves. He signed free agents Gary Mathews and Andy Messersmith and clashed with Bob Horner, who had made the big-league club right out of college. He fired Bobby Cox in 1981, only to bring him back as the general manager five years later. In fact, one of Turner's best quotes of all time came at the press conference when Cox was let go. Asked who was on his short list to be the Braves' manager, Turner said, "It would be Bobby Cox if I hadn't just fired him. We need someone like him around here."

Perhaps Turner's best can-you-believe-this moment happened soon after he bought the Braves. With the ballclub mired in a sixteen-game losing streak, Turner ordered manager Dave Bristol to take a leave of absence. With Bristol out of the way, Turner decided to manage the team himself, wearing uniform number twenty-seven. The stunt lasted only one game, as it was found to be a violation of a major-league rule that prohibits players and managers from owning shares of a team. Although Turner lost his only contest in uniform, a 2–1 defeat to the Pittsburgh Pirates, he does remain an owner with a managerial record, duly noted in the record books and at 0–1.

"[Pitching coach] Johnny Sain probably was the only person in Pittsburgh who didn't know what was going on," Braves broadcaster Pete Van Wieren said. "He finally said, 'Where's Dave?' He had no clue."

The defeat was the Braves' seventeenth straight, and coach Vern Benson was the manager the following day when Atlanta snapped its losing streak, with a 6–1 victory.

"Well, I'd like be down there to take some credit for this," Turner told the *Washington Times*.

Soon enough Bristol returned from his owner-imposed vacation, and things returned to normal in a season that would see Atlanta finish with a 61–101 record. With Bristol back at the helm, the Braves were shut out by the St. Louis Cardinals.

Despite such antics, Turner's flair impressed ballplayers elsewhere, especially in locales that were fast becoming small-market have-nots. "The Braves had the resources to keep people, and we didn't," said Andy Van Slyke, who had joined the Pittsburgh Pirates in 1987 and would lose to Atlanta in consecutive National League Championship Series. "They, and the Cubs with WGN, were becoming America's teams. Ted Turner wasn't afraid to spend money. That certainly wasn't the case in Pittsburgh."

————

The Braves had chances to pull ahead in Game Three, but they were admittedly playing a few bricks shy of a load. Their running game, which had been a chief weapon during the regular season, remained stuck in neutral during long stretches of the postseason. The major reason? Otis Nixon, who led the team with seventy-two bases, was sidelined after testing positive for drugs.

Back in July the Braves' center fielder was first caught for cocaine. Commissioner Fay Vincent studied the results and decided not take any action at that point because the data was inconclusive. "The test was very, very marginal," Vincent told *USA Today*. "We looked into it, interviewed Otis, and concluded the best course was to give him a chance which it seemed to us he had earned by his conduct over the years."

Unfortunately for Nixon and, ultimately, the Braves, the superb center fielder soon failed a subsequent random drug test, and Vincent had no choice but to suspend him for sixty days. That meant Nixon missed Atlanta's final eighteen games of the regular season as well as the playoffs and World Series.

"We coped with the loss of a lot of key players this year," Braves general manager John Schuerholz said at the time. "We'll try to do the best we can to cope with this."

With Nixon atop the batting order, the Braves offered an effective blend of speed and power. Not only did he steal seventy-two bases in 1991, but the switch-hitter also hit .297, with an on-base percentage of .371. On this ballclub he was the perfect table-setter for the big bats of Terry Pendleton, Ron Gant, David Justice, and Sid Bream.

When Pendleton signed with the Braves during the offseason, coming to Atlanta after seven seasons with the St. Louis Cardinals, he did so because the Braves' young pitching staff impressed him, and Schuerholz and Cox had assured him that the ballclub "would go out and get the pieces that were necessary to compete."

"[The Braves] had a young Ron Gant, a young Jeff Blauser, a young Dave Justice," Pendleton said. "Probably the final piece to the puzzle came when we got Otis Nixon. That was huge, because we really needed a leadoff hitter."

With Nixon out of the lineup for the 1991 postseason, Ron Gant took over defensively in center field, and Lonnie Smith moved into the leadoff role. The latter was nicknamed "Skates" for his misadventures in the outfield and on the basepaths. In addition the Braves were missing another valuable cog with the postseason in full swing, as two-sport star Deion Sanders had to report to the Atlanta Falcons' football camp. During the Braves' stretch run for the divisional title Sanders came through, though, especially with a pivotal home run against Pittsburgh in late July. Ironically, Sanders would rework his contract in 1992 so he could play the entire season with Atlanta and participate in that year's World Series against Toronto, in which he would bat .533 with two doubles and four runs scored despite playing with a broken bone in his foot. "Neon Deion" may have been a part-timer in baseball, but the Braves certainly could have used him in the 1991 World Series.

Sanders, for one, came to Nixon's defense after the suspension made headlines. "This man was having the best year of his career, a free-agent year, the team's winning, he had an outside chance at the MVP and the man already gets drug tests three times a week," he told the *New York Post*. "They were on his bandwagon just a couple of days ago when he was driving in runs and doing it for the team and now they say it was drug-aided."

Speed can be the great equalizer in any sport. Deployed correctly, a fast team has the definite edge over a slower one. Yet many coaches seemingly distrust the concept, fearful that speed will disappear when a team needs it the most. The Orioles' Earl Weaver, for example, believed in pitching, defense, and the three-run homer. Rolling the dice on hit and runs, stolen bases, and putting the runners in motion wasn't his way. Perhaps that's why somebody like Alan Wiggins didn't fit in during his final seasons when he was in Baltimore. Or perhaps it was simply that drugs had already eaten away too much of him by that point in his career.

No doubt that Wiggins had wheels. In his seven-year career, 1981–1987, he hit only .259 but stole 242 bases in 631 games for a 38.4 percentage. In comparison, all-time stolen-base leader Rickey Henderson stole 1,406 bases in 3,081 for 45.6 success rate. But, of course, Rickey was unabashedly the greatest of all time. Among the game's top base stealers of all time, Lou Brock stole 938 bases in 2,616 games for a 35.9 percentage, whereas Ty Cobb sported a 29.6 rate, and Honus Wagner 25.9. The Braves' Otis Nixon would finish his seventeen-year career with a mark remarkably similar to Wiggins': 36.3 percent.

Only a few years before, on the 1984 San Diego Padres, another manager, "Trader" Jack McKeon, had seamlessly employed Wiggins's talent. With Wiggins as the leadoff batter on that team, Tony Gwynn hit .351 behind him and secured his first National League batting title.

As a team, the Padres won the pennant, advancing to the World Series, where they lost in five games to the Detroit Tigers and Jack Morris, then their staff ace.

McKeon said that Wiggins "became our catalyst in 1984. He was a good kid who ran into problems. When we lost him it took three years to find another second baseman [Roberto Alomar] and five years to find another leadoff hitter [Bip Roberts]."

Former Padres shortstop Garry Templeton later told the *San Diego Union* that Wiggins "was one of the best sparkplugs any club ever had."

Unfortunately, Wiggins missed the 1985 opener at Dodger Stadium and was soon admitted to a drug rehabilitation center. When Padres owner Joan Kroc refused to allow Wiggins to rejoin the team, McKeon was forced to trade his speedster to Baltimore.

From a baseball standpoint, Kroc's stand made little sense and ran counter to the working agreement between the players and owners. Yet she remained adamant that Wiggins had to go, that he would never play in a Padres uniform again.

"The game of baseball was not something she was very familiar with. The business side, even less," Padres executive Dick Freeman once told *San Diego Magazine*. "If I said, 'Oh, she was great to work for and it was a piece of cake,' I wouldn't be telling the truth."

On the East Coast Tony Attanasio, Wiggins's agent, said his client's new teammates soon ostracized him, and as a result, he turned to drugs anew. The Orioles would finish the 1986 season with a 73–89 record. As they began to struggle, Weaver told his players to steer clear of the media; he would do all the talking with the Fourth Estate. At the same time in world events Libyan leader Muammar al-Qaddafi had drawn an imaginary "Line of Death" in the Mediterranean Sea, telling US forces to stay away. Wiggins, who regularly read the *Wall Street Journal* beyond the sports section, joked around the batting cage that Weaver had drawn a line of death between the Orioles' ballplayers and the media. For his trouble, Attanasio said, Wiggins was literally beaten up by his new teammates.

"After that Alan said he couldn't play for them, and who could blame him?" said Attanasio, whose clients have included Goose Gossage, Bobby Valentine, Reggie Smith, Steve Howe, and Ichiro Suzuki. "Here was a guy who could have been the best second baseman Baltimore ever had. A guy who could run and field and hit. Instead, they didn't want anything to do with him. They shunned him."

Soon Wiggins was back doing drugs, and he shared needles as part of his addiction. His family believes that's what led him to become the first major-league player to die of an AIDS-related illness (acquired immune deficiency syndrome), which took him in early 1991. Wiggins's death was another pebble thrown into the vast pool called sports that soon sent major waves throughout society by the end of that particular year. Even among those playing on the biggest stage later that season, Alan Wiggins's death wasn't forgotten.

The Braves' Terry Pendleton remembered that he would speak with Wiggins when either one of them were on base—the one taking up his defensive position in the field, the other looking to stretch his lead. "It was, 'How you doing?' That kind of thing," Pendleton said. "I really didn't know him, but I knew him as a player, the speed and talent that he brought to the game. Unfortunately, he got into the wrong thing. He could have had a great baseball career.

"I was saddened by [his death]. It shocks you when anybody—ex-player, ex-teammate—passes away. It shocks you because we all think we're still twenty-five years old. But we're not."

Former teammates Steve Garvey and Lee Lacy as well as Attanasio and Freeman attended Wiggins's funeral. Although Candice Wiggins was just three years old at the time, the day remains one of her earliest memories. She can still close her eyes and see the Calvary C.M.E Methodist Church in Pasadena, California, packed to overflowing, and she will never forget how frightened everyone was.

Although the initial reports said her father had died of respiratory failure from lung cancer, many in attendance knew better. Soon it came out that her father was the first major-league ballplayer to die because of AIDS.

"It was a very scary time," Candice recalled. "There was a lot of fear because of AIDS, and people back then knew so little about it. Back then some people felt you could get it by breathing. Just breathing."

———

Looking back on Otis Nixon's absence from the Braves' lineup, his suspension underscored a growing problem the national pastime had with drugs during this period—performance enhancing or otherwise—and the owners' and players' inability to agree on a way to effectively test for them. Steroids wouldn't make major headlines for a few more seasons. Yet the signs were there, with little in place to curb their escalating use. According to José Canseco's book *Juiced,* steroids were being used in baseball as early as the mid-1980s. His Oakland Athletics, with fellow Bash Brother Mark McGwire, would soon become a major focus for such activity. No matter that Peter Ueberroth proclaimed baseball to be drug-free before he stepped down as commissioner in 1989, PEDs were becoming a huge part of the sports scene overall, and they would soon be blamed for football player Lyle Alzado's premature death in 1992. Through it all Major League Baseball couldn't agree on an effective formal policy. In most cases the Major League Baseball Players Union opposed random testing. For example, the only way Nixon was caught for cocaine was because he tested positive as part of an earlier rehab program. Originally arrested in 1987 while playing at Triple-A Buffalo, Nixon had pled guilty to obstruction. Those drug charges were dropped, but the ballplayer was required to begin a rehab program that later resulted in the sixty-day suspension.

"The only thing I know is we knew [Nixon] was on an aftercare program when we acquired his contract," Braves GM John Schuerholz said in 1991.

In large part baseball wasn't able to focus on steroids and drugs because of the growing labor storm. Owners and players couldn't agree on the framework for a new collective bargaining agreement, let alone a standardized drug policy. In testimony years later on Capitol Hill, MLB executive vice president Rob Manfred said, "No one believed that there was significant steroid use in the game at the time," adding that "economic issues" took precedence over a stronger drug policy.

Canseco recalled that the owners' attitude bordered on, "Go ahead and do it."

As a result, more players took the overall dysfunctional situation as permission to dabble with steroids. In the summer of 1994 the owners would lock out the players, resulting in the World Series to be canceled for the first time in ninety years. "It really, really spread like wildfire after that," Andy Van Slyke said. "Very few people say this, but steroids saved baseball and made a lot of players rich today. And everybody, it seemed, was drinking from the juice by the midnineties."

Well, maybe not everybody. Rickey Henderson, Canseco's teammate and the game's all-time base stealer, claimed he didn't know about steroids back then. "They kept that [stuff] a secret from me," he told the *New Yorker* in 2005. "I wish they had told me. My God, could you imagine Rickey on 'roids? Oh, baby, look out!"

(Henderson was the first professional athlete I ever encountered who talked about himself in the third person, as in "Rickey is in a bit of a slump, but he'll be good" or "Rickey slides head first because it's closer to the ground. That way Rickey doesn't get hurt.")

In the spring of 1991 I had been in the Phoenix area, making the rounds of the training camps. I finished the American League previews I was responsible for and, more importantly, established better contacts throughout the league. I told anybody who would listen that I was writing for a new publication, *Baseball Weekly*, which would be published nationwide beginning in a few weeks by *USA Today*.

But through those days in the desert one baseball star eluded me. In fact, he wasn't sitting for interviews with anyone. And he was the guy I needed the most—Rickey Henderson.

Even though the A's outfielder would soon begin the regular season only three bases away from breaking Lou Brock's all-time stolen base record, Henderson had gone public earlier in spring training about wanting to renegotiate his contract. As a result, Henderson said crowds booed him throughout Arizona early in 1991. The superstar blamed the media for this debacle and refused to talk with any of us.

That was well and fine with most writers. After all, speaking with Rickey Henderson could be a bit like listening to a combination of hip hop and haiku. But I needed fresh quotes from the "Man of Steal." The premiere issue of *Baseball Weekly* would have Henderson on the cover, and I had been assigned the story. Everybody else could wait out Henderson's latest snit—except me.

That afternoon in Phoenix Municipal Stadium, the Athletics' spring home, Henderson started the game in left field against the Seattle Mariners. By the middle innings Oakland manager Tony La Russa began to sub out his regulars, replacing them with rookies or journeymen who needed another audition under the Arizona sun before their station for the season was decided upon. Henderson ran in from left field to a smattering of boos and cheers. As he did so, I slowly walked to the back of Municipal's open-air press box. I was trying to be nonchalant, acting like I was heading to get another hot dog or ice cream swirl. But my notebook was in my back pocket, and as soon as I came down the steps of the press box I picked up the pace, heading for a door behind the stands that led down to the A's clubhouse.

Downstairs nobody was in sight at first. But then coming around the corner was Rickey Henderson himself. He had a towel fastened around his waist and another draped around his neck. Even though he was thirty-three years old at the time, he had the physique of a guy in his midtwenties—defined torso, thick shoulders, and thick, cable-like legs.

When Henderson saw me he turned in one movement, ready to escape to the areas of the clubhouse that were off-limits to the media.

"Rickey," I shouted.

But he kept going.

"I don't want to talk about your contract. I want to talk about you about to break Lou Brock's record."

Thankfully, Henderson stopped in his tracks and looked over his shoulder back at me.

"Nothing about the contract?"

"That's right," I replied. "I just want to talk about you and Brock's all-time stolen base record."

Henderson considered this for a moment.

"Just about Rickey and Lou?"

"That's right," I said. "Just about you and Lou—the two greatest base stealers of all time."

"Rickey and Lou?"

"Yes, this is for *USA Today*," I said, not wanting to complicate things by explaining about a publication that hadn't made the newsstands yet.

"Rickey and Lou," Henderson again said, pulling up a stool in front of his locker. He motioned for me to sit down next to him. "Rickey would like that."

So we spent the next half-hour talking about Rickey's upbringing in the rough streets of Oakland and how in high school he sometimes raced the team bus to the next neighborhood game to build up his legs. Once he was between the lines he remembered to come home with a dirty uniform or else his mother wouldn't believe that he had even gone to the game. As a result, if he hadn't done much on the basepaths on a particular afternoon, he would go back out on the field, "sliding in the dirt" after the final out.

In the early 1990s the national pastime once more mirrored the world around it. Even when the conversation wasn't about money, it somehow came back to the all-mighty dollar. Although I kept my word and didn't bring up the contract hubbub, Rickey Henderson couldn't help but comment on the booing he had heard an hour or so earlier. Granted, it was hard to feel sorry for a guy making $3 million annually. Yet Henderson wasn't among the top twenty-five in salaries as this season began. He felt he had no choice but to complain—even threaten to hold out for a higher wage.

"This should be my golden moment, but I've gotten so much heat about my contract," Henderson said as more of his teammates began to file into the A's clubhouse. "I'm not even thinking about Lou Brock or his record. This is maybe the most important thing of my life. What I've played years for. But with all this other stuff going on, breaking Brock's record could be kind of hollow."

He glanced around the room before adding, "The last year and half I was the best anybody can be. They say they can't renegotiate, but that's crazy. In baseball right now there are no rules when it comes to money and contracts. No rules about anything except what happens out there on the field."

———

Without Otis Nixon and Deion Sanders in uniform, no high-quality speedster like Rickey Henderson at the top of the lineup, the Braves needed new heroes in the 1991 Fall Classic. With novelist Stephen King looking on in Atlanta, the bottom part of the Braves' lineup began to step up. Catcher Greg Olson, second baseman Mark Lemke, and shortstop Rafael Belliard would eventually go 4-for-11 in Game Three, with three runs batted in, as the heart of the Braves' order batted only 2-for-16.

Heading into the postseason Lemke decided that he had no reason to worry. "We had other superstars, so right away that took a lot of pressure off me," he told the *Atlanta Journal-Constitution*. "I would, in turn, look out at the pitcher say, 'The pressure's on you. We all know who the big bats are. You have to get me out.'"

In the middle innings of Game Three it appeared that the Braves could ride starting pitcher Steve Avery to their first World Series victory. After the fielding mishap in the first inning, which resulted in the Twins' first run, Avery cruised into the seventh inning with a 4–1 lead. That's when Kirby Puckett, who had struggled to this point, drove the second pitch he saw well out to left field. The blow was only a solo shot and the Braves retained a two-run lead, but the Twins' bats were on the verge of waking up.

An inning later, after Twins pinch-hitter Brian Harper reached on an error by Terry Pendleton, Atlanta manager Bobby Cox decided to go to his bullpen. Managers point out that they make so many choices in any game that it can be easy to second-guess. Although Cox could have kept Avery in the game—he had set down fifteen in a row at one point—the left-hander did seem to be tiring. Into the game came right-hander Alejandro Peña, who had come over from the New York Mets during the regular season and recorded three saves in the NLCS against Pittsburgh. A hard-throwing right-hander, Peña worked the count to 1–1 on another Twins pinch-hitter, Chili Davis.

But as they say, baseball is a game of adjustments, ones often made on the fly. When Davis found he couldn't get around on Peña's fastball over the inside half of the plate, he opted to hit the next one he saw the other way. "Right after that he threw me a fastball up and away, and I fouled it straight back," Davis recalled years later. "That's when I said to myself, 'Man, if you throw that one more time, I ain't missing it.' Then he threw it again. I couldn't believe it."

Davis got his arms extended and was able to drive the ball out the opposite way to left field, tying the game at 4–4. "That stadium in Atlanta was a great place to hit in," Davis said. "If I'd played in that ballpark instead of Candlestick Park, I might have four hundred or more home runs today."

As Terry Pendleton watched Davis's home run sail into the seats, he couldn't believe how the tables had been turned once again in the Series. "Just when you feel like it's under control, they come back and tie the ballgame," he recalled. "It's not a good feeling. But that's what that series soon became all about. You never felt easy with where you stood, even when you had the lead."

After this new swing in momentum, Peña was fortunate to hold Minnesota to just two runs scored in the inning. The Braves' reliever gave up singles to Chuck Knoblauch and Kent Hrbek, and the Twins appeared poised to take the lead and seize control of the series. At this point Peña bore down, going with hard stuff to strike out Puckett and Shane Mack. The contest was now tied at 4–4.

After the Braves went down in order in the bottom of the frame, both teams put men in scoring position in the ninth inning, but neither squad could score. With that, Game Three headed into extra innings in search of a hero, and an unlikely one would soon emerge.

More baseball in Atlanta meant that the chant of the Tomahawk Chop became ever-present, loud, and obnoxious, the new soundtrack of this Fall Classic and soon to be on the greatest hits playlist for postseason action. Legend has it that Deion Sanders brought the cheer to Georgia after the chop became a hit at Florida State in the eighties. Sanders was a two-time All-American cornerback for coach Bobby Bowden at FSU, whose nickname is the Seminoles. To properly perform the cheer one needs to swing an arm, hinging at the elbow, in rhythm with the OHHH, a-ooooo cadence of those around you. Go ahead—it's easy to follow along.

Once The Chop took hold in Atlanta, many fans really got into the swing of things, so to speak, by wielding Styrofoam tomahawks back and forth in time with the chant. Such accessories were found at the souvenir stands inside the Atlanta stadium. No matter that the Tomahawk Chop and the war chant had no basis in Native American history or in the South itself, The Chop was here to stay.

In fact, the cheering and chanting soon became so controversial that protests greeted fans outside of both stadiums during the Series. "We want Ted Turner to meet with us and put a stop to this stupid, ignorant, racist behavior," Clyde Bellecourt, founder and chairman of the American Indian Movement (AIM), told the (Baltimore) *Sun*. "Why don't they just call them the Atlanta Bishops? They don't issue crucifixes when people come in the gate. They don't wave crucifixes when someone hits a homer. Why don't they call them the Klansmen, so they all wear sheets? How would the American people feel about that? During the seventh-inning stretch, they could hang Jews and blacks."

The protests, which many consider the first united opposition to Indian sports nicknames, certainly put Jane Fonda in an uncomfortable position. The onetime activist sat alongside Turner, her husband, cheering for the Braves, despite that she had been arrested as part of an AIM protest in Seattle in 1970. When asked how he felt when he saw Fonda doing The Chop, Bellecourt replied, "I feel betrayed."

The chanting became louder as the Braves put two men on with two out in the bottom of the tenth, only to see pinch-hitter Jeff Blauser line out to Chuck Knoblauch at second. As the innings went by, Twins manager Tom Kelly kept a parade of pinch-hitters going up to the plate. Disgruntled about the lack of a designated hitter in the National League ballparks, Kelly was still determined to deploy his deep bench and keep his pitchers from being a laughingstock with a bat in hand. Here in Game Three, Kelly used his pinch-hitters in the following order: Gene Larkin (sixth inning), Brian Harper (eighth), Chili Davis (eighth), Mike Pagliarulo (ninth), Randy Bush (ninth), Paul Sorrento (tenth), Al Newman (eleventh), and Rick Aguilera (twelfth). Yes, that last guy is a pitcher.

Near the end of the regular season Kelly ordered his pitchers to take batting practice under the watchful eye of hitting coach Terry Crowley. Aguilera, who had come over from an occasional at-bat in the National League, remembered the sessions becoming pretty competitive, reminding him of times with the Mets when Dwight Gooden, Ron Darling, and even Sid Fernandez swung away for team bragging rights. For his part, Kelly wasn't nearly as impressed with most of the Twins' pitchers when they had a bat in hand. "We got through [Game Three] with only one pitcher getting embarrassed," Kelly said.

That was starter Scott Erickson, who struck out on three pitches in the third inning.

"We saved everybody else from that, and I felt good about that," the Twins' manager added. "I didn't want my pitchers to go up there and have to hit. It was a joke. [They] had no chance."

With so much mixing and matching, Kelly used a record eight pinch-hitters and a record number of twenty-three players in the ballgame. The only guys who didn't see action in Game Three for the Twins were pitchers Kevin Tapani and Jack Morris, who was scheduled to pitch the next evening.

Aguilera was warming up to pitch the bottom of the twelfth when the bullpen phone rang, asking whether he wanted to swing the bat too. Aguilera said sure, and moments later he ran down to the Twins' dugout to put on a helmet and try to find a bat. "I grabbed the lightest bat that I could find," he said. "To this day I don't recall whose bat it was."

As the top of the twelfth inning unfolded the Twins had another major opportunity to go up three games to zip in the best-of-seven series. With one out, Gladden singled to right, and Knoblauch reached on an error by Braves second baseman Mark Lemke. Kent Hrbek, who was being constantly jeered by the Atlanta fans for his tussle with Ron Gant in Game Two, struck out in short order. When the Braves intentionally walked Kirby Puckett, that left the bases loaded with two out and the pitcher's spot coming up. Kelly figured his closer, Aguilera, could do a better job at the plate than Mark Guthrie, who had never swung a bat in a big-league game to this point in his career. Even though Aguilera had last batted in 1989, he did have a .203 career average, with three home runs and eleven RBIs, and he was originally signed as a shortstop. As a result, the Twins' closer became the first pitcher to pinch-hit in a World Series game since 1965, when the Dodgers' Don Drysdale faced the Twins' Jim Kaat. In addition, Aguilera was the first pitcher to pinch-hit in the Fall Classic since the advent of the designated hitter in 1973.

As Aguilera stepped into the batters' box—Aguilera and Greg Olson had once been in the Mets' organization together—he jokingly asked catcher Olson what Braves reliever Jim Clancy was going to throw him. Olson replied that they planned to come right at him, and, indeed, Clancy's first pitch was a hard slider.

"Believe it or not, I felt pretty comfortable in that at-bat," Aguilera recalled. "I was seeing the ball."

Clancy's first pitch, a slider in the dirt, was blocked nicely by Olson. The second offering was a fastball on the outside corner. Years later Aguilera wondered whether he should have swung at that one, perhaps flared it to right field. But the bat sat on his shoulder for that offering. Clancy's third pitch was another fastball, moving over the inside part of the plate, and Aguilera went for it.

"I got a decent swing on it, but I got jammed a little bit," he said. "Not enough to get it in the gap. I knew that I made pretty good contact, so it was not going to bloop in over the shortstop's head. It was hit better than that. But I also knew it probably wasn't hit hard enough to get in the gap or get over Ron Gant's head. So it was decent contact and put your head down and run to first base. [Clancy] just got a little bit inside on me."

In the end Aguilera gave a good account of himself, driving a ball fairly deep to center field, where Gant had to make a running catch. Still, it went down as nothing more than another out in the scorebook, and the Twins had left the bases loaded.

"I surprised a few people," Aguilera added. "I know Crowley was impressed. I didn't embarrass myself, and I didn't embarrass TK for putting me in there. In looking back on it I'm more disappointed about how I did on the mound in the next inning."

Kelly added, "We tried to win the game within a nine- or ten-inning structure, and we couldn't get the job done. We had our chances. We had the hitters we wanted up in those situations, but they just couldn't get the job done."

Chili Davis, one of the few pinch-hitters to deliver on this night, added, "We get those opportunities again, and I guarantee you we get some runs."

Aguilera's well-hit out also got Mark Lemke off the hook. The Braves' second baseman had stood with his head down, pawing the dirt with his feet after making the error on Knoblauch's grounder that put the winning run in scoring position in the top of the twelfth. When Cox went to the mound to make a pitching change, Lemke tried to push the word "goat" out of his mind. Teammates told him not to worry about it—keep his head up. Still, Lemke knew he had put the Braves "in a real tough situation."

Now that the Braves had wriggled out of the jam, Lemke would soon have the chance to redeem himself and, possibly, end Game Three. During the regular season Lemke had batted just .234, with a pair of home runs and twenty-three RBIs. He remained a utility guy who struggled so much that he sought out the advice of Terry Pendleton, the National League's Most Valuable Player in 1991, who told Lemke to put the regular season behind. "When the playoffs start nobody cares what you did back then," Pendleton said. "They only care about what you do in the playoffs and the World Series. That's what people remember."

Lemke took the veteran's advice so much to heart that he began using Pendleton's bats when the third baseman wasn't looking. "I guess you could say he had open range to them," Pendleton said. "Mine was a bigger bat than the one he'd been using—thirty-six inch, thirty-two ounces. With my bat he started to do what he was capable of doing."

Lemke remembered that he "was getting out on too many balls tailing away. So Terry and I talked, and he suggested that I go with a bigger bat, so I tried his. It was about two inches longer and several ounces heavier than mine, and sure enough I was able to get good wood on those outside pitches. With that bat I began to flair them the opposite way, and with each hit that postseason my confidence really grew."

The twelfth inning soon became one curious situation heaped upon another for Aguilera. Not only had the Twins' closer pinch-hit, almost giving the Twins the lead, but now he began the inning of a tie game— not with the lead, which closers usually prefer. Also, he was making his third appearance in a row, realizing that he would probably need to keep pitching until the game was decided. Aguilera knew that he was in it for the long haul, ready for "two, three, or more innings," he said. "I knew I was the last guy."

Later Aguilera admittedly became too fine with his pitches.

With one out in the bottom of the twelfth, David Justice singled and stole second after Brian Hunter popped out. The theft was the Braves' first stolen base of the series, underscoring Nixon's absence. Olsen drew a walk off Aguilera, and that brought Lemke up with two on, two out, and the hometown Chop crowd raising a real ruckus now.

Batting left-handed against Aguilera, Lemke worked the count to 1–1. Aguilera threw him a pitch on the outer half of the plate, and Lemke stroked it the opposite way. As the crowd roared, the ball dropped in front of Twins left fielder Dan Gladden, who came up throwing. Charging around third base, Justice cut to the inside and slid in just ahead of Harper, who was trying to apply the tag.

Safe at the plate, Justice had won the game for the Braves, and Lemke's hit had given the hometown team its first World Series victory ever in the South.

"We've been on such a roller coaster ride," Olson said afterward. "We really felt if we could win this game, we could win the Series. But if we lost, who knows what would happen."

"The weirdest thing in this game is that Clancy gets the win for getting out a pitcher," said Kevin Tapani, one of the few Twins who didn't play in Game Three.

The Twins' Randy Bush added, "It could have been a storybook ending for Aggie. But nobody here is down. If anything, you can't wait to play again after a game like that."

That said, the Twins knew they had missed a golden opportunity to go up three games to none in the Series. In battling back to win in extra innings, the Braves had guaranteed that a more boisterous crowd of Tomahawk Choppers would be back tomorrow night.

———

**FINAL SCORE: BRAVES 5, TWINS 4**

|     | 1 | 2 | 3 | 4 | 5 | 6 | 7 | 8 | 9 | 10 | 11 | 12 | R | H | E |
|-----|---|---|---|---|---|---|---|---|---|----|----|----|---|---|---|
| MIN | 1 | 0 | 0 | 0 | 0 | 0 | 1 | 2 | 0 | 0  | 0  | 0  | 4 | 10 | 1 |
| ATL | 0 | 1 | 0 | 1 | 2 | 0 | 0 | 0 | 0 | 0  | 0  | 1  | 5 | 8 | 2 |

ATTENDANCE: **50,878**     LENGTH OF GAME: **4 HOURS, 4 MINUTES**

# Game Four

WEDNESDAY, OCTOBER 23, 1991
AT ATLANTA-FULTON COUNTY STADIUM
ATLANTA, GEORGIA

Less than twenty-four hours after the Braves' extra-inning victory the two teams were ready to go back at it, with a pitching matchup between youth and experience. Atlanta's John Smoltz was eager to take on his boyhood idol, Jack Morris. Interested parties, though, couldn't quite leave last night's game in the rearview mirror. Twins manager Tom Kelly said that if Game Three had gone on much longer, he would have had outfielder Dan Gladden pitch and shifted reliever Rick Aguilera to the outfield.

"If I'd gone to the mound," Gladden said, "I would have been the most underpaid pitcher out there."

Commissioner Fay Vincent declared that Game Three had been one of the best ever played in postseason history, comparing it with Carlton Fisk's home run in the 1975 World Series, the 1986 National League Championship Series between the New York Mets and Houston Astros, and Kirk Gibson's dramatic homer off Dennis Eckersley in the 1988 World Series.

Vincent added that the World Series coming to Atlanta and the South for the first time gave this series "a freshness. The tomahawking, the chanting makes it special."

Undoubtedly, the Twins disagreed.

In Game Four Minnesota again took the early lead as Mike Pagliarulo singled in Harper, who had doubled to lead off the top of the second inning.

In the bottom of the third inning Morris was sailing along, striking out Smoltz and Lonnie Smith. He seemed to be in control until Terry Pendleton smacked a 3–1 fastball, driving it out for a home run to right-center field. The game was tied at 1–1 and promised to be another tense one.

"That's the way almost every game of that Series was," Scott Leius remembered. "Soon you just kind of fell into it, just going from pitch to pitch, inning to inning, knowing you'd come out the other end—someday, somehow."

By the bottom of the fifth Morris was falling behind too many Atlanta batters. Smith led off the inning with a single to left field. In the stands Jane Fonda sat alongside Braves owner Ted Turner, both of them wearing Atlanta ballcaps, and to Turner's left was former president Jimmy Carter. They cheered as Smith stole second base, moving into scoring position for Pendleton, who had homered two innings earlier. The National League MVP smoked a line drive to center field, which sailed over Kirby Puckett's head. In a baserunning blunder and a harbinger of what was to come, Smith mistakenly tagged up. As a result, he was at least a step late rounding third base as Braves third-base coach Jimy Williams waved him toward home.

Chuck Knoblauch took the relay throw from Puckett and briefly appeared surprised that Smith was even trying to score on the play. Knoblauch collected himself and threw accurately to Harper at home plate. The ball arrived on a difficult in-between hop the instant before

Smith ran headlong into Harper, who was on his knees. The force of the collision knocked Harper onto his back, with Smith flying over the top of him.

"I thought Kirby [Puckett] was going to catch it, so I got a few steps down the line," Smith recalled. "When I saw it drop in I knew I had to kick in the speed. I came around third, and I saw Brian catch the ball. I couldn't go around him and I couldn't go under him because he was down."

A close play at the plate ranks among baseball's classic moments. Home runs certainly linger in the mind, often due to their unexpected nature, that dry crack of a branch in the woods. Great pitching performances, shutouts, no-hitters, and alike can creep up on us over the course of a game, with the magnitude of what's at stake revealing itself only in the late innings when everything is on the line. In comparison, a play at the plate remains easily understood by the most casual of fans and certainly appreciated by longtime observers. The base runner rounds third, here comes the throw, and so much is at stake. Game Four of the 1991 World Series offered three magnificent plays at the plate involving Twins catcher Brian Harper. "I think back now, look at the replays, and I became the guy in the right place at the wrong time," he said. "Or maybe it was the wrong place at the right time."

Although Harper spent the game becoming part punching bag, part hockey goalie, part hit-and-run victim, he later said he was never really hurt on any of the key plays in Game Four. "Maybe it's the adrenaline of playing in a game like this," he said. "But I never saw stars. Not on any of them."

Ray Fosse, Rick Dempsey, Buster Posey, and Buck Martinez are a few of the catchers who have been seriously injured in collisions at home plate over the years. In Martinez's case he suffered a broken ankle and somehow hung in there long enough to make not just one but two putouts. It happened on July 9, 1985, with the Toronto Blue Jays visiting Seattle. With the Mariners' Phil Bradley on second base,

Gorman Thomas singled to right field. In a violent collision at home, Bradley was out as he ran over Martinez, breaking the catcher's ankle.

As the play continued, Thomas rambled for third base. Despite being unable to stand up, as the broken ankle was incapable of bearing any weight, Martinez attempted to throw Thomas out. For his trouble he saw his errant throw sail into left field, where Blue Jays outfielder George Bell retrieved it. Now, a real teammate would have perhaps hung on to the ball or thrown it to somebody else. But with Thomas now heading for the plate, Bell decided to peg it home. Thanks for nothing, right? Martinez somehow caught the ball while still sitting down, and finally somebody showed some heart or simple common sense as Thomas didn't slide into his friend. (He and Martinez had been teammates in Milwaukee.)

That meant the Blue Jays catcher could tag his old buddy for the final out of the inning—to boos from some in the crowd—and then be removed from the field on a stretcher. Martinez went on to be the team's broadcaster and, for a brief time, the Blue Jays' manager. He also wrote a couple of books, including *Worst to First*, about Toronto capturing its first division title in 1985.

"Sometimes playing catcher means putting yourself out there," he said. "Then you're praying something terrible doesn't happen."

In Game Four of the 1991 Series Harper's teammates were left to marvel at their catcher's courage and lousy luck. "He's going to be sore tomorrow," Kirby Puckett said. "I guarantee you."

"We hit straight on," Harper said of his first collision with Smith. "We pretty much hit shoulder to shoulder. He got me pretty good."

Somehow the Twins' catcher held on to the ball—jumping to his feet and gripping it in his bare hand.

"How did I hang on to the ball?" Harper later said. "I still don't really know. It's being in the moment, I guess."

Tim McCarver, a former big-league catcher, told his television audience, "That was as about a tough a collision as you'll see in a baseball game."

On the play Pendleton moved to third base, and with Ron Gant coming to the plate, the Twins had no choice but to bring their infield in, trying again to cut off the go-ahead run. When Gant walked, the Braves had two men on with one out—a situation that put Harper back in the spotlight again.

Morris bounced an 0–1 pitch to David Justice and Pendleton headed for home, looking to score. In hindsight the ball didn't bounce far enough from the plate for Pendleton to take this kind of chance. Harper scrambled after the ball, and with Pendleton coming down the line, he dove to the opposite side of home plate, tagging out the Braves' base runner. Knowing he had made a mistake, Pendleton walked to the Braves' dugout, muttering to himself.

Harper, a guy who several ballclubs deemed didn't catch all that well, had made a pair of defensive gems in the same inning. Drafted by the Angels in 1977, Harper performed exceptionally in the minor leagues, hitting .293 at Quad Cities and .315 in El Paso. Inexplicably, after he hit .350 with 122 RBI at Salt Lake City, the Angels traded him to Pittsburgh, which already had established catchers in Tony Peña and Steve Nicosia. With no room on the roster, Harper tried unsuccessfully to play first base and the outfield. When that didn't work out, Harper began a magical mystery tour of the majors, seeking a job. By the time he reached Minnesota, Harper was a bona fide journeyman after failing to catch on with St. Louis, Detroit, and Oakland. "He lost a lot of his career to other people's stupidity," statistician Bill James later wrote. "He was slow, didn't have real power, didn't walk and didn't throw well, but he could hit .300 in his sleep."

Growing up in southern California, Harper had also played football in high school, and he remembered being tackled "a lot"—nothing on the gridiron compared to the pounding he would take in Game Four, though.

They say playing catcher gives one "God's view" of the game of baseball. Everything plays out in front of you, and nobody is more involved in the action. Being front and center can come with a price. Not only are there the balls in the dirt, bouncing off all parts of your body, a catcher also needs to become part shrink, part confidant in calling the pitches for a staff that invariably comes with individuals of various temperaments and personalities. Then, to top it all off, you're a target. A guy who's supposed to stand in there no matter what, even if the other guy, the base runner who just barreled into you, will often be the one the crowd cheers after the play at the plate.

"A catcher must want to catch," Hall of Famer Bill Dickey once said. "He must make up his mind that it isn't the terrible job it is painted, and that he isn't going to say every day, 'Why, oh why with so many other positions in baseball did I take up this one?'"

Harper had long ago made his pact with this devil. He didn't care about the price of playing behind the plate as long as he could win a place on a major-league roster. "By the time I got to the Twins I was satisfied if I could just be a backup catcher," he said. "I had almost given up being an everyday player. So to have a chance to catch, to be in the everyday lineup in the World Series, I knew how precious that was by that point in my career."

Other players acknowledge, perhaps begrudgingly, what a catcher goes through on a daily basis. "I knew that Brian was strong because I played with him in St. Louis," Lonnie Smith said. "I found how strong he was that night, in that game."

But there are always a few who will take advantage of the situation, twist the meaning of old school and hard ball to their own advantage. In part that's why some old-timers don't think much of Pete Rose. In the 1970 All-Star Game, in what many consider an exhibition, or a "friendly," to use soccer terminology, the Reds' star plowed into catcher Ray Fosse in a play similar to the Smith-Harper collision. The media hailed Rose for scoring the game's deciding run. Fosse, who played for the in-state rival Cleveland Indians, was never the same player after fracturing his shoulder. "I knew I was hurt, but didn't know to what extent," Fosse said decades later. "I don't care if someone is a hundred and fifty pounds or three hundred pounds—if they are coming full blast at you while you are standing still and they hit you, you are going to feel it. There was no fake about it."

———

A few seasons after I joined *Baseball Weekly* I wrote that it was time to allow Rose, baseball's all-time hits leader, into the National Baseball Hall of Fame and Museum in Cooperstown, New York. Although Rose had gambled on baseball, we should let bygones be bygones. After all, he had just served five months in prison for income tax evasion in January 1991. Rose had suffered enough, I wrote. In the days after that column I heard from several Hall of Famers. Pretty much they told me I was dead wrong and didn't know what I was talking about. Several urged me to have an audience with John Dowd, the one who had investigated Rose's activities for Major League Baseball.

Back then Dowd's office window overlooked New Hampshire Avenue, just off Dupont Circle in a high-rent section of Washington, DC. The man who busted Rose was waiting for me that morning. Moments after shaking hands he handed me a 225-page report—the boiled-down version of the Rose investigation.

"The actual report is up here," he said, pointing to the top shelf of his bookcase. "What you have there is the summary. I must have sent out at least five thousand copies of this over the years, trying to set people straight."

Born in Brockton, Massachusetts, the mill city that produced boxers Rocky Marciano and Marvin Hagler, Dowd brought a similar combative style to the courtroom. "It's all crap, and crap goes nowhere" was how he once characterized a rival's case against a recent client. To Dowd, law was a full-contact game. Although such an approach didn't make many friends, his peers did admire how much evidence he could assemble effectively in a hurry.

Early in 1989 Commissioner A. Bartlett Giamatti and his number-two man, Fay Vincent, met at the Hay-Adams Hotel in Washington. For months it had been rumored that Rose was deeply involved with gamblers in the Midwest and New York City. Rose had already appeared before Peter Ueberroth, the previous commissioner, to discuss such accusations and whispers. In that meeting Rose flatly denied that he had bet on baseball or that he had any problems at all with any bookies. Ueberroth may have doubted Rose's claims of innocence, but with only months left in his tenure the ongoing commissioner didn't appear eager for a full-scale investigation. That left it to Giamatti, the former president of Yale University and a distinguished scholar of Renaissance literature, to pick up the pieces and decide what to do about Peter Edward Rose.

At the Hay-Adams Giamatti asked Vincent whether he knew somebody who could get to the bottom of this Rose mess and do it in a hurry. Vincent suggested Dowd.

The two of them had first met during a trial years earlier in Richmond. While initially put off by Dowd's take-no-prisoners approach, Vincent came away convinced that Dowd would do anything and everything to ferret out the truth. From the Hay-Adams Giamatti phoned Dowd at his home in suburban Virginia. The next morning, backed up by a dozen other investigators, including Kevin Hallinan, Major League Baseball's director of security, Dowd was on his way to Cincinnati to begin the Rose inquiry.

Dowd grew up a big baseball fan. He, like Giamatti, followed the Boston Red Sox as a boy. Even though Dowd knew Rose only from afar, he liked what he saw. "The impression in my mind was a guy who didn't have natural ability but was Charlie Hustle," Dowd recalled. "I admire people like that. There are people a lot smarter than me out there, but I can outwork anybody."

And once his plane landed in Cincinnati, that's what Dowd proceeded to do: outhustle the Hit King. Within weeks Dowd and his investigative team had assembled an impressive stack of circumstantial evidence. Dowd participated in every interview. Key witnesses, such as Paul Janszen and Ronald Peters, were interviewed a minimum of three times each. Rose himself was interviewed over two days at a nuns' convent in Dayton, Ohio. Through it all Dowd allowed Rose and his lawyers to see every bit of evidence against Charlie Hustle. "That was Bart's doing," Dowd said of the former commissioner. "The idea was not to grill [Rose] but to let him see all the evidence and let him have a chance to answer. It's unlike anything I've ever done in my life.

"I told [Rose] everything. That was the brilliance of Bart's plan. We had no secrets. We weren't going to play a normal detective-prosecutor kind of game. The way we did it took away any complaint of unfairness."

Giamatti's hope was that sooner or later the amount and detail of the evidence against him would overwhelm Rose and he would throw himself upon the commissioner's mercy. "We wanted him to come to Jesus," Dowd said. "[Then] we could have worked with him."

If Rose had come forward, Dowd later said, Giamatti "would have sat him down for two to five years." After that Rose could have returned to baseball. Today he would be enshrined in the Hall of Fame, with his bronze plaque hanging with the game's other immortals.

Looking back upon the investigation Dowd recalled only one incident in which Rose appeared ready to acknowledge his widespread and deep gambling involvement. The two-day session at the convent took place in the nuns' cafeteria. First, Dowd revealed to Rose that the investigation knew about the huge sums he was putting down on games, especially baseball games.

"We're talking about two, three, four thousand a game," said Dowd, who cut his teeth busting racketeers. That led to the $500,000 Rose owed to bookies in New York. "The wise guys in New York owned him," Dowd added. "Essentially what you had was the manager of the [Cincinnati] Reds indebted."

Handwriting experts and a wealth of phone records supported this assertion. Calls were made to the same numbers, to the same bookies, before home or away games involving the Reds. It was at this point that Dowd remembered Rose "turning a little green." Still, the Hit King refused to admit at the time that he had done anything wrong or had a gambling problem. Dowd pushed Rose's attorneys to let him talk with Rose alone.

"We would have taken a walk on the beach or in the woods, some kind of private meeting," Dowd recalled. "I would have said to Pete, 'We've got you. We've got you cold. Look, why don't you just come in?' All Pete had to do was say, 'Help me.'"

But Rose's representatives nixed a private meeting with Dowd or any other member of the investigative team.

In May 1989 Dowd delivered his 225-page report, with more than two thousand pages of transcribed interviews and supporting exhibits, to Giamatti. The commissioner read over it three times in one day. Except for the questionable use of a semicolon, he told Dowd it was perfect. The report cost $3 million to produce. Over roughly the same time period Rose spent nearly $2 million on attorneys. This high-priced game of legal chicken soon backed both sides into their respective corners. Rose still refused to admit that he had a problem with big-stakes gambling. Giamatti, armed with Dowd's exhaustive report, had no choice but to play hardball with the all-time hits leader. Since 1919, when the "Black Sox" conspired to throw the World Series, betting on baseball has been the game's worst and most feared sin, a mistake that can harm the very integrity of the game.

In August 1989 the two sides began settlement talks. It was agreed that Rose would be placed on the ineligible list. His suspension would be called permanent, but he could apply for reinstatement after one year. Rose's attorneys were able to insert a key sentence in the five-page report. "Nothing in this agreement shall be deemed either an admission or a denial by Peter Edward Rose of the allegation that he bet on any major league baseball game," it read.

Dowd, who was present at that final meeting, emphasized that even though Giamatti allowed such language to be in the settlement papers, the commissioner told Rose and his attorneys that, if asked, he would acknowledge that Rose had gambled on baseball. Sure enough, the first question at the news conference that followed was, "Did Rose bet on baseball?"

Giamatti began, "In the absence of a hearing and therefore in the absence of evidence to the contrary . . . " He paused, before continuing, "I am confronted by the factual record of Mr. Dowd. On the basis of that, yes, I have concluded he bet on baseball."

Afterward, back in Giamatti's office, Dowd recalled the phone "ringing off the hook. Ballplayers were calling in from all over the country, telling Bart that he did the right thing."

Eight days after that news conference at the New York Hilton, Giamatti died of a heart attack. He was succeeded by Vincent, who would be forced from the commissionership by the owners a year after the 1991 World Series—an event that set the stage for the pending labor war.

With Giamatti dead, Vincent soon to be shown the door by the owners, it was left to Dowd to give the counterpoint to Rose's ongoing campaign to be reinstated. To this day Dowd considers the Rose situation to be a tragedy of major proportions. "He had several openings," Dowd said. "Even when Fay became commissioner, he still could have walked in there and said, 'I've got a terrible, terrible habit. By God, I've gambled on the Reds.' I think baseball would have acted very positively. But every year we are treated to what I call the PR wave. He goes on radio and television, and then I go back on radio and television and pull out my old reports."

In 1990 Rose pled guilty to two counts of filing false tax returns. He was released early the next year and performed one thousand hours of community service in the Cincinnati inner-city schools. Also in 1991, the board of directors for the National Baseball Hall of Fame and Museum in Cooperstown, New York, barred Rose from appearing on the Hall's ballot. Still, he received forty-one write-in votes. Six years later Rose applied for reinstatement, but it wouldn't be until 2002 that he admitted his gambling activities to Commissioner Bud Selig.

Since then some former ballplayers, including old teammates, decided Rose had suffered enough. "I think if you're going to allow guys with PEDs on the ballot," former teammate and Hall of Fame second baseman Joe Morgan told *USA Today*, "then we have to allow him to be on the ballot. . . . I think they have to take a second look at Pete now that this has come out."

In September 2013 Rose was allowed to join with the starting lineup of the Cincinnati Reds' back-to-back champions in 1975–1976 for the unveiling of a bronze sculpture of Morgan.

———

Growing up in central New York, Mark Lemke collected baseball cards, with his favorites being of Reggie Jackson, Johnny Bench, and Pete Rose. For the longest time those cards appeared to be as close as the utility infielder would ever come to being in the major leagues. A twenty-seventh-round draft pick by the Atlanta Braves in 1983, Lemke spent five-plus seasons in the minor leagues. Listed generously at five-foot-ten, 167 pounds, the switch-hitting infielder was often sent down in spring training. Although such demotions grated on him, Lemke played on, even if his teams were a long way away from the parent club in Atlanta.

"I wanted to play this game," he said. "I'd heard that I wasn't big enough. But I'd always been able to pretty much block that all out. Being a major league baseball player, that's what I thought I always wanted to be ever since I can remember. I always wanted to make it to the big leagues, but more than anything I just wanted the chance to see how far I could go in this game."

His approach began back home in Utica, a town of sixty-two thousand between Albany and Syracuse. In these parts one learned to just play even if it meant basketball (Lemke's other favorite sport) outdoors in freezing temperatures when the school janitor refused to unlock the gym. Or learning to switch-hit because the field where Lemke and his buddies played pickup games had too many trees in left field and drives in that direction were deemed long outs. That ballpark was on the grounds of the Mohawk Valley Psychiatric Center, beside the trees in left field, and sometimes games were halted so the mental patients could take a stroll. "I go back to that field sometimes now, and I laugh," Lemke told the *New York Times*. "It looks so small, and we used to think it was so big. It was a lot of fun. It was a beautiful place."

Back then sports moved with the seasons in this part of the world, and Lemke later realized this was becoming increasingly unusual. "When it became spring," he recalled, "warm enough to play ball, you were really excited about it. Sometimes I feel sorry for kids today, especially the ones in a warm-weather climate. They get overexposed to one sport too often, and then it's not much fun. I can safely say I was more interested in basketball than baseball growing up, but you're never sure how things are going to work out.

"I believe I was in eighth grade when Andy Van Slyke got drafted in baseball, and we couldn't believe it. Sure he was from Utica, but we knew Andy Van Slyke as a basketball player, not a baseball player. Back then you played everything."

Playing just for the joy of playing became about the only thing Lemke had going for him early in his pro career. After several solid seasons in the minors, including winning All-Star honors in the Gulf Coast League, Lemke's trajectory stalled. In 1985 he hit .216 in the South Atlantic League and his professional career appeared to be coming to an end. But then Lemke hit a team-best eighteen home runs the following season, and by 1990 he had somehow climbed through the Braves' minor-league system to become a part-time player with the big-league club in Atlanta.

As with Brian Harper, being a backup in the big leagues was just fine with Lemke. He worked hard at becoming a proficient pinch-hitter and late-inning defensive replacement. In 1991 he hit a .333 as a pinch-hitter and made only ten errors in 136 games. When Jeff Treadway, the Braves' regular second baseman, was sidelined with a wrist injury, Lemke moved into the starting lineup. During the final weeks of the 1991 regular season, as the Braves surged past Los Angeles, Lemke had several key hits, and his performance continued into the postseason.

Atlanta manager Bobby Cox often called Lemke "Dirt," a term of affection and accuracy because Lemke loved to get his jersey dirty, perhaps as much as his boyhood hero, Pete Rose.

"It doesn't shock anyone on this team that he has hit," Cox said. "He's paid for his defense, sure, and in that role he can turn the double play as well as anyone. But he can hit. He hit in the minors, he's hit in spots here."

When it came to the 1991 Series, when he became a household name Lemke explained that every "player is going to have a hot streak in a season. I guess I waited all season for mine."

———

In the seventh inning of Game Four the Twins and Braves traded solo home runs. Mike Pagliarulo homered to right field. The run batted in was Pagliarulo's second of the evening and a mistake by John Smoltz. Using his curveball to get ahead in the count, Smoltz came inside with a fastball, and Pagliarulo turned on the pitch, driving the ball out of the park. For a moment it appeared that the Twins would capture their first World Series road victory since 1925, when they were the Washington Senators and Walter Johnson pitched them to victory against the Pittsburgh Pirates. Yet that tenuous grasp on the past soon slipped away. Minnesota starter Jack Morris, who, with his bushy moustache and prickly disposition, looked like he could have pitched in the Roaring Twenties, had already been lifted from the game. Seeing a chance to open up a bigger lead, Tom Kelly pinch-hit Gene Larkin for Morris in the top of the seventh inning. So it fell to the Twins' bullpen to bring this one home, with Carl Willis now taking the mound.

This right-hander was rumored to throw an occasional spitball, and he got two outs before the Braves' Lonnie Smith stepped in. Smith blasted the first pitch he saw from Willis out to straightaway center field, and the game was tied again, this time at 2–2.

Without the interest of the Atlanta Braves and, specifically, manager Bobby Cox, Smith probably wouldn't have been in the major leagues in 1991. Due to a series of disastrous personal decisions and actions, the outfielder had worn out his welcome in Philadelphia, St. Louis, and Kansas City. For here was a guy who once tackled the Phillie Phanatic because the mascot wouldn't stop poking fun at him, testified against a teammate or two in a well-publicized drug trial, almost died from a cocaine overdose in a hotel room, and once seriously considered shooting his general manager.

The last incident occurred in 1987 after Smith was summoned to testify in the trial of Curtis Strong, the one-time clubhouse caterer convicted of dealing drugs to major leaguers. Heading into a new season, the only offer Smith received was a low-ball one from John Schuerholz, then the Royals' general manager. Smith appeared in just forty-eight games in the majors in 1987, hitting .251, and was released by Kansas City at the end of the year.

Back home in South Carolina, seemingly out of baseball for good, Smith plotted his revenge. He purchased a 9mm pistol at a pawn shop and schemed about how he could go to Kansas City and shoot Schuerholz in the stadium parking lot. Even though Smith didn't care whether he spent the rest of his life in prison, he held off and began to call teams, looking for a job instead. Only Atlanta general manager Bobby Cox showed any interest, so Smith began the 1988 season in the Braves' minor leagues. After hitting .300 with nine home runs in Richmond, the Braves' Triple-A affiliate, he was called up to the parent club and became the team's starting left fielder.

Cox once told explained that Smith "was a special player. He had absolutely no fear. He stood up on top of the plate and dared a pitcher to come inside. Then when they did, he didn't say a thing. And he'd knock the shortstop halfway into left field" to break up a double play.

Of course, when Cox became manager the following season Schuerholz was hired as the Braves' new general manager. For the most part
Smith steered clear of his old nemesis. Yet when the Braves clinched
the National League West in 1991, Smith and Schuerholz found themselves next to each other in the victorious clubhouse. Amid the champagne and celebration they hugged, even though Smith later said that
he "hated it. It was something that had to be done. It was a joyous time,
and I didn't want to disrupt it."

———

Before the series began, most experts graded the Minnesota bullpen
ahead of Atlanta's relief corps. But that hadn't proven to be the case
in the Fall Classic itself. Except for Alejandro Peña's gopher ball to
Chili Davis in Game Three, the Braves had come through in a big way.
They would again tonight, as Mark Wohlers and Mike Stanton kept
Minnesota off the scoreboard as the game headed to the bottom of the
ninth. The Twins went down in order in the top of the frame, thanks
in large part to David Justice's sliding catch in right field.

Needing to rest closer Rick Aguilera, Kelly turned to Willis and
then Mark Guthrie to close things out. The plan worked at first, but
Guthrie got into trouble when Lemke tripled to the gap in left-center
field. After driving in the winning run the night before, the Lemke hit
parade continued, as he now had three hits (single, double, and now
a triple) in Game Four.

"Mark Lemke, Mark Lemke," Gene Larkin repeated years later.
"Forget about Ron Gant or Terry Pendleton or even David Justice.
Mark Lemke was the hitter for the Braves that just wore us out."

———

Near the end of the 1991 regular season Jim Lefebvre reached me at
*Baseball Weekly*'s office in Rosslyn, Virginia.

"You trying to get me fired?" he asked.

"No," I replied, confused by what he was talking about.

"Because that last column of yours made me look pretty bad," he continued.

"I'm not trying to make anybody look bad," I replied.

"It's lousy enough that the local writers have it out for me," Lefebvre said. "You learn to expect that, but to get it from the national media just makes things that much worse on my end."

For the life of me I couldn't remember what I had written that was so awful in this manager's eyes.

"Do me a favor," Lefebvre added. "Before you write anything more, call me, okay?"

"Well . . . "

"Call the direct number to the team. I'll leave your name with the switchboard. They'll pass you right through to me."

With that, he hung up.

Curious, I looked at the previous week's issue, and all I found was a short item in which I second-guessed Lefebvre's use of his bullpen in a recent loss. What was going on to have Jim Lefebvre so concerned about what I was writing? After all, he was a colorful guy who knew the game. If anything, the powers that be in Seattle could have marketed him as the face of the franchise.

During his playing days in Los Angeles Lefebvre enjoyed playing minor characters on such popular television shows as *Gilligan's Island* and *Batman*. In 1965 he joined Wes Parker, Jim Gilliam, and Maury Wills in the Dodgers' all switch-hitter infield, and the courtship of his wife had demonstrated real determination. Lefebvre first glimpsed the beauty with long black hair and dressed in a purple miniskirt at a hotel coffee shop in Los Angeles the day after Christmas in 1968. He returned to the hotel for three consecutive mornings until he saw her again. Jean Bakke told Lefebvre that she didn't recognize him and didn't follow his team. "I was a Braves fan," she later explained, "and I hated anyone who'd beat them." But that didn't deter the ballplayer nicknamed "Frenchy." The two began dating and were married the night before the All-Star Game.

When Lefebvre's major-league playing career ended he signed with the Lotte Orions and became the first player to win a championship in America and Japan. After his playing days were over he was named batting coach for the Dodgers until he ran afoul of manager Tommy Lasorda and was replaced by Manny Mota before the 1980 season. The Lasorda-Lefebvre feud made headlines in Los Angeles when the two crossed paths during a taping at KNBC-TV. After his interview Lasorda waited for Lefebvre, calling him disloyal to the Dodgers. When Lasorda tried to take a swing at Lefebvre, the former coach split his old boss's lip.

"Lasorda left with blood on his face, and Lefebvre left with a smile on his," said sportscaster Steve Somers.

Lasorda later claimed that Lefebvre had sucker-punched him. Yet Lefebvre told the *Los Angeles Times*, "Well, I'll tell you what, it was the sucker who got punched all right."

Lefebvre recalled that his former manager took off his watch and suit jacket before trying to land the first punch in a vacant studio in Burbank. "Then I decked him. His lip was bleeding, and it definitely wasn't bleeding Dodger blue. He kept saying, 'Look what you've done to me, look what you've done to me. I'll sue.' The only regret I had then was that I knew I'd never be able to wear a Dodger uniform again."

Few regrets, a guy willing to stand on principle—Jim Lefebvre was the kind of manager who could really rally a ballclub. Certainly he couldn't be worried about holding on to his job, could he? But then I looked at the latest standings, with the Mariners a half-dozen or so games behind the Twins in the American League West. In 1991 more and more major-league managers found themselves under the gun. A major shift was taking place in how they were judged and, ultimately, rated. Ownership arguably held them to higher standard—perhaps an unfair one.

A record fourteen managers would be fired in 1991. The Cubs went through two skippers all by themselves this season. The long list of dismissals had begun in April, only a few weeks into the season, when Philadelphia let go Nick Leyva. The pink slips really started to fly when three managers—the Cubs' Don Zimmer, the Royals' John Wathan, and the Orioles' Frank Robinson—were fired on consecutive days a month later. By midseason seven teams had decided to make a change.

"With free agents, owners put out a lot of money and expect instant results," Robinson told *Baseball America* after his dismissal. "But there's no guarantee. These people still have to execute, but what we have now is a society syndrome of win or else."

Despite leading the St. Louis Cardinals to a winning record (84–78) after Whitey Herzog quit the season before, Joe Torre knew that he wouldn't be cut any slack. "If we don't do well next year, if we start out under .500, guys are going be out for my scalp," he said at the time. "I understand that. It goes with the job. It has nothing to do with being fair."

As the national pastime gained a corporate identity, with Disney and the Tribune Company buying big-league franchises, the new bosses often couldn't understand why what worked in other areas of industry regularly fell flat in baseball. "You have people in ownership who aren't around baseball," Detroit manager Sparky Anderson said. "They understand tire companies or department stores."

Second-guessing and the concept of "win now or else" spread throughout the game, with managers becoming the convenient fall guys. After all, it's easier to blame and fire the manager than reconstruct an entire twenty-five-man roster. As Don Zimmer explained, the new wave of ownership didn't really want to understand the game's nuances. On paper, for example, Ryne Sandberg certainly had the numbers to bat third in the Chicago lineup. Yet the All-Star second baseman was more comfortable batting second, so that's where Zimmer put him despite second-guessing from on high.

In many ways this was the beginning of "Moneyball," in which numbers and formulas superseded hands-on experience and personal insight. In fact, the first time I ever saw the term *Moneyball* was on the cover of *Baseball America* in late 1991, with the subhead, "Managers, GMs and Scouting Directors Come Under the Gun." In 1991, however, baseball had not quite fallen into two distinctive camps—the haves and the have-nots. Believe it or not, the Oakland Athletics, the ballclub that would eventually usher in the new days of "Moneyball," had one of the biggest payrolls in the game this season, at almost $34 million. The San Francisco Giants, California Angels, Boston Red Sox, New York Mets, and Los Angeles Dodgers were right up there at $30 million-plus, with the New York Yankees close behind. If you took away the Houston Astros at $12.8 million or the Baltimore Orioles at $15 million, most teams were still in the ballpark financially.

"This time was the end of payroll balance in baseball," said Ted Robinson, who was the Twins' television voice in 1991. "In that era you had Pittsburgh, Cincinnati, Oakland, and Minnesota winning division titles. Back then the financial disparity in terms of team payroll wasn't nearly as wide between teams as it is today."

One could argue this trend mirrored a growing rift in our society when it came to compensation and job security. Between 1982 and 2003 the top 5 percent of music acts took home 90 percent of all concert revenues. On the home front the richest households, the top 1 percent, doubled their share of the national income over roughly the same time frame, going from taking 10 percent to 20 percent of the riches. "We're increasingly becoming a winner-take-all economy, a phenomenon that the music industry has long experienced," said Alan Krueger, chairman of the White House Council of Economic Advisers, in an address given at the Rock and Roll Hall of Fame in Cleveland. He could have just as easily given the address at baseball's Hall of Fame in Cooperstown.

"Over recent decades technological change, globalization, and erosion of the institutions and practices that support shared prosperity in the US have put the middle class under increasing stress," he added. "The lucky and the talented—and it is often hard to tell the difference—have been doing better and better, while the vast major-ity has struggled to keep up."

Even after leading their respective teams to the World Series, Bobby Cox and Tom Kelly realized they didn't have much job secu-rity in this ever-shifting economy. The baseball world was changing too fast for any guarantees, especially for a pair of baseball lifers. Not only were fourteen managers fired in 1991, such longtime baseball men as Davey Johnson, Syd Thrift, Dallas Green, and Jack McKeon were shown the door too.

"It used to be if you became a general manager or a club presi-dent you'd have it for life if you wanted, you'd die with your boots on," Green told the *New York Times* in the fall of 1991. Green had led the Philadelphia Phillies to their first title in 1980 and tried his best to rebuild the Chicago Cubs before being let go. "But times have changed, feelings have changed. That's why I think it's almost impos-sible to conceive of there ever being dynasties or long-term managers or long-term general managers."

Baseball's new reality left Thrift, a former general manager with the Pittsburgh Pirates and New York Yankees, wondering about loy-alty and whether he had been played for a sap. "It used to be you'd turn down jobs to stay," he said. "I did that in Pittsburgh, turning down a five-year job with the Orioles. I wanted to stay because I thought I'd get to finish what I started. But I got fired. I guess that makes me loyal—and an idiot—doesn't it?"

Even Tom Kelly couldn't help thinking that the deck was becom-ing increasingly stacked against him too. Although he may have led his team to another World Series, what did the future really hold for a guy with only a high school degree, with corporate types becoming as thick as loons on a Minnesota lake in his sport?

"I always was encouraged to read more growing up," Kelly said, "but I spent more time in the pool hall and playing ball. I used to sit on the buses when we would travel as minor leaguers. There'd be guys reading. And there'd be guys doing some crossword puzzle. There'd be guys shooting the bull. And there was a card game. Well, I was in the card game. I wish I did more reading."

After Seattle ownership didn't land another right-handed bat, Lefebvre's Mariners couldn't keep pace with the Twins in the American League West in 1991. Although the Mariners improved in each of Lefebvre's three seasons at the helm, setting new attendance records, they didn't come close to winning the division. Even with an 83–79 record, the franchise's first winning season ever, Lefebvre was fired.

"I came to Seattle with a mission to make the M's a winner and build fan support," he said in a statement. "I feel that we've accomplished these goals."

It wasn't good enough. Not with the way things were changing in 1991.

———

With runners at first and third, with one out, the Twins brought in right-hander Steve Bedrosian, who, in 1987, had won the National League Cy Young Award with Philadelphia. Stepping in against him was journeyman Jerry Willard, who was more expendable than Mark Lemke within the Atlanta system. The catcher had spent ten years in the minors and been demoted to the Braves' Triple-A team in Richmond three times in this season alone. Now, with everything on the line and Lemke standing at third base as the potential winning run, the guy coming to the plate had collected only fourteen at-bats for Atlanta this season.

"I'd been with several clubs, and it just seemed for a long period of time like I never got a break from 1987 until now," Willard later explained. "I never got a chance to either be an everyday catcher, a backup catcher or something."

After falling behind 1–2 in the count, Willard lofted a high fly ball to right field, and the game appeared to be over, to be remembered as a gritty comeback victory by Atlanta against the Twins' bullpen.

As Lemke tagged up at third base, Minnesota outfielder Shane Mack retreated three steps. He squared nicely up on the ball and had it in his possession only for an instant before making a great throw through to home.

To everyone's amazement the ball and base runner seemed to be converging at the plate at nearly the same time. Lemke decided he wouldn't follow Lonnie Smith's example and try to mow Brian Harper over. Frankly, he wasn't big enough for that kind of play and he knew it.

Instead, Lemke dodged to the outside, away from the Twins' catcher. In a much closer play than many expected, when Willard first hit the ball, Harper caught Mack's throw and edged across the plate, trying to tag Lemke out. The pair definitely made contact, with Harper doing everything he could to cut Lemke off.

In a bang-bang play, home plate umpire Terry Tata ruled that Harper didn't touch Lemke with the glove or ball. Instead, the only contact occurred when Harper's elbow brushed against Lemke.

"He's out," Jack Buck told his television audience, "safe, safe, safe."

It didn't matter that Harper ended the close play sprawled out, holding his glove up high, showing the umpire that he still had the ball. The call was safe, and the hometown crowd roared the Braves' 3–2 victory.

Lemke remembered that when he "looked for Mack, somebody was blocking my view. When I finally got a glimpse of him, he already had the ball. I knew it was going to be close, and the only chance I had was to go around [Harper].

"We made contact, but he hit me with his arm. I knew there was no way I could knock him over. I knew it would take a perfect throw to get me."

Jogging up the first-base line, Willard realized how close he came to not being a World Series hero after all. "When I hit it I thought it was deep enough," he said, "but then I looked back at Lemke, and it looked like he got a bad jump. I couldn't see the play at the plate, but I saw the umpire give the safe sign, and I just said to myself, 'Thank God.'"

Upon Tata's safe call, Harper jumped in the air and threw his mitt to the ground in disgust. Later, in the Twins' clubhouse, he was more subdued and said if the replays indicated that Tata's call was correct, then "it was a helluva call."

Yet Harper maintained he had gotten such calls in the past. "I made contact and hung on to the ball," he said. "Often that's enough."

Across the visiting clubhouse Twins leader Kirby Puckett added, "I thought he was out. In a collision like that, where two players make contact, you're out most of the time. It was just like Smith's play. I've been called out on plays like that, right here in the big leagues."

Meanwhile, Jack Morris grumbled about Kelly lifting him for a pinch-hitter after six innings. "TK screwed up by taking me out," he later told *Sports Illustrated*. "We would have won it."

With the Series now tied at two games apiece, with another contest remaining in Atlanta, everybody was feeling the pressure.

———

### FINAL SCORE: BRAVES 3, TWINS 2

|     | 1 | 2 | 3 | 4 | 5 | 6 | 7 | 8 | 9 | R | H | E |
|-----|---|---|---|---|---|---|---|---|---|---|---|---|
| MIN | 0 | 1 | 0 | 0 | 0 | 0 | 1 | 0 | 0 | 2 | 7 | 0 |
| ATL | 0 | 0 | 1 | 0 | 0 | 0 | 1 | 0 | 1 | 3 | 8 | 0 |

ATTENDANCE: **50,878**     LENGTH OF GAME: **2 HOURS, 57 MINUTES**

# Game Five

THURSDAY, OCTOBER 24, 1991
AT ATLANTA-FULTON COUNTY STADIUM
ATLANTA, GEORGIA

When Chili Davis came to the Minnesota Twins he was told to put away his glove. His days of patrolling the outfield, which he had done with some flair earlier in his career with the San Francisco Giants, once leading the National League in assists, were now behind him. At thirty-one, Davis didn't run like he used do, and the switch-hitter was assigned to be the team's designated hitter for the season, playing 150 games at DH and making only two appearances in the field.

Back on September 29, the same day after the New York Mets fired manager Bud Harrelson, the eighth manager to be canned so far that year, the Twins found out they had clinched the American League West title while heading to the airport in Hamilton, Ontario, Canada. Hours earlier Minnesota had lost 2–1 to Toronto, the team they would soon defeat in the league championship series. When they received word that Seattle had downed second-place Chicago, the Twins were officially division champs and the first team in major-league history to go from last place to first place. The team buses pulled over on the Queen Elizabeth Way between Toronto and the Hamilton airport, and the players briefly congratulated each other. The next day, as the team finished its road trip in Chicago, Davis told manager Tom Kelly that he was open to playing some outfield in preparation of the team advancing to the World Series.

"I knew the National League parks from my days with the Giants," Davis recalled. "I told him, 'We've got a week now with nothing on the line, let me play the outfield, get some games at that position again.' I remember him looking at me and saying, 'Nah, we don't need you. You're our DH, and that's it.'"

A few weeks later, as the World Series began, Kelly was asked whether he was tempted to put Davis in the field, with the designated hitter unavailable for the games in Atlanta. "I wouldn't do that in a tie or close game," he replied, "because of the defensive liability."

Yet after the second consecutive close loss for the Twins in Atlanta, Kelly decided to roll the dice. Davis remembered that he and Kirby Puckett were walking out of the visitors' clubhouse after the 3–2 defeat in Game Four when Kelly shouted out, "Get your rest."

Davis turned and asked, "You're talking to Puck, right?"

Kelly shook his head. "No, you, number forty-four," he told Davis, "because you're in there tomorrow. You're starting in right field."

In that off-hand way, it became official: Davis would replace Shane Mack in the Twins' lineup and defensive alignment.

Before Game Five got underway Davis tried to make light of the situation, saying he was back in the field because Kelly "got sick and tired of seeing me on the bench."

When asked about his troublesome back Davis replied, "You don't know this, but three years ago I had surgery to remove my whole back. And now there's nothing left."

Decades later, though, Davis admitted he didn't get much sleep the night before Game Five. "This guy—I told him to work me into outfield at the end of the regular season," he said of Kelly. "And now he's going to stick me out there in friggin' Game Five of the World Series.

Until that point in that season about the only time I'd touched the outfield was during BP, shagging flies."

Game Five's starters, Kevin Tapani for the Twins and Tom Glavine for the Braves, were sharp early, and the contest remained scoreless into the bottom of the fourth inning. That's when Tapani fell behind Ron Gant, who laced a 2–0 fastball into left field for a single. David Justice followed by poking a Tapani fastball the opposite way, where it hit off the top of the fence and bounced into the seats for a home run. After Sid Bream walked and Greg Olson singled, Mark Lemke continued to be the man of the hour, lofting a fly ball deep to right field, out in Davis's direction.

As they like to say, the ball will find you in this game, often when you don't want to see it come calling. At first Davis appeared to be in a good position to make a rather difficult catch. But then Lemke's blast continued to carry, sailing closer to the fence. When Davis tried to chase down the ball, he never really caught up to it. As he neared the wall the ball glanced off his glove and dropped to the ground. Bream and Olson easily scored, and Lemke ended up on third base.

"I was playing him shallow, but that Lemke was hitting everything in sight," Davis remembered. "I had to go back after the ball. It hit the glove, and I almost caught it against the wall, only to see it pop out. Some people dogged me after that, saying any good outfielder would have made that play. But it was a tough play."

The official scorers agreed and awarded Lemke a triple. That said, Davis would soon face his share of criticism. "Thankfully, Johnny Bench came to my defense," Davis said, "reminding everybody that I'd once played center field at Candlestick Park. Bench told anybody who would listen that I was a good outfielder. I just hadn't been out there the whole season."

After Davis's adventure in right field, Tapani battled to finish the inning and left, trailing the game, 4–0. The Twins' starter didn't return for the bottom of the fifth inning.

"I had my chance to make a great play," Davis said. "I just didn't come through."

———

In 1991 what was going on away from the field sometimes superseded the action between the lines. Teams scrambled to fill out their rosters in large part because few ballplayers remained with a franchise for the entirety of their careers. In the growing era of free agency big money usually trumped any sense of team or civic loyalty, especially when even rookies were afforded high-powered counsel. In this new era Scott Boras soon became the most powerful sports agent in baseball and one of the most powerful individuals in sports. From 1983 to 1991 twenty-five of his clients were chosen in the first round of baseball's amateur draft, with most going in the top ten for soaring contracts and signing bonuses.

The son of a dairy farmer, Boras grew up in Elk Grove, California, just south of the state capital of Sacramento. From a young age he excelled at playing baseball and attended the University of the Pacific on a baseball scholarship, going on to play four seasons in the minor leagues. When bad knees ended his playing career Boras returned to school, first earning a degree in pharmacy and then a law degree back at Pacific. His first clients in baseball were Mike Fischlin, a former high school teammate who played infield for the Cleveland Indians, New York Yankees, and Houston Astros, as well as relief pitcher Bill Caudill, whom Boras met during his years in the minors.

From the start Boras proved to be adept at leveraging the marketplace, and he soon became a major headache for team owners. Big contracts and landmark deals were his signatures, in large part because Boras remembered when scouts had low-balled him when he was a minor-league player. The team representatives, whether they were a scout, a general manager, or even the owner, were never to be fully trusted, Boras told his clients. A ballplayer only had several key times in his entire career when he could compete on close to equal footing with management at the bargaining table—hence, the talk of leverage and waiting for the right moment to really strike a deal. Boras wasn't reluctant to tell a high school player to go to college if that meant possibly a larger payday—in essence more leverage down the road.

In the seasons leading up to the 1991 season Boras put together a series of deals that turned heads within the game. He negotiated a $1.5 million contract for his old friend Caudill that made the pitcher the second-highest paid reliever in the game at that time. In 1988 he represented a pair of young-gun pitchers (Andy Benes and the Braves' Steve Avery). They were among the top in the amateur draft, and Benes signed for a record $235,000 bonus. A year later Boras got a landmark $350,000 deal for pitcher Ben McDonald with the Baltimore Orioles, and in 1990 he scored a stunning $1.2 million package for Todd Van Poppel, another top-prospect pitcher, with the Oakland Athletics. With the high-powered agent calling the shots, Van Poppel received that kind of money, even though he was taken thirteen players after Atlanta made shortstop Larry "Chipper" Jones the top selection in 1990.

Some teams tried to avoid players Boras represented. They disliked spending so much and having their negotiations often stretch past the eleventh hour. "Ask anyone in the business: It's called The Boras Factor," San Diego Padres general manager Joe McIlvaine told *Baseball America*. "Almost every Boras client underachieves in the major leagues, and that's no accident. He takes the focus away from playing and puts it on the money."

Padres scouting director Randy Smith added that some ballclubs were ready to draw a line in the sand. "Boras changed the industry with the Van Poppel and McDonald deals," he said in August 1991, "but the industry is ready to say enough is enough."

That proved to be easier said than done, as most ballclubs found that sooner or later they had to deal with Boras because he represented many of the top prospects. That became only more apparent in 1991 as four of the top eight selections, including pitcher Brien Taylor, were Boras clients. A six-foot-three left-hander with a fastball clocked in the midnineties, Taylor was just the kind of arm big-league scouts fall in love with. Ironically, the Taylor family decided to go with Boras as its representative only after a phone call from an anonymous base-ball executive told them to steer clear of the high-powered agent. "Right then, I knew he was the man for us," said Bettie Taylor, Brien's mother.

Boras told the Taylor family that the marketplace had been set by the $1.2 million deal he had completed the year before for Van Pop-pel. The Taylors agreed and told the Yankees that they wouldn't set-tle for a penny less. The negotiations soon became a high-stakes game of chicken. At the time Commissioner Fay Vincent had banned New York Yankees owner George Steinbrenner from day-to-day involve-ment in his team's operations for paying a gambler named Howie Spira to dig up "dirt" on Dave Winfield. But that didn't stop the "Boss" from weighing in from the sidelines. With Boras telling the Yankees that Taylor would enroll in college, put off turning pro, if he didn't get the right deal, Steinbrenner went public with his frustration. Days before the deadline for Taylor to sign or go to college, Steinbrenner said that if the Yankees let the pitcher slip through their fingers, those respon-sible "should be shot."

Boras couldn't have planned it any better. The Yankees soon caved, giving Taylor a record $1.55 million signing bonus. The deal rippled throughout the amateur draft, with number-two choice Mike Kelly, an outfielder, receiving $575,000 from Atlanta. Meanwhile, the ask-ing price for the remaining Boras clients skyrocketed. Pitcher Kenny Henderson wanted $1 million and eventually enrolled at the Univer-sity of Miami when Milwaukee offered only $500,000. Pitcher John Burke did likewise after refusing $360,000 to sign with Houston.

As always with Boras, the negotiations were all about leverage. "The truth is this is not a risk," he said of the Taylor deal specifically and his philosophy overall. "If the player has a level of certainty, then pay for it."

———

In the bottom of the fifth inning of Game Five the Braves tacked on another run against Twins' reliever Terry Leach, a journeyman reliever who had seen his salary rise from $190,000 to $500,000 in recent seasons. In comparison, Atlanta starter Tom Glavine was destined to soon become the highest-paid player on the Braves and would see his salary triple from $775,000 to $2.9 million by the start of the next season.

In any event Glavine was staked to a 5–0 lead in Game Five and appeared ready to bring it home when he suddenly couldn't throw a strike to save his life.

With one out, the Braves' left-hander walked Chuck Knoblauch. After Puckett singled to right, Glavine walked Chili Davis and then Brian Harper. With one run already across, Glavine walked Scott Leius, and Minnesota was back in it, and the Atlanta ace was out of the ballgame.

In the sixth inning Glavine faced six batters, walking four of them. Although Kent Mercker did a quality job in relief, the Twins had cut the lead to 5–3 by the time the dust settled. "Tommy threw the ball great," Atlanta manager Bobby Cox said. "But he got the five runs and forgot to pitch."

Thankfully for the Braves, Twins pitching soon followed suit. David West, who had thrown well in the American League Championship Series, came into the game in the seventh and proceeded to one-up Glavine. He allowed two hits and a pair of walks without getting anyone out. From there the game dissolved into a laugher, the only lopsided game of this epic series, as the Braves scored six runs in the inning, taking an 11–3 lead.

Such meltdowns on the mound can be more frequent than many would think. Over the years the list of prominent pitchers who overnight couldn't throw a strike no matter how hard they tried includes Steve Blass, Pat Jordan, and Steve Dalkowski. A future victim of such ineptitude was in the Braves' bullpen during the 1991 series. Mark Wohlers's fastball may have been clocked at 103 miles per hour, making him a valuable closer on the Braves' future championship team in 1995, but too soon he would forget how to throw a strike too.

Early signs of trouble came in the midnineties when Wohlers began to have difficulty throwing to first base on routine fielding plays. Braves pitching coach Leo Mazzone feared that such wildness would carry over to Wohlers's deliveries to the plate, and sure enough that was the case. Wohlers began to walk more batters, and his pitches sometimes sailed past the catcher to the screen. Ironically, Wohlers's wild streak affected only his fastball. His other pitches, the slider and split-finger fastball, remained accurate enough, especially for some-body coming out of the bullpen. Hitters, however, soon realized that the hard-throwing right-hander couldn't throw his best pitch, the fast-ball, for a strike, and they began to wait on the slower stuff.

After saving ninety-seven games in three seasons Wohlers was sent down to the minors in 1998, and his career never really recov-ered. When asked what went wrong, Wohlers replied, "I wish I knew."

Nolan Ryan, who suffered through epic bouts of wildness early in his career, believed that the real measure of a pitcher couldn't be found in wins and losses or earned run average or any other statistic, for that matter. Instead, the pitcher nicknamed "The Express" said it came down to "Can you deliver the pitch you need to throw, with little margin for error, in the place you need to put it with the whole world watching you? That's the mark of a quality pitcher."

In 1991 Ryan rose to the top level of the game one last time. On May 1 of this memorable season Rickey Henderson made history in the afternoon by breaking Lou Brock's all-time steals record of 938. The whole event was staged to the hilt with Henderson holding the record-setting base aloft to show the crowd at Oakland-Alameda County Col-iseum and proclaiming himself now the greatest of all time.

That evening we were closing on the next week's issue of *Baseball Weekly* when the buzz spread that Nolan Ryan had a no-hitter going in Arlington, Texas, against the Toronto Blue Jays. Despite the approaching deadline, we began to redo pages, demoting Henderson's accomplishment, which had been expected for some time, and giving more space to Ryan, if the no-no happened. There was a connection between the two superstars, as Henderson had been Ryan's five thousandth career strikeout victim and one of the final outs in Ryan's previous no-hitter.

"If he ain't struck you out," Henderson said years later, "you ain't nobody."

Reports from Texas said people continued to file into Arlington Stadium as Ryan mowed down the Blue Jays in order on his way to sixteen strikeouts in the game. Once more things had fallen into order for the laconic right-hander, he was able to place his epic fastball precisely where he wanted.

Ryan secured his record seventh no-hitter when he struck out Roberto Alomar to end the game. Coincidentally, Alomar's father, Sandy, had been the second baseman behind Ryan in his first two no-hitters with California in 1973.

"Normally you say that luck is involved in pitching a no-hitter," former manager Bill Rigney said of Ryan. "But there's no luck involved with him anymore."

"No contest, it's Ryan," Frank Robinson told the *New York Times* when asked what was the bigger baseball story on this historic Wednesday in May. "The thing that I admire most is that he's a complete pitcher, 150 percent better than he was at any other time in his career. Hitters go up there, now, with hardly a chance."

The ability to throw a ball, one going nearly a hundred miles per hour, for a strike can elude the best of them. Yet as Ryan's evening in 1991 demonstrated, the baseball gods aren't necessarily fickle and cruel all the time. Occasionally they can be open to epiphanies and sometimes revelation. Almost three decades before Ryan's final no-hitter, in a spring training game in Orlando, the Dodgers took the field with Sandy Koufax on the mound. Until this point in his career Koufax had been a disappointment. Everyone knew the promising left-hander could throw hard, but he didn't throw many strikes or quality pitches for outs. Until this point in his career he was 36–40 in six seasons at the major-league level.

Before the game began, Koufax told Norm Sherry, who was catching for the Dodgers that day, that he wanted to work on his breaking stuff. After walking the first two batters, Koufax decided to rear back and fire only fastballs, throwing them as hard as he could. Soon enough the bases were loaded with nobody out.

Sherry came to the mound and told the stubborn left-hander, "Sandy, we've only got nine or so guys here to play this game. If you keep this up, you're going to be here a long time. Why don't you take something off the ball? Lay it in there. Let them hit it. We'll catch the ball, get some outs, and maybe we'll get out of here at a decent hour. Nobody is going to swing the way you're going now."

Koufax followed Sherry's advice and promptly struck out the side.

A few days later, back at the Dodgers' spring complex in Vero Beach, the buzz was that the fireballer had somehow turned the corner—gone from wild prospect to a pitcher with real control. In "the string area," a series of practice mounds with strike zones of various heights, Koufax pitched with command to Sherry. As the Dodgers' brass looked on, Sherry covered the plate with dirt. Then the catcher drew a line at the outside of the plate, with another for the inside part. With that Sherry moved his mitt from one corner of the plate to the other, and Koufax had no trouble hitting the target. "It was unbelievable how much he changed," Sherry remembered decades later. "The previous years he couldn't have come close to that. Heck, the previous week he couldn't have done it."

That season Koufax broke through for good, going 18–13 and leading the National League with 269 strikeouts. He pitched the first of

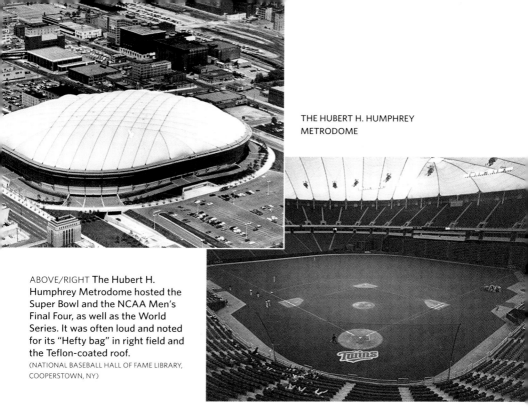

THE HUBERT H. HUMPHREY
METRODOME

ABOVE/RIGHT **The Hubert H. Humphrey Metrodome hosted the Super Bowl and the NCAA Men's Final Four, as well as the World Series. It was often loud and noted for its "Hefty bag" in right field and the Teflon-coated roof.** (NATIONAL BASEBALL HALL OF FAME LIBRARY, COOPERSTOWN, NY)

LEFT/BELOW **Nicknamed "The Launching Pad," this was where the Braves' Hank Aaron broke Babe Ruth's career home run record in 1974. After opening in 1965, Atlanta Stadium soon became home to the first major-league team in the Deep South.** (NATIONAL BASEBALL HALL OF FAME LIBRARY, COOPERSTOWN, N.Y.)

ATLANTA-FULTON COUNTY
STADIUM

Few had more fun playing the game than Rickey Henderson. Many considered him to be the top leadoff hitter of all time. When he retired, he was baseball's career leader in stolen bases. (JOSE LUIS VILLEGAS)

TOP For a guy who didn't want to be a reliever, Dennis Eckersley made the most of opportunity, finishing with 390 career saves. (JOSE LUIS VILLEGAS)

BELOW LEFT Tony La Russa won World Series titles with Oakland in 1989 and St. Louis in 2006 and 2011. (JOSE LUIS VILLEGAS)

BELOW RIGHT In Oakland, pitching coach Dave Duncan, left, helped La Russa put together one of the top staffs in the game. (JOSE LUIS VILLEGAS)

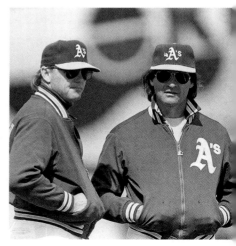

ABOVE The Hall of Fame's board of directors voted unanimously in 1991 to bar ineligible individuals. That included Pete Rose, baseball's all-time hit king. (NATIONAL BASEBALL HALL OF FAME LIBRARY, COOPERSTOWN, N.Y.)

BELOW/LEFT Jim Lefebvre, center, made the Seattle Mariners into a winner, but it wasn't enough to save his job as a record number of managers were fired in 1991. (JOSE LUIS VILLEGAS)

BELOW/RIGHT Oakland's Jose Canseco tied with Cecil Fielder for home-run honors in 1991 as each hit 44. (JOSE LUIS VILLEGAS)

ABOVE Candice Wiggins with her siblings and father, Alan Wiggins. (THE WIGGINS FAMILY)

LEFT Alan Wiggins struggled to find a home in Baltimore after leaving San Diego. (NATIONAL BASEBALL HALL OF FAME LIBRARY, COOPERSTOWN, NY)

BELOW In September 1991, baseball's Statistical Accuracy Committee officially put Roger Maris's sixty-one home-run season ahead of Babe Ruth's sixty. (NATIONAL BASEBALL HALL OF FAME, COOPERSTOWN, NY)

TOP Born in Minneapolis, first baseman Kent Hrbek became a local hero to Twins fans. (JOSE LUIS VILLEGAS)

ABOVE An aggressive hitter, Dan Gladden would score the winning run in the 1991 World Series. (JOSE LUIS VILLEGAS)

RIGHT A key offseason addition, Chili Davis settled in as Minnesota's designated hitter. (JOSE LUIS VILLEGAS)

BELOW Closer Rick Aguilera solidified the Twins' bullpen and ranked among the best relievers of his era. (MINNESOTA TWINS)

RIGHT After being with five teams, Brian Harper arrived in Minnesota looking for a job. He ended up becoming the full-time catcher. (MINNESOTA TWINS)

BOTTOM With Gary Gaetti gone to the California Angels, Scott Leius helped fill the void for Minnesota at third base. (MINNESOTA TWINS)

ABOVE/LEFT **Kirby Puckett surprised himself by being able to hit for power after reaching the major leagues. He had friends seemingly everywhere he went.**
(JOSE LUIS VILLEGAS)

OPPOSITE/ABOVE **With one swing of the bat, Puckett joined the ranks of those who have homered with everything on the line in the World Series.**
(MINNESOTA TWINS)

OPPOSITE /RIGHT **Puckett's career ended prematurely after the 1995 season due to irreversible retina damage in his right eye.**
(MINNESOTA TWINS)

ABOVE Rookie Chuck Knoblauch took over for the Twins at second base in 1991. (MINNESOTA TWINS)

RIGHT The addition of Scott Erickson rounded out the Twins' starting rotation in 1991. (MINNESOTA TWINS)

BELOW Veteran Greg Gagne would join with Knoblauch to turn a fake DP for the ages in the 1991 World Series. (MINNESOTA TWINS)

RIGHT Tom Glavine reached the twenty-victory plateau for the first time in 1991 and was named the National League's Cy Young winner. (NATIONAL BASEBALL HALL OF FAME LIBRARY, COOPERSTOWN, NY)

LEFT Terry Pendleton, the National League's MVP in 1991, still contends that the Braves were the best team in baseball in 1991. (JOSE LUIS VILLEGAS)

BELOW David Justice supplied power for the Atlanta Braves' attack, helping lead the ballclub to the first of fourteen consecutive visits to the postseason. (JOSE LUIS VILLEGAS)

RIGHT The Braves' Mark Lemke saved his best at-bats for postseason play. He remains a favorite in Atlanta.
(JOSE LUIS VILLEGAS)

ABOVE Pitcher John Smoltz turned to mind visualization to right his career, and in doing so he assured that Atlanta would have arguably the best rotation in baseball.
(JOSE LUIS VILLEGAS)

RIGHT In building his media empire, Ted Turner transformed the Braves into "America's team."
(NATIONAL BASEBALL HALL OF FAME LIBRARY, COOPERSTOWN, NY)

TOP Dan Gladden's hard slide upended Braves catcher Greg Olson and set the tone for a no-holds-barred World Series. (MINNESOTA TWINS)

RIGHT No lead was safe in the 1991 World Series, which saw four walk-off endings and three games go to extra innings. (MINNESOTA TWINS)

ABOVE When Twins first baseman Hrbek became entangled with the Braves' Ron Gant, the umpires found themselves back in the postseason spotlight. (MINNESOTA TWINS)

BELOW Some protesters put together this banner in a response to the Braves' nickname. (MINNESOTA HISTORICAL SOCIETY)

ABOVE Atlanta's baseball nickname, the Braves, brought out demonstrators at both World Series venues. (ASSOCIATED PRESS)

BELOW The controversy about the Braves' nickname only made many in Atlanta cheer louder as this was the season when the Tomahawk Chop took hold. (ASSOCIATED PRESS)

TOP Mark Lemke was safe at the plate in Game Four, which knotted the World Series at two games apiece. (ASSOCIATED PRESS)

BELOW The Braves prided themselves on their rally caps, which they felt had helped them turn the tide throughout this season. (ASSOCIATED PRESS)

LEFT Several costly mistakes, especially in games Six and Seven, left the Braves wondering what could have been (ASSOCIATED PRESS)

BELOW Nobody had a bigger postseason than the Twins' Kirby Puckett. After being named the MVP of the American League Championship Series, he was interviewed by announcer Jim Kaat. (MINNESOTA TWINS)

Minnesota workhorse Jack Morris pitched ten scoreless innings in Game Seven and was named the 1991 World Series MVP. (MINNESOTA TWINS)

his four no-hitters the next season and led the league in victories and strikeouts in 1963, 1965, and 1966.

Jeff Torborg, who caught Koufax's perfect game in September 1965, agreed with Ryan's assessment of quality pitching. Sooner or later the key becomes "Can they harness their stuff?" he said. "That's not an easy thing to do. Sometimes it can take years. Just ask Nolan or Sandy."

———

By the time Steve Bedrosian replaced David West in the bottom of the seventh inning, Game Five had turned into a laugher for the home-town team. The Braves put up six runs in the frame and then tacked on three more in the bottom of the eighth inning.

The Twins' offense was still swinging for the fences as Minnesota scored five runs over the last four innings. But with the bullpen unraveling fast, the Twins simply couldn't keep up on the scoreboard. West gave up four earned runs without recording an out. Bedrosian lasted an inning and allowed two more earned runs, and Carl Willis finished off the evening with three earned runs of his own in one inning of work.

"Some nights you just have to forget about it," Willis said, "and try to turn the page."

———

"[Build it to be] compatible with the warehouse and Baltimore's civic buildings in terms of scale, configuration, and color. . . . [Build it] so the fans can see the city.

"Reduce the height of the second deck. Reduce the height of the third deck. . . . Trees, plants, and other greenery are critical to designing this facility *as a ballpark, not a stadium.*"

Even today, after so many copycat ballparks have arisen, the words still jump off the page. The memo written by Baltimore Orioles vice president Janet Marie Smith to HOK Sport ranks among the most important documents ever penned regarding stadium design in this country.

In the fall of 1991 the Orioles raced to finish their new jewel of a ballpark in time for Opening Day the following season, and they had to be a little like the Beatles before the release of *Sgt. Pepper's Lonely Hearts Club Band*. Others may have forgotten about what they were up to, but everybody in the band knew they were about to shock the world. Even today, when it comes to baseball stadiums in this country, one can separate the eras into Before Camden Yards and After Camden Yards.

Before the Baltimore ballpark, which did open to acclaim in 1992, most stadiums were multipurpose facilities. They were not only home to baseball games but also football, rock shows, monster truck shows, and on and on. The emphasis was on a quick turnaround, maximizing the calendar to fill as many dates as possible. Where the Braves and the Twins called home in 1991 fell into that category. Atlanta-Fulton County Stadium was as cavernous and as soulless as Three Rivers in Pittsburgh, old Busch Stadium in St. Louis, or Riverfront in Cincinnati. The Metrodome in Minneapolis may have been domed, putting it at first glance into the same company as the Astrodome in Houston or SkyDome in Toronto, yet when it came to sightlines and general ambience, the Metrodome had more in common really with the cookie-cutter, multipurpose stadiums. For here was a domain in which a Hefty garbage bag, stretched taut and true, stood in for the outfield wall in right field, and the fence in dead center was sported by a stretch of Plexiglas straight out of a local hockey rink, and it was all topped off by that Teflon roof.

In the decade leading up to the 1991 World Series many in the game realized that oval concrete bowls, which could host so many events, didn't truly serve the national pastime. The search began for something more memorable and appropriate to showcase the game. With construction costs escalating, cities and sports franchises only had to look north to Canada for a pair of vivid demonstrations about what was now at stake.

In Montreal Olympic Stadium had replaced Parc Jarry, where the Expos played from 1969 to 1976. Located in north Montreal, Jarry was hardly an ideal place for the first major-league baseball franchise outside of the United States. Less than thirty-thousand fans could cram into the place, and initially the makeshift ballpark was supposed to be the ballclub's home for only a season or so. Thanks to political haggling, however, construction of a new stadium was delayed for years. Despite the minor-league-like digs, outfielder Rusty Staub, nicknamed "Le Grand Orange" for his reddish hair, helped the new team draw a following.

After suffering through eight seasons at Jarry, the Expos and their fans went upscale in 1977 when they moved into Stade Olympique, which had been the main venue for the 1976 Summer Olympics. On paper the new facility was stunning, with a retractable roof that was supposed to rise up like a giant handkerchief in good weather. Unfortunately, the apparatus rarely worked, and the roof soon began to leak. Eventually, the ballclub replaced the roof with a permanent lid.

Built in a hurry for the 1976 Games, the new ballpark soon began to fall apart. During the 1991 season a fifty-five-ton piece of concrete fell onto an exterior walkway. Although nobody was injured, the Expos were forced to play their final thirteen home games on the road. In the ensuing years part of the roof collapsed in a snowstorm, and as recently as 2012 another concrete slab fell in the facility's underground parking garage. Called "The Big O" when it opened for the Olympics, the stadium soon became known as "The Big Owe."

As Gary Gillette and Eric Enders wrote in their classic book *Big League Ballparks*, "By the time the stadium was finally fully paid off in 2006, the Olympics were gone, the Expos no longer existed, and interest and repairs had driven the stunning final price tag to an estimated $1.61 billion."

In the world of ballpark design Olympic Stadium became a real cautionary tale. So when Toronto followed them to the drafting board a few years later, also with a retractable dome in mind, the first goal was not to duplicate Montreal's folly. The improbable design team of Roderick Robbie and Michael Allen won the contract for Toronto's new stadium along the Lake Ontario waterfront. Though neither one of them had ever attended a baseball game in their lives, they certainly did their homework, even talking with the team's beat reporters about what they liked in particular stadiums around the league. But it was left to Allen to eventually solve the riddle of how to move the roof back and forth economically and efficiently.

As Allen remembered it, he was on a flight to Ottawa, sitting in the front row, when it was time for a beverage and snack. (Yes, this was back in the day when domestic carriers still served complimentary meals.) With no tray table to pull down from the back of the seat in front of him, Allen was instructed to snag the table out of his armrest. As he did so, Allen realized here lay the answer—how to solve the riddle of the great dome roof. As the flight attendant waited, he repeatedly folded the table in and out of the armrest in amazement by what he saw. "That was it," Allen recalled. "The answer to how we could put it all together."

When completed, the SkyDome roof towered thirty-one stories into the sky, more than twice the height of Houston's Astrodome. The roof was divided into four sections, and to open to the heavens the larger ones moved back along tracks, with the remaining smaller section swinging in underneath, mirroring that airline tray on the flight to Ottawa. In the early days the roof's opening and closing sometimes drew more applause than the teams on the field. Pretty much everyone was impressed, and some were left to wonder what could have been. "It's great," pitcher Mike Flanagan told *Sports Illustrated*, "but I was kind of hoping they'd have retractable fences."

With its plethora of restaurants, wide concourse, and a hotel with rooms overlooking the field, the Toronto stadium came with a slew of modern-day bells and whistles. And unlike Montreal, its retractable roof actually worked—opening or closing in about a half-hour. Although truly functional, some still didn't care for the overall ambience. Michael Janofsky of the *New York Times* compared SkyDome to "an airplane hangar or merchandise mart or a place in which Crazy Eddie might hold a giant warehouse sale."

When Larry Lucchino, then the Orioles' president, first saw Toronto's SkyDome, he said, "They built the eighth wonder of the world. We're just building a nice little ballpark."

Baseball had yet to see the best in ballpark design, so the door remained ajar for the Baltimore Orioles to turn back the clock and throw in a few novelties at the same time.

Guidelines and standards—baseball has plenty of both. So much so that the line between such designations can become blurred at times. The pitcher's mound lies sixty feet, six inches from home plate. That's a rule, of course, as is the ninety feet between the bases. "The ball field itself is a mystic creation, the Stonehenge of America," Roger Kahn once wrote.

As the Orioles began work on their new ballpark, though, they realized that perhaps too much was set in stone when it came to ballpark dimensions. Major League Baseball's guidelines called for 330 feet down either line, a symmetrical outfield of equal proportions. Certainly that made it easier for baseball and football to share the same venue. Such formulas remained perfect for multipurpose facilities. Yet in Baltimore the Colts had already fled to Indianapolis in the middle of the night in 1984, leaving the Orioles as the only professional team in town at the time. That meant "the stars were aligned" to try something new and distinct, remembered Janet Marie Smith, the team's vice president for planning and development.

At the time recent industry standards for baseball stadiums were Kansas City's Royals Stadium and Chicago's new Comiskey Park. The former was located off a freeway, a fair distance from downtown, and Comiskey had a steep upper deck that many fans found challenging and, god forbid if you suffered from vertigo. Baltimore's new ball-park would be downtown and baseball only. As a result, the Orioles decided to embrace the game's past and emulate such old-style structures as Ebbets Field in Brooklyn, Fenway Park in Boston's Back Bay, and Wrigley Field in northern Chicago. What did these places have in common? An asymmetrical outfield, seating low and close, and light towers instead of banks of lights ringing the stadium's upper lip. "We wanted our ballpark to be old-shoe comfortable," Smith said, "even if it was brand new."

This nod to the past extended to the small touches at Camden Yards. The flags above the right-field wall flew in descending order of the team standings and are changed each game day to reflect the current rankings. A small silhouette of Wee Willie Keeler can be seen in the chairs. The bullpen areas remain visible so most fans can view who is warming up. Seven-foot walls, instead of the eight-foot ones MLB guidelines called for, line the outfield, which makes it easier for leaping catches that take away would-be home runs. After much debate and local opposition, the famed B&O warehouse, which stands fifty feet wide and a thousand feet long, became part of the overall design. Amazing to think that it was slated to be demolished in the original plans.

"It was fitting that the new age of the retro-park was celebrated in Baltimore, a provincial, blue-collar, crabcakes-and-beer town with thick roots and a thicker accent," wrote Tim Kurkjian of *ESPN The Magazine*. "It is a neighborhood town, a brick town, which is why the ballpark was built of brick and steel, not of concrete like the flying saucers that landed in too many major league cities."

Oriole Park at Camden Yards opened in April 1992, with the hometown team edging the Cleveland Indians, 2–0.

"I made sure I took in the whole experience on my way to the ballpark that day," recalled Charles Nagy, the Indians' starting pitcher that day, "and when I got to the park hours before the game, I went on the field to soak it all in.

"It was very exciting. When Jacobs Field [in Cleveland] was built, I saw a lot of Camden Yards. It was special to be a part of the opening of a great new ballpark. I just wish we'd won."

The new ballpark in Baltimore would usher in a new era in stadium design and change industry standards forever. "If you look at three-quarters of the ballparks built since Camden Yards, they have been built in a downtown setting," Smith said. "It's been part of an urban renaissance, which is nice because there are not a lot of things that bring people into a downtown today.

"We don't have any need for a central banking center or central anything really anymore. But we're still social animals, and it's good to have cities alive. Sports has found a way to help this process with its newer ballparks."

———

When the dust settled in Game Five, the Braves had trounced the Twins, 14–5. Right fielder David Justice finished with five runs batted in, with Mark Lemke right behind him with three RBIs on a pair of triples. With his home run in the seventh inning, outfielder Lonnie Smith became only the fifth player and the first from the National League to drive one out of the park in three consecutive games. He joined Lou Gehrig, who did it in 1928; Johnny Mize (1953); Hank Bauer (1958); and Reggie Jackson (1977). Yes, all the others were members of the New York Yankees when they accomplished the feat.

Atlanta's fourteen runs stood as the most in a World Series game since the Yankees scored sixteen runs in Game Two of the 1960 World Series against the Pittsburgh Pirates. Lemke's two triples tied a World Series record last accomplished by the Dodgers' Tommy Davis in 1963. More puzzling was that Lemke had continued the grand tradition of second basemen—yes, second basemen—stepping up big in postseason play.

Usually second base is home to one of the smaller guys on the team, somebody who doesn't exhibit the best of arms. That's not to denigrate second basemen, but take a look at any team, even one on the sand-lot: the best arms are in center field, right field, third base, and short. Big guys who can hit but don't have much range are often put at first base. Second sackers? They're usually the last ones chosen when picking up teams, and perhaps that's why Atlanta fans embraced this little guy named Lemke.

"My two favorites on that team were Mark Lemke and Ron Gant," recalled Larry Taylor, a former major general in the Marines who attended the games in Atlanta. "Lemke because I've always been partial to smallish second basemen, the position that usually attracts the guys with the least natural baseball talent. Smallish and not much natural baseball talent, that pretty much describes me."

For some reason in the postseason, though, second basemen often step up. Back in 1953 the Yankees' Billy Martin had twelve hits in the World Series. Seven years later Pittsburgh second baseman Bill Mazeroski homered off Ralph Terry in the ninth inning of Game Seven to give the Pirates a 10–9 victory and the title over New York. In 1961 another Yankee second baseman, Bobby Richardson, collected nine hits in five games as New York downed Cincinnati.

The Amazin' New York Mets in 1969 wouldn't have upset the Baltimore Orioles without Al Weiss hitting .454 in the series and delivering a key home run. Then there was Brian Doyle, another Yankee, who hit .438 in the 1978 World Series. A fill-in for the injured Willie Randolph, Doyle helped New York defeat Los Angeles. "If it happened for a few games during the season, they would just say you were lucky," Doyle said. "But everything is so magnified in the World Series that they start comparing you with Babe Ruth and Joe DiMaggio."

The coronation was underway for Lemke, and if the Braves could close things out in Minneapolis, he had the inside track to be the series MVP. Heading into Game Six back in Minneapolis, he stood one triple away from tying Tommy Leach's World Series record for four, which was set in 1903. "There's a phenomenon at second base,"

Commissioner Fay Vincent said. "The World Series is the coming out of second basemen."

Justice's five RBIs marked only the fifteenth time anybody hit that many in the history of World Series. The last guy to do it was the Twins' Dan Gladden in 1987.

Justice admitted to feeling pressure to come through in the clutch. "From the team standpoint this has been a lot of fun," he said. "But from a personal standpoint it has been something else. I feel like I've got a thousand knife marks in my back."

Ron Gant added, "Everybody expects you to do well. But what happens is then you try to do too much and try to play over your head. What you need to do is learn how to relax. You just have to try to do the best you can, and you will be better off."

After the game Atlanta fans lingered in the stands, some still doing the Tomahawk Chop. The mind-numbing chant could be heard well below the stands, echoing through the corridors outside the team clubhouses.

"It's all about home-field advantage," said Atlanta pitcher John Smoltz. "The Twins play inside a place they call the Thunderdome. And now we have this cheering to remind us that we're home, in front of our crowd."

That the Braves had anything to call their own, even if it was just a rousing cheer, after so many years in the baseball wilderness was something to behold—perhaps even indicative of the season at hand. In the two decades leading up to the 1991 Series the Braves had only five winning seasons. Now, after sweeping the Twins at home, the Braves stood one victory from a championship many thought was downright impossible when this season began.

"I remember that the Braves were in third place at the All-Star break, only one game under .500 and nine and a half games out of first at the time," said Terry Sloope, a longtime member of Atlanta's Magnolia Chapter of the Society for American Baseball Research. "For the

Braves that was great. I remember thinking the Braves were actually playing decent ball that year, were actually competitive. Over the previous seven years or so they had been just horrible. A third-place finish somewhere near the .500 mark would have been just fine for most fans."

Of course, Atlanta manager Bobby Cox believed his ballclub could reach higher, could be the first ballclub to go from last place to the world title in a single season. The Braves had fired him after the 1981 season only to put him back at the helm in Atlanta nine years later. He had returned in large part because he saw the potential in this organization. Still, if anybody understood how baseball could break a guy's heart, it was Cox.

Born in Tulsa, he grew up in Fresno County, California, and signed with Los Angeles for $40,000 after attending Reedley Junior College. He spent five years in the Dodgers' minor league system before eventually going to the Braves in their first year in Atlanta. Cox never made that big-league team as a player, but he did catch on with the New York Yankees in 1968 and was named to the Topps' Rookie All-Star Team. A year later he lost his job in New York to Bobby Murcer and, as a result, soon turned to managing.

In 1971 he guided the Yankees' farm team in Fort Lauderdale, Florida, and had a winning record in each of his six years in the minors. He became Billy Martin's first-base coach in 1977 in New York as the Yankees won the World Series. That's when Atlanta hired him to assist with such promising young players as Bob Horner and Dale Murphy. Cox led the Braves to their first winning season in six years in 1980. But that didn't keep owner Ted Turner from firing him the next season.

Cox returned to the American League, taking over as manager for another young team on the rise, the Toronto Blue Jays. Cox nearly led them to the World Series in 1985, as the Blue Jays lost in seven games to the Kansas City Royals for the American League pennant. That fall Turner lured Cox back to Atlanta, this time as the Braves' new general manager. Throughout baseball the Braves were considered to have plenty of young stars—on the major-league roster and especially down on the farm—so when manager Russ Nixon failed to get results, Cox stepped in as manager in 1990. John Schuerholz was named as the new GM, and the two became one of the most successful duos in baseball history.

"It wasn't only the Xs and Os and knowing all the strategy with Bobby," remembered pitcher Mark Grant. "Somehow he stayed a humble human being through it all. I can guarantee you the day he stands at the podium in Cooperstown, one of the first things out of his mouth will be something like, 'One of the reasons I was here was that I had such great talent.' He's not afraid to recognize that. He's so humble. He was a guy who got along with everybody, but he didn't play favorites."

Terry Pendleton said he loved playing for Cox because the manager "had the patience of grandma out there. The rest of us could be in a mean, crazy panic and Bobby would be saying, "No, no, we're good. Things are going to be just fine. You wait and see.'

"When a player is struggling, he knew that Bobby would stick with him, and sooner or later the player would break out of it. Often Bobby had a better idea of how good his players could be then they did. Also, some guys want to manage before the first pitch is ever thrown. Bobby would let the guys play and manage when he had to manage. He never got ahead of the game and what needed to be done at the time."

As a baseball lifer, Cox knew that warm and fuzzy stories didn't carry the day as much as some people wanted to believe. Baseball was like everything else now—it was "What have you done for me lately?" And how long a manager stayed in his job had little to do with how loud folks cheered on a particular evening in October. During his two decades already in baseball Cox had seen it all and could detail the broken hearts and find the dead bodies as well as anyone. Carlton Fisk waving the ball fair at Fenway Park during the 1975 World Series, for example, was replayed over and over again on the TV this time of year. But the Red Sox had lost to the Cincinnati Reds in seven games in that Fall Classic, and their manager, Darrell Johnson, was soon sent packing. Few remembered that, but Bobby Cox did. A decade later Boston again had the championship within its grasp after winning the first two games over the New York Mets and later holding a three-to-two games lead. They had to win, right? But they didn't, did they?

After Game Five Cox tried to tell those around him that the St. Louis Cardinals had once held a one-game lead heading back to the Twin Cities against the Twins. Those 1987 Cardinals were then the best team in baseball, in his opinion, with a quality pitching staff and superb team defense. Another veteran manager, Whitey Herzog, led them. Yet in the din of the Metrodome the Cardinals came unhinged and lost the remaining two games and the World Series.

As Cox briefly surveyed his victorious clubhouse, he knew that the same thing could happen to his ballclub. When the media began with questions about being on the brink, being only one win away from baseball's promised land, Cox refused to play along.

"There's no place like it," Cox said of the Metrodome as the Tomahawk Chop continued several levels above him. "There really isn't. Our job is to focus on the next game up there. That's all there is for us."

———

"We play this game every day."

That's a bromide often bandied about in baseball. I'm told Earl Weaver and Sparky Anderson said it, often to new reporters on the beat who were too excited, too intense for a sport that delivers a box of score results almost daily for half of the year.

San Francisco Giants Roger Craig gave me the following piece of advice my first year covering baseball in the Bay Area, back when I tried to interview half the team in a single afternoon at Candlestick Park for a sidebar that eventually ran in the back of the sports section: "Son, we play this game every day."

In essence, like any piece of advice, it remains equal parts wisdom and warning. A reminder that baseball will never be like football, where a week of mind-numbing practices culminates in a game seemingly always bigger than the one the week before, and to win or lose it means the world. No, a baseball team can look downright terrible one night and terrific the next; it's which identity that eventually emerges over the course of another long season that eventually decides things. Ballclubs rarely reveal themselves in grandiose star turns; instead, it's the little moments, what happens every day that defines everything by the end of the season.

One of the things I've come to appreciate about baseball is how methodical it can be. How such due diligence can add up over time.

In those early years at *Baseball Weekly* I didn't have much time for other things I dreamed about doing. Besides doing my part to get a new publication off the ground I also had two young kids at home. Decades later it's strange to look back on those days, with both of my children now in their twenties and moved out of the house, and remember how little free time there once was to even think about and ponder other projects.

That's how I came to write on my commute to work on the Washington, DC, subway. It wasn't much time, only twenty-five minutes from the parking garage where I left my car to the long escalator ride back above ground at the Rosslyn station and face to face with the USA Today skyscraper headquarters for another day. Yet I began to write in a spiral notebook that I brought along—a page at best in an unruly scrawl, and that was enough for now. Soon it was either time to go to work or, on the evening commute back home, time to do my best to be a family man with all that it entails. Back in the day there were major responsibilities at either end of that subway line.

The summer after starting at *Baseball Weekly* I made my first trip to Cuba, and the level of play there stunned me. The starting infield for their national team back in the early 1990s, Orestes Kindelan, Antonio Pacheco, German Mesa, and the great Omar Linares, ranks as one of the best I've ever seen.

Even in such an exotic, star-crossed place the game could still be the same. Before one contest several of us were speaking with Linares, hinting to him how much more money he could make in the major leagues, what a star he could be in America. But the third baseman, who could field like Brooks Robinson and hit like Mike Schmidt, only smiled and said, "But there's another game here to play tomorrow."

In his own way Linares was staying as true to things as Roger Craig or Earl Weaver or any other wise baseball man. He was reminding us that one always had to be mindful, that it was necessary to stay in the moment. To be successful you had to remember, "We play this game every day."

———

After Game Five, with Atlanta now holding the upper hand, the buzz among both teams was remarkably similar. Everyone was reminding everyone else that this Series was far from over, that it would ultimately go to the team that stayed focused on the next game and didn't allow its attention to waver.

Down the corridor from the Braves' clubhouse, past the swells hanging around owner Ted Turner and his wife, Jane Fonda, was the visitors' clubhouse. Inside Twins skipper Tom Kelly appeared to be as relaxed as Cox was wound tight. Kelly talked about the state of his team as though he were viewing a wreck on the highway from a good distance away. Perhaps that was the correct approach to take, seeing as his ballclub had lost by nine runs on this night in Atlanta.

Kelly, like any good manager, focused on what could turn things around for his team. As he reminded everyone, the remaining games of the 1991 season, whether it was one contest or two, would be back in Minneapolis, an American League venue. Prior to 2003 home-field advantage alternated between the American League and National League. So, like in 1987, the Twins could enjoy the last two games at home. After 2002 the home-field advantage went to the winner of the All-Star Game, a change made by Commissioner Bud Selig in the wake of the Midsummer Classic ending in a 7–7 tie when both teams ran out of pitchers. Even under Selig's new guidelines, the Twins would have been going home with a chance to turn the tables as the American League won the 1991 All-Star Game, 4–2, at Toronto's new SkyDome, with Cal Ripken the game's MVP.

Returning to an American League city meant that the designated hitter was back in play. Shane Mack, even with seven strikeouts so far in the Series, would be in the outfield. Kelly said he was confident that Mack could turn it around. "We've hidden all the razor blades," the manager said. With Mack back in right field, Chili Davis would again be the designated hitter.

"There are just some things Chili just can't do," Kelly told the press.

"Like what?" he was asked.

"Catch the ball," Kelly tersely replied.

As Kelly saw it, the Twins' hitting attack had been shut down for long stretches during the first five games of the series. How much this had to do with lack of a DH in Atlanta or the impressive trio of Braves starting pitchers—Tom Glavine, John Smoltz, and Steve Avery—was left to hang in the air.

"And we've been in this situation before," the manager said, again alluding to 1987. "The way it works out, we got to play three games here but have a chance to play four at the American League park. It looks like we're going to need all four to get the job done. Hopefully, it works our way."

Twins closer Rick Aguilera remembered being impressed by Kelly's calmness through it all. "Many of us kept waiting for this big team meeting prior to the playoffs or even during the World Series, that kind of thing. But he just went along like it was business as usual. Why make this bigger than it is? We already knew how big playing in the World Series was.

"In keeping things going along, he didn't create anxiety for the players. That's what I saw from TK and the staff back then. I don't remember sensing any panic after the games in Atlanta. There was no more anxiety. We battled well. We almost won Games Three and Four, and we got blown out of Game Five. Now we were going home to the Dome, which was already in the Braves' heads. So we knew there was a little bit of advantage there for us. Why panic? That was really TK's message to all of us."

Certainly what nobody wanted to hear about in the visiting clubhouse was that the franchise, between its tenure in Washington and the Twin Cities, had now lost fourteen consecutive World Series games on the road. That dated back to 1925 and Walter Johnson's Washington Senators.

Instead, Kelly was asked whether he could convince his players that a defeat, either by 1–0 or 14–5, was still just one loss. "I don't think it's easy," he replied. "We're off track."

The Twins' players would agree with their manager's assessment. Team leader Kirby Puckett said he didn't fault Kelly for trying to get Davis's bat (with its twenty-nine home runs and ninety-three runs batted in the regular season) into the lineup despite the accompanying defensive liabilities.

"You can't blame TK," he said. "You can't take anything away from him. He's done this sort of thing all season long."

Kent Hrbek, who put up twenty home runs during the regular season, had only three hits in sixteen at-bats so far against Braves pitching. For his trouble, Kelly had demoted him to the seventh spot in the Minnesota order.

"Maybe we win at home because of the fact that we don't have a pitcher in the lineup and we get to use the lineup that got us here," Hrbek said. "We'll be fine once we get home. That's what I think anyway."

Asked whether the Twins could pull off a repeat of 1987, Hrbek replied, "I certainly hope that déjà vu strikes again."

Throughout the three-game stretch in Atlanta, Hrbek had received threatening phone calls at the team hotel, and in the stadium Braves fans chanted his name and continued to boo him because of the wrestlemania incident with Ron Gant back in Game Two.

"I know he has been a little quieter the last few days," Kelly said. "I don't know if it's affected him, but I know it's affected his family."

Certainly Tina Hrbek, Kent's mother, had had her fill of Atlanta. She became especially rankled by signs at Atlanta-Fulton County Stadium that read, "Hrbek is a Jrk."

"You know, every player gets hassled now and then," she said, "but I didn't like them picking on the family name."

Organizations pride themselves on turning over every stone in the search for talent. Yet sometimes the best players can be found right next door. Such was the case with Kent Hrbek. Perhaps that's why he was as eager as anybody in a Twins uniform to return to Minnesota.

Born in May 1960, the season before the franchise vacated Washington, DC, and headed north to become the Twins, Hrbek grew up in Bloomington, Minnesota, so close to the old Metropolitan Stadium that he could see the lights from his bedroom window. Despite the proximity, a young Hrbek usually attended games only on Mondays because on those days tickets were just a dollar. Growing up, Hrbek watched such Twins stars as Tony Oliva, Zoilo Versalles, and Harmon Killebrew. Like most kids back in those days, Hrbek played several sports, eventually deciding to concentrate on baseball. He didn't enjoy football's five days of practice to play just one game a week, and with basketball he seemed destined to foul out most of the time. (Undoubtedly, Ron Gant would agree.) Even though Hrbek played a ferocious left wing in hockey, his father, Ed, urged him to go with baseball. It helped that first base opened up on the Kennedy High squad in Bloomington about the same time.

Although the left-handed slugger often hit for power, few scouts took notice. It wasn't until a concessions manager at the old Met told scout Angelo Giuliani about the homegrown talent that the Twins decided to draft Hrbek in the late rounds of the 1978 draft. "He was a seventeenth-round pick who would have been a first-rounder if people would have known about him," Giuliani said.

Indeed, Hrbek didn't stay in the minor leagues for long. He hit .379 for Visalia, at that point the best average anywhere in professional baseball, and led the California League in slugging and on-base percentage too. Those numbers resulted in Hrbek becoming one of the few players to make the jump from Class A ball to the majors. He made his Twins debut in Yankee Stadium, where his twelfth-inning home run defeated New York. His meteoric rise soon got everyone's attention in the baseball world, with even Reggie Jackson chatting him up.

In 1982, Hrbek's first full season with the Twins, he hit twenty-three home runs, with ninety-two RBIs, and finished behind the Orioles' Cal Ripken for American League Rookie of the Year. Unfortunately, by the end of his storybook season amyotrophic lateral sclerosis (ALS), better known as Lou Gehrig's disease, had claimed his father's life. Years later Hrbek described that season as "a high point and low point for me."

By the 1991 World Series Hrbek could see the end of a fourteen-year career that had made him a fan favorite in the Twin Cities. As a free agent, he signed for millions less to stay in his hometown. Whereas the Twins of this era were often considered Kirby Puckett's team, Hrbek played a strong role in the clubhouse. "He was the hometown guy," Greg Gagne remembered. "We were in his town, playing in front of his fans, and it gave all of us kind of a comfort zone. For a long time he was the heart of the Minnesota Twins."

Gene Larkin added that Hrbek "just tried to enjoy every minute of his time in the big leagues. Obviously, he felt pressure being the hometown boy helping the Twins win. When he got to the park he thought baseball, and when he left the park it was over. He had done what he could do. Then he would try to forget about it and not think about it until he came to the park again the next day."

That proved to be increasingly difficult, however, in the 1991 Series. Not only did the lumbering first baseman hear the catcalls in Atlanta, but he and rest of the Twins knew they were on the verge of losing four consecutive games and, with it, the world championship. In the postgame discussions Kelly spoke briefly about how he hoped the Twins fans would "retaliate" in kind for Game Six for the abuse that Hrbek had received in Atlanta.

"In the games that we've been here, there's been a lot of flash-bulbs going off when we were at bat and calling Hrbek a cheater," the manager said. "They're trying to do whatever they can to distract us. Hopefully, our fans will counter in a similar way when we get home."

Now things were beginning to sound like a professional cage match.

Still, as it grew late after Game Five in Atlanta and both teams packed up to return to the Twin Cities, the discussion turned to a more pressing concern—the Twins' slumbering attack. One game away from elimination, Puckett was hitting only .167. As a team the Twins were batting .218 after averaging .276 in defeating the Toronto Blue Jays in the American League Championship Series.

"All I have to do is hit one ball hard," said Puckett, one of the last Twins to leave the visiting clubhouse that evening.

How he hungered to once again hear the distinctive sound of a base-ball well hit and dare to wonder whether it had enough to clear the outfield fence. For Puckett knew as well as anybody that if he could square one up, it could make all the difference now.

———

**FINAL SCORE: BRAVES 14, TWINS 5**

|     | 1 | 2 | 3 | 4 | 5 | 6 | 7 | 8 | 9 | R | H | E |
|-----|---|---|---|---|---|---|---|---|---|---|---|---|
| MIN | 0 | 0 | 0 | 0 | 0 | 3 | 0 | 1 | 1 | 5 | 7 | 1 |
| ATL | 0 | 0 | 0 | 4 | 1 | 0 | 6 | 3 | X | 14 | 17 | 1 |

ATTENDANCE: **50,878**    LENGTH OF GAME: **2 HOURS, 59 MINUTES**

# Game Six

SATURDAY, OCTOBER 26, 1991
AT HUBERT H. HUMPHREY METRODOME
MINNEAPOLIS, MINNESOTA

By the bottom of the eleventh inning things had gotten to the point at which Kirby Puckett believed he could predict the future. Leading off the inning, Puckett told teammate Chili Davis, who was in the on-deck circle, that his services would no longer be needed in this game, one that would be remembered as one for the ages. If Atlanta's latest reliever, left-hander Charlie Leibrandt, got his changeup up in the strike zone, he told Davis he was going to end it right here and now.

Legend has it that Puckett said something like, "You listening, Dog? It's going to be all over. We can't have another game like we did down in Atlanta, where TK runs out of players and has to ask poor Aggie to bat. I'm going to take pitches, I tell ya, Dog. Take pitches until that changeup of Leibrandt's rides up in the zone. It's going to rise, I tell ya, Chili Dog, and when it does I plan to do something about it."

With that, Kirby Puckett stepped up to the plate, with the score tied at 3–3. No matter that until this point in the 1991 World Series the Twins' star had just five hits in twenty-one at-bats and hadn't demonstrated much patience at the plate. He had struck out twice against Leibrandt back in Game One. Yet as Chili Davis and the rest of the baseball world looked on, Puckett did begin to wait Leibrandt out. Waiting for that changeup to rise in the zone.

Decades later Davis remembered that he and Puckett were indeed jawing with each other before this epic World Series at-bat. But it is funny how things can be played up, warped beyond recognition over the years, especially when something of real consequence takes place. Davis, who was as close to Puckett as anybody on the 1991 Twins, recalled their conversation quite differently from what was later chronicled, even by Puckett himself.

"We were barking at each other," Davis agreed. "But we were barking at each other because at first Puck wanted to bunt."

Bunt?

Davis and I were speaking across one of the tables in the Oakland Athletics' clubhouse, where the ex-slugger now worked as the team's hitting coach.

"You heard what I said," Davis smiled. "Puck at first was all set to bunt his way on. Believe it or not, he came up to me and said, 'Dog, I've got this game plan. Tell me what you think. I don't hit these soft throwers like Leibrandt very well.'

"Now you have to remember that Puck could really bunt. He had a good chance of bunting for a hit. So he's all excited and telling me, 'I'll get one down and then I'll steal second. You hit these guys—better than me. Take it to the gap, and I'll score the winner. That will be the ballgame.'"

With that Davis leaned back in his chair, remembering this moment from decades ago, and shook his head. How did he respond after hearing Puckett's grand plan? This scheme to get on with a bunt?

"I told him, 'That's a bad plan, Puck. These people didn't come here to watch you bunt. Not now. Not on this night.'"

Emphatically Davis urged Puckett to swing away. Telling him that one good knock could end this ballgame, here and now. That is what the two of them are seen discussing in the footage of Game Six. Davis recalled ending the conversation by telling the Twins' star not to swing at anything down in the strike zone.

"Look for something up," he told Puckett. "Don't chase that changeup of Charlie Leibrandt's. Don't try to pull him. Just try to put the ball in the gap."

Soon enough Puckett began to believe in what Davis was saying. For a moment Puckett became the flock and Davis the preacher man until those roles suddenly pivoted, with the Twins' superstar breaking into one of his legendary riffs, telling his friend Chili that of course he could hit that fickle changeup, especially if it dared rise up in the strike zone.

The whole plan and brash talk almost went out the window when Leibrandt's first pitch—a changeup, naturally—sailed low across the plate, only to have home plate umpire Ed Montague call it a strike.

"That pitch really scared me," Davis recalled. "It was maybe knee high, maybe, and it got the strike call? So now I'm worried that I gave Puck the wrong advice. I'm thinking if Leibrandt throws you another one of those, you've got to swing, Puck."

Somehow the Twins' slugger remained patient at the plate, even with so much on the line. After that first pitch sailed in low for a called strike, the next one was too high. Ball one. Then came another changeup from Leibrandt, and this one, thankfully, was called low for ball two by Montague.

With the count 2–1, Leibrandt tried to fool Puckett with another changeup, this time on the outside half of the plate. Puckett was waiting on it, though, and he put a good swing on the offering. As the ball began to carry toward left-center field, the sellout crowd and the Twins in their dugout rose, with everybody trying to gauge whether it would have enough power to carry out of the ballpark.

From his vantage point in the on-deck circle, Davis couldn't believe what his friend had pulled off. "Puck waited him out," he said more than twenty years later, drumming his fingertips briefly on the clubhouse table. This particular at-bat remained as clear as anything that ever happened to him in the game. "Leibrandt puts a ball up in the zone, and the next thing I knew Puck hit it.... Whether or not it would clear that Plexiglas atop the outfield fence, that was the question from where I was watching. That was the only question in my mind."

Confident that he had hit it hard but unsure how far the ball would carry, Puckett took off, running hard out of the batter's box, heading toward first base. Thus began a journey around the diamond that many will never forget and one that the Twins' best player would arguably never recover from.

———

If ever a game was a story unto itself, Game Six was. In Puckett the Twins had a leader in talk and action. In the first inning he had tripled home a run and later scored. In the third inning, with a runner on, he made a terrific leaping catch up against the Plexiglas fence, denying the Braves' Ron Gant of a home run.

"If he hadn't made that catch," teammate Gene Larkin said, "we might have lost the World Series right there."

Before Game Six, after the Twins had been swept in Atlanta, now one loss from elimination, Puckett called an impromptu players-only meeting back in Minneapolis. There he told his teammates, "Jump on board, boys. I'm going to carry us tonight. Don't even worry about it. Just back me up a little and I'll take us to Game Seven."

Larkin recalled the Twins being "in a bad way" after the three consecutive losses in Atlanta. "Not many guys can talk the talk and walk the walk, but Kirby always could for us. We knew he was going to do something special and here it was—on the biggest stage."

Puckett's interactions with his teammates were rarely so serious. When he was around one of the team mottoes was, "Everybody has a price," said Dave Winfield, who came to the Twins in 1993. One time, after a game in Oakland, Puckett bribed the driver of the team bus to take everyone to a barbecue place "right in the middle of the ghetto,"

Winfield remembered. Chicken and ribs never tasted so good, and everyone got back to the hotel safely.

Once, the Twins had a bat boy Puckett nicknamed "Little Snoop." The Twins' star offered the kid $600 to shave off his large Afro. At first Little Snoop refused, but Puckett kept passing the hat in the Twins' clubhouse until the pot climbed to $800. The bat boy agreed to the haircut, and Puckett took the first pass at that head of hair and then pretended that the electric clippers had somehow broken.

"The kid looks in the mirror, and this big Afro has a strip right down the middle," Puckett recalled. "Little Snoop says, 'Oh, my mamma's going to kill me . . . she's going to kill me.'"

Raised in south Chicago, the youngest of nine children, Puckett loved to play baseball and said that the game kept him off the mean streets. Despite being a star third baseman for Calumet High School, he received only one scholarship offer, from Miami-Dade Junior College in Florida, which he decided was too far away from home. Instead, he found work for a time putting down carpet for the new Thunderbirds, which rolled off the line at the local Ford plant. At a tryout camp he caught the eye of Dewey Kalmer, the coach at Bradley University in Peoria, who offered him a scholarship. With the Bradley infield already set for the season, Puckett moved to the outfield and led the team with eight home runs in his lone season at the school. When Puckett's father died, the ballplayer transferred to Triton Junior College in River Grove, Illinois, so he could be closer to home. But before really getting started at Triton, Puckett played for Quincy in the Central Illinois college summer league.

Baseball was barely operational in the summer of 1981, as the major leagues were on strike. Owners wanted compensation for the loss of free-agent players to other teams. The players considered this an attempt to undercut the recent gains in free agency. Play stopped for fifty days, costing 712 major-league games, and as a result most clubs didn't pay for their scouts to do any traveling.

Jim Rantz, the Twins' assistant farm director, spent his free time watching his son, Mike, play for Peoria in the summer league. That's how he happened to be in stands when Puckett's Quincy team took the field. Rantz remembered Puckett collecting several hits and making a great throw from center field to nail a runner at the plate. The best part? No other scouts were in attendance.

Rantz compiled a glowing report about Puckett, and the Twins made the neophyte outfielder their first pick (the third overall) in that year's draft. Puckett rose through the Twins' farm system, leading the Appalachian League in batting average and hitting safely in his first sixteen games in the Single-A California League. From there, in 1984 he jumped two minor-league rungs to the Triple-A Toledo Mud Hens. Although Tom Kelly, who was a minor-league coach at the time, told the front office that Puckett was ready to play in the majors right now, the Twins waited until May, when the Mud Hens were in Maine and the Twins were in southern California to call the prospect up officially. When Puckett's connecting flight in Atlanta was delayed, he landed at Los Angeles International Airport several hours late. He took a cab to Anaheim, where the Twins were about to take the field against the Angels. With less than $20 in his pocket, Puckett had to beg for more change in the Twins' clubhouse to pay the $83 cab fare. As they say, everyone has his price.

Due to the delay, Minnesota manager Billy Gardner had already scratched Puckett's name from the starting lineup. After sitting that night Puckett made the most of his major-league debut as he singled four times the next day, becoming only the ninth big-league player in the twentieth century to break in with four hits. From there Puckett never looked back, hitting .296 his rookie season and leading the American League in hits in his fourth season, quickly becoming an integral member of the Twins' World Series run in 1987. Standing only five-foot-eight, willing to chat up anybody about just about anything, Puckett became a crowd favorite, both home and away.

"Everywhere we went Kirby got as many cheers or sometimes more than the teams we were playing," Greg Gagne said. "People loved to watch him play and just carry on."

Brian Harper added, "Kirby was an unbelievable hitter. We would shake our heads at some of the things he would do. He loved to practice and work hard. And he also made it easy for TK to manage because he hustled all the time. Here was the star of the team and running everything out, so it was easy for the manager to make sure everybody else did their jobs."

Kent Hrbek added, "When things aren't going well, sometimes it's tough to go to the ballpark. But when you'd walk into the park and Puck was there, you'd have to smile. When he was in a room he brightened it up."

Back in the spring of 1991 I made deadline with the Henderson profile, and the inaugural issue of *USA Today Baseball Weekly* was on newsstands, with a scowling picture of Rickey sharing the cover with a smaller one of Bo Jackson and an even smaller one yet of President George "Poppy" Bush, whose Yale baseball teammates remembered him in our "Nostalgia" section.

From Arizona I returned east, spending the last two weeks of spring training in Florida. To this point my only experience covering baseball had been as the "swing man" for the *San Francisco Examiner*, switching back and forth between the local Giants and Athletics. Truth be told, I knew much more about the National League, but my initial beat for *Baseball Weekly* was the junior circuit. So the remaining weeks of spring training were more of a fact-finding mission, a quick effort to get up to speed on the teams in the American League.

On the recommendation of Paul White, the esteemed editor of *Baseball Weekly*, I flew into Tampa, drove down the Gulf Coast, and stopped by the White Sox's longtime spring home in Bradenton and then the Texas Rangers' complex in Charlotte, Florida. But Paul urged me to reach Fort Myers as soon as I could and check out the two teams there, the Boston Red Sox and the Minnesota Twins. He felt the Red Sox, who had won the American League East the previous year, would certainly contend again in our first season of publication. The Twins, however, were more of an afterthought after having finished last in the AL West, twenty-nine games behind Henderson's Athletics.

I arrived in Fort Myers the following evening. After setting up at the local Holiday Inn I decided to swing by the Lee County Sports Complex, where the Red Sox and Twins played their spring home games that season. The place was brand new, as the Twins had moved over from antiquated Tinker Field in Orlando and were on their way to posting a 21–10–1 record that spring.

Even though no games were scheduled that evening, I heard the rat-tat-tat of a bat hitting a ball after I parked the rental car. Somewhere, somebody was taking some serious after-hours batting practice. No lights were on above the grandstand, and the noise came from deep inside the ballpark. Curious, I walked to the front gate, which was locked down tight. Yet just up the first-base line I found an open door. Following a dark corridor, I heard the smacks of a bat hitting horsehide.

Up ahead of me was a hint of light, which grew brighter as I drew closer. Eventually I turned the corner into a small room, where netting hung down from the ceiling and the whir of a pitching machine systematically propelled the next baseball to the far end of the batting cage. A half-dozen ballplayers were gathered around the far end, hooting and hollering as they took turns hitting in the cage. I recognized Kent Hrbek, Chili Davis, and Dan Gladden. Taking huge cuts, seemingly too big a swing for a guy his size, was Kirby Puckett.

"Who are you?" Puckett shouted at me, letting the next ball pass by, where it hit with a dull thud against the protective matting.

I told them I was with *Baseball Weekly*, the new national publication. Perhaps they had heard of it.

"I've seen it," Hrbek said dismissively. "You have to do better than putting that piss-ant Rickey Henderson out front."

"They're going with the familiar faces," Puckett said, labeling the next pitch into the mesh above my head. I wondered whether he was aiming for me.

"Same old, same old," Davis complained.

"Don't give the man a hard time," Puckett said, ready to take another swing. "That's probably who your bosses assigned you to do, ain't that right?"

"Well, sort of."

"Guys, I hate to say it," Puckett continued. "But we're nothing until we do something again."

"We won it all in '87," Hrbek said.

"And finished dead last year," Puckett said, lacing another line drive. "It's like anything these days—we have to prove ourselves all over again."

Puckett exited the batting cage and Hrbek took his place.

"But *Baseball Weekly*, man, you have to ask yourself something," Puckett continued.

I shrugged, not sure what he was talking about.

"How many teams are taking BP at this hour?" Puckett asked.

"Probably none," I replied.

"Exactly," Hrbek said, tattooing the ball with the same efficiency that Puckett had demonstrated moments earlier.

The Twins began to laugh among themselves.

"We are sick pups," Hrbek said. "No night life for us."

"It's because we love to rake, hit that ball," Puckett said. "Look at my hands," he said, holding up a paw. "Blister upon blister."

For the most part Puckett loved to play this role—the bubbly, exuberant guy who was just happy to be here, playing baseball for a living. Ted Robinson, the Twins' television play-by-play man in 1991, can recall only a few times when Puckett lowered his guard. One such instance occurred that season in New York, where the Twins played the Yankees soon after Los Angeles police had repeatedly beaten Rodney King.

147

"The ballclub had been told to ride the team bus, no cabs or subway, to Yankee Stadium in the Bronx. It was a precaution after what happened in LA," Robinson said. "On the field before the game Puckett was asked about the incident and he said, 'Why they'd have to hit him so many times?'

"Kirby didn't talk about serious politics that much. But I couldn't help thinking he just gave us a small glimpse into his life. What it's like to be a black man, a prominent black athlete, in this world."

Years later Robinson said that Puckett was "one of those great half-full people," meaning that "the glass was always half-full with him."

Others sometimes weren't as convinced. Ann Bauleke, who chronicled the Twins so well for the *City Pages* in Minneapolis during this period, recalled Puckett as being "most generous with his time. He spent hours with me." Still, she added that the Twins' star "always kept up a wall. . . . I don't think he let many people in. He was big hearted and really did carry the team with his bat and his glove, and he was fun—quick-witted, a smart tease, not with the usual sophomoric stuff that can go on."

Rick Aguilera remembered that Puckett was the first Twins player he met after coming over in the midseason trade with the New York Mets in 1989. The pitcher will always treasure that moment. "The Twins were on the road, playing the Yankees in the Bronx, and the game had already started by the time I got there," Aguilera said. "I went in the clubhouse and got my uniform on. I walked down the runway to the dugout and stood there on the ground level, right where you have the two or three steps up to the dugout.

"I was standing there, watching the game, and Puckett had just grounded out. He ran back to the dugout, disgusted with himself, and then he saw me standing there. He walked down the steps and shook my hand, called me Aggie, and welcomed me to the Twins. I couldn't believe it. Here was the face of the Twins. He had just grounded out, pretty upset with himself, and then he went out of his way to bring me on board."

That's one of things we expect from our heroes, isn't it? A common touch that transcends the every day and can reach out to so many. Perhaps this is why some individuals step so easily into the hero's role, whereas others battle for admiration and rarely receive much adulation or even respect.

About a four-hour drive away from the Metrodome in downtown Minneapolis, north by northwest along Interstate 94, lies Fargo, North Dakota, where Roger Maris grew up. The slugger was born in Hibbing, Minnesota, the most famous native son after Robert Zimmerman, a.k.a. Bob Dylan. Whereas the enigmatic singer-songwriter and cultural icon adroitly kept fame at arm's length and somebody like Kirby Puckett, at least when he was in uniform, seemed to revel in all the attention, Maris never really warmed to the flame of celebrity. The E Street Band guitarist and SiriusXM disc jockey "Little Steven" Van Zandt once said that the home run hero "may be textbook on how not to handle to fame."

Early in Maris's life the family moved to Fargo, and driving across the northern Plains, it can be easy to dismiss the region as flat and somewhat predictable—little more than a patchwork of September wheat and sugar beets. Yet down here at ground level the land can rise and fall like waves out on an inland sea. The wind echoes down from the Canadian border, rippling everything that stands in its path.

In 1991 Maris was given a measure of respect as baseball's Statistical Accuracy Committee moved his sixty-one home run season of 1961, once and for all, ahead of Babe Ruth's sixty home run campaign accomplished in 1927. Commissioner Ford Frick supposedly hung an asterisk on Maris's accomplishment because it occurred in a season with twelve more games that Ruth's. Actually, there was no real asterisk. The two magnificent seasons—sixty-one and sixty—were simply listed separately in the record book.

The debate assured that fans knew more about the record and supposed controversy than they ever did the man. No matter that Maris played in the World Series seven times or that he was a fine all-around player, as good with the glove as he was with a bat in his hands. Or that despite hitting sixty-one home runs in 1961, an accomplishment that some once again consider the all-time record for the most home runs in a season, dismissing the steroids era of McGwire, Sosa, Bonds, and others, Maris didn't find his way into the Hall of Fame. In all likelihood he never will be enshrined in Cooperstown. That seemingly goes with the territory for a guy who was never comfortable in the spotlight, never as quick with a joke or a quote as such Yankee teammates as Yogi Berra and Mickey Mantle.

To catch a glimpse of Maris, one must walk the wide streets of Fargo and talk with old friends and family members, who are sometimes as reluctant as he was to rehash the glory days and what could have been. Although this slugger retired to Florida and died in Houston at the age of fifty-one, he came home to be buried in a small cemetery on the northern edge of town. There he lies under a Manchurian ash tree, close to Kenny Hunt, his boyhood friend and another major leaguer from these parts. In the Holy Cross Cemetery Maris's tombstone is in the shape of a ball diamond, with the inscription, "61 in '61—Against All Odds." "My heart has always been close to Fargo and North Dakota," Maris once said.

A museum to the man can be found at the West Acres Shopping Center, a few miles from downtown Fargo. A seventy-two-foot-long, ten-foot-high showcase stands along the hallway to the parking lot, around the corner from the Sears store. The display includes Maris's Gold Glove and Sultan of Swat awards. The West Acres mall had 2 million visitors a few years back. How many came to view the Maris memorabilia and watch the footage of him hitting his record-breaking home run and how many came to shop at the CVS remains anybody's guess.

Born Roger Maras in Hibbing on September 10, 1934, the family changed the spelling of the family name when he was eighteen years old. "I was told it was because of the last two letters, A and S. You know how you put them together and how it sounds," said Orv Kelly, who knew the home run hero in high school and, in later years, helped organize the annual charity golf tournament in Fargo that bears Maris's name. "Nobody wants to be teased like that from the fans. The family changed it, and that was it."

Don Gooselaw, another boyhood friend, remembered being in the Navy and searching for Maras, not Maris, in the *Sporting News*. "It threw me that I couldn't find him," Gooselaw said. "But when I came home on leave, somebody told me the family had changed the spelling. That was all I ever made of it."

Once asked about the name change on a team questionnaire, Maris simply answered, "Immaterial."

Maris once said that his brother, Rudy, really had "more enthusiasm about sports than I did." Rudy Maris was a year older and Roger would tag along to sandlot games in the empty lots near the train tracks and roundhouses in the area. At Shanley High School the brothers played football, basketball, and baseball. Shanley ran a single-wing offense, patterned after the famed University of Michigan attack of the time. Rudy threw the ball and Roger ran it. In fact, Roger set the state record for five touchdowns in a single game, against Devils Lake in 1951. The scores came on an eighty-eight-yard run, ninety-yard kickoff return, forty-five-yard punt return, thirty-two-yard run, and a twenty-five-yard interception return. "God, he loved to hit," Kelly recalled. "Rog was a cornerback [on defense], and nobody I ever saw could come up to the line [of scrimmage] as fast as him and just rip people. It got to the point where other teams simply stopped running the ball to his side of the field."

Such play attracted the attention of legendary football coach Bud Wilkinson at the University of Oklahoma. Maris was offered a scholarship to play football for the Sooners, and he rode the bus for an entire day from Fargo down to Norman. One story has it that when no one from the university was there to meet him, Maris boarded the next bus back home. But several high school friends maintained that Maris did stay in Norman, at least for a day or so, before he decided more time in the classroom wasn't for him.

Fresh out of high school Maris signed with the Cleveland Indians and broke in with the hometown Fargo-Moorhead Twins, where he was the rookie of the year. Four seasons later he reached the majors, playing in Cleveland and then in Kansas City. He was traded from the Athletics to the Yankees—one of fifty-nine players involved in fifteen different deals between the two ballclubs in the late 1950s. His first year in New York (1960), Maris hit 39 home runs, drove in 112 to lead the American League, and won his first Gold Glove. He and Mickey Mantle suddenly were the best one-two punch in baseball, with the Yankees reaching the World Series the next four seasons. But none of it could compare with the year Maris put together in 1961.

Incredibly, through the first ten games of that memorable season, Maris hit just .161. Mantle, the favorite of the New York fans and the front office, already had six home runs before Maris hit his first, the only one he would hit in the month of April. Management asked Maris whether he was having trouble at home. Maris told them no, and besides, it was none of their business. The front office had his vision checked. When the results showed nothing unusual, Maris was told that the organization didn't care how many hits he got—after all, there were plenty of singles hitters in the game. No, what the brass wanted were homers, dingers, the precious long ball. Give us the sweet snap of the bat hitting that ball.

Maris got the message, and throughout the rest of the season he was remarkably consistent. Maris hit eleven home runs in May, fifteen in June, thirteen in July, eleven in August, and with the press now dogging his every move and hanging on his every word, he hit nine in September and one more to break the Babe's record in October.

"The only peace I had by the end was in-between the lines," Maris said years later. "As a ballplayer, I would be delighted to do it again. As an individual, I doubt if I could possibly go through it again."

Back at the museum inside the West Acres Shopping Center, a boy stood with his father, taking in the showcase exhibit. The kid stared at the flickering black-and-white image of Maris circling the bases after his record-breaking hit, head down, running at a machine-like clip. The kid leaned in closer, fogging the glass.

If some careers are as regular as tomorrow's dawn, then Maris's was like a comet flashing overhead. For a few months it filled the night sky with brilliance, and then it was gone. In essence, Maris had several good seasons and one stellar one. His sixty-one home runs were twenty-two more than his next best season. In fact, Maris averaged less than twenty-three home runs over his twelve-year career. But what he accomplished, though it was so fleeting, had a certain solidness and even class to it. Too many ballplayers today seem to gaze a bit too long after the ball is sent soaring toward the fence, acting as though they were atop of the world when, of course, nobody enjoys such a vantage point for very long.

———

With his leaping catch against the Plexiglas and driving in two of the Twins' first three runs, Kirby Puckett had certainly backed up his big talk before the game. But one thing he couldn't do was pitch the ball. Slugger of the moment? Sure thing. A starting pitcher who could carry Minnesota far into the game? That fell to Scott Erickson on this night. The Twins, with only a three-man rotation, came into Game Six desperate for an extended performance from their starter. Kevin Tapani had gone only four innings in the last loss in Atlanta, and the Twins' bullpen was extended, perhaps overly so.

Though Erickson was a shadow of his midseason self, the twenty-game winner went six-plus innings, surviving on breaking stuff, with help from some great defense behind him. Not only did Puckett make a leaping catch for the ages on Ron Gant's blast, but left fielder Dan Gladden ran down Sid Bream's opposite-field line drive with two on, and third baseman Scott Leius leaped to snare Brian Hunter's line drive.

"This was the last game of the year for me," Erickson said, "so I tried to go out there and give it all I had."

Twins pitching coach Dick Such said Erickson "didn't have his good stuff. But Junior [Ortiz] kept saying that his ball was moving, so we stayed with him."

Puckett's great catch made that decision easier. "It went farther than I thought it would," Erickson said of Gant's blast. "He hit a breaking ball. I was just happy the way it turned out, that Kirby caught it."

Sometimes we don't fully comprehend or acknowledge the power of time. We want to believe that it remains regimented, methodical, always logical in how it unfolds on the land. But often time runs away from us, speeding up in a heartbeat, gazing back at us like a mischievous child, and before we realize it the years have flown away from us. Perhaps that's what happened to Kirby Puckett.

"You have to remember that for so long Minnesota was the land of the also-rans," said John Rosengren, a local writer and Minnesota native. "From the North Stars to the early Twins to the Vikings, this was the land of second place. We were always the bridesmaid, never the bride.

"That changed when the Twins first won in 1987, and then it changed forever when they won again in 1991. And who was the guy at the center of both of those teams? That teddy bear of a guy, Kirby Puckett. The player who always had a smile for everybody.

"So when the sad, sad ending happens to Kirby Puckett it just breaks your heart that much more. Because here's the guy who helped give us that wonderful feeling in 1987 and again in 1991, in particular his performance in Game Six when he almost single-handedly won it for us. When he's the one who falls from grace, it really hurts."

The way Puckett played that evening, the capacity crowd chanting his name, waving those white Homer Hankies, anybody with a heart would freeze-frame it all. In a perfect world this would be the lasting memory of a Hall of Fame player who so many in baseball loved.

Unfortunately, this moment of greatness and grace ran away from us far too soon as well, leaving things in a jumbled mess between this night and the events to come.

Stew Thornley grew up in Minneapolis, becoming a noted baseball historian and the Twins' official scorer. For him, Puckett and Mickey Mantle, another larger-than-life baseball star, share so many similarities, good and bad.

"Mantle was my hero growing up," Thornley said, "just like Puckett was the hero for so many in this part of the country years later. I think that sometimes it's as much the fault of the fans as it is the players when it comes to these things. We want to believe so much. That's what we fell into with [Mark] McGwire and [Sammy] Sosa, before the revelations about steroids came out.

"Both Puckett and Mantle were far from perfect, as we found out. And sometimes the fans have difficulty accepting such transgressions, especially by their heroes."

Thornley assembled a thorough, often-moving biography about Puckett for the Society for American Baseball Research. Near the end he wrote, "Learning the truth wasn't easy for many, particularly those in Minnesota, and some had trouble reconciling the Puckett they had chosen to envision and the real Puckett—a human being with many virtuous qualities as well as some flaws."

Thornley acknowledged those words were as much about his boyhood hero as the star he later covered. "I was thinking of Mantle," he said. "How torn I was after reading *Ball Four* and hearing the other stories that showed that he was just another gifted athlete trying to be a man while playing a boy's game."

After the 1991 World Series Puckett would have other memorable times at the plate, leading the American League in hits in 1992 and in RBIs in 1994. But he would never again play in the postseason, and his career would end with the 1995 season. On September 28 Puckett was trying to drive in Chuck Knoblauch for his hundredth RBI of that season when a pitch from Cleveland right-hander Dennis Martinez sailed inside. It caught Puckett square in the face, breaking his jaw. This time his teammates ran from the dugout to find him lying in a pool of blood. "I still can't believe how much he was bleeding," Knoblauch said.

The next spring Puckett returned to action, and a week before Opening Day he batted against the Atlanta Braves once again, this time in Grapefruit League action. It would be Puckett's last appearance as a player. The next morning he awoke with blurred vision. A black dot had appeared in his right eye, and the diagnosis was a central retina vein occlusion in that eye and glaucoma in both eyes. Despite three surgeries his vision didn't return to the point at which he could hit big-league pitching anymore. As a result, Puckett's career was over at the age of thirty-six.

On July 12, 1996, he made the announcement at the Metrodome that he was leaving baseball. "I never took the game for granted," he said, a bandage over his eye. "I loved it and treated it with respect, but my life isn't over. The world hasn't come to an end."

Puckett told his teammates that he loved them and would miss them. He added that he didn't plan to put on a baseball uniform again.

"Considering what's happened in the last few years, with the labor problems and everything else, the game can hardly afford to lose a player of Kirby's ability and personality," Twins manager Tom Kelly told the *Los Angeles Times*. "We saw how much he'll be missed this year when we'd go into Boston or Baltimore or New York, and fans would have banners for him or would chant, 'We want Kirby.'"

Scott Leius's time with the Twins had ended the year before Puckett's abrupt retirement. Now playing for Cleveland, he attended the sullen gathering as the Indians were the visiting team in Minneapolis that day. "It was a tough day," he said. "But being there I realized how lucky I was. I played for three teams at the big-league level [the Twins, Indians, and Royals]. But there was something about that

Minnesota team. Hrbek, TK, Kirby—I'd run through a wall for those guys."

———

Some of the most famous home runs ever hit didn't sound exactly right. They didn't quite have that dry snap of a branch out in the woods as they left the bat. Mark McGwire's sixty-second, which broke Roger Maris's mark for the most homers in a season, came with a violent crack, leaving those in attendance wondering at first whether it had enough height to carry over the outfield fence. The same with Joe Carter's World Series–winning home run in 1993. He didn't start jumping for joy until the ball cleared the left-field fence.

If a hitter isn't careful, he can fall in love with the sound of a well-hit ball. His mind can play tricks on him and make it sound better than it perhaps is. That drives veteran ballplayers crazy when they watch the superstars of today standing there, admiring a ball that doesn't quite go out of the ballpark. For the sweet sound can be as illusory as any mirage in a desert.

When Puckett homered in Game Six he wasn't sure he had really connected.

"The good ones you know right away," he said years later. "But that one in the World Series wasn't really a good one. We just happened to have close to sixty thousand people in the place, and when you get that many people in there it gets hot, and the ball tends to carry."

Perhaps it had some help too. For years opposing teams grumbled about how the Twins' long flies often carried to the seats whereas theirs died on the warning track. The Metrodome was air conditioned, and in 2003 Dick Ericson, the stadium's longtime superintendent, confirmed that blowers behind home plate were sometimes turned on high when the Twins were at bat and throttled back when the opposing team stepped up. "It's your home-field advantage," Ericson told the *Minneapolis Star-Tribune*. "Every stadium has one."

Between the sound of the bat and whatever he knew about the stadium's internal workings, Puckett bolted out of the box in Game Six. "I was running hard because I thought it was going to hit the Plexiglas above the fence," he said. "I was looking to get a double, or maybe it bounces off the glass and does something weird and I can get a triple. I don't want an inside-the-parker. That's too much work. But then it landed six or seven rows up, and that's because there were so many people. They helped put it out."

Any hitter will tell you that there's a real Zen thing to hitting home runs. Try too hard and you'll surely fail—pop one up to the outfield at best. But begin to relax, try to believe that it's simply a science, and occasionally a lightning bolt shows itself in the heavens.

Puckett reached the majors as a leadoff hitter and was scared to death when Ray Miller, the Twins' manager before Tom Kelly, began to bat him third in the Minnesota lineup. "I wasn't a home run hitter," Puckett said. "I told Ray that. I didn't think I'd ever be a home run hitter. But he told me to relax and just hit the ball hard, and you know something? It was the strangest thing. The homers? They happened. They were there when I needed them."

Our last conversation about the yin and yang of home runs took place in the autumn of 1998, almost seven years to the day after Puckett went deep against Atlanta, extending that epic World Series to a seventh and final game. We were in Puckett's executive office with the Twins, overlooking downtown Minneapolis. On the wall hung framed newspaper front pages and colored drawings from the Twins' glory days. We spoke excitedly about the 1998 recent season that saw McGwire and Sosa break Maris's single-season home run record, how the whole shebang seemed almost too good to be true.

"I'm happy as an ex-player," Puckett told me, "but mostly I was excited for everybody in the country who is a sports fan. My kids are taking about it. They're eight and six, and before, they didn't even watch baseball. But with this, they knew what was going on.

"Even Rip took a day off this season. He's about the same age as I am, but he looks like he's a hundred years old. I asked him this year, 'Was it worth it?' And he said it was. But I said, 'Look at you, man, you look terrible.' For me, an off day was good. But Cal Ripken never saw it that way.

"It was all unbelievable. I know, after the strike in 1994 it was ugly at a lot of ballparks. If I didn't sign autographs for everybody, somebody would yell, 'Hey, Puckett, we pay your salary.' But with this '98 season, we've healed the past."

Puckett's discourse was equal parts jazz riff and state-of-the-union speech, and in listening to the tape of our conversation years later I still want to believe so much about this sweet spot in time. I remember it being a sunny day in Minneapolis, with the wind gusting out of the west, off the prairie. Not cold enough yet that you couldn't go down to the local sandlot and see whether you could get a game going. I almost mentioned that to Puckett. Hey, let's get out of here and see if kids were playing somewhere in town. Because as he spoke about hitting that home run in Game Six and just dingers in general, the words just tumbled out of his mouth, rapid-fire style, punctuated with "man" this and "man" that. A barrage that once prompted Sparky Anderson to ask, "Do you ever shut up?"

But, of course, when Puckett got on a roll nobody wanted him to shut up. For we were witnessing one of baseball's wonders: a guy who could play the game and loved to do so too.

If I had known what was on the horizon when it came to Puckett and the revelations of his private life, I would have begged him to come with me. Let's drive around town and look for the game or go down to the field here at the Metrodome and perhaps run around those bases again. For Puckett had made good on his vow. Except for a day or two in spring training, he hadn't put on the uniform to coach again. Instead, he went to work in an office and was a public relations emissary as a team executive vice president. If we had known what would soon unfold, I would have asked, and I like to believe that Puckett would have said,

"Sure thing, man. Let's go see if we can scare us up a game. There's got to be someplace a guy can still swing a bat in this town."

———

Some of Puckett's teammates believe he didn't coach because his weight embarrassed him. An issue when he was playing, his weight got him when he ballooned up in retirement and refused the team's offers to be a regular hitting coach in Florida or when the ballclub returned north for another season. After retirement he spent a lot of time fishing, a pursuit he had fallen in love with during his decade-plus in the Twin Cities. Sometimes he went with ex-teammates, like Kent Hrbek, but usually he kept company with guys outside his old circle of baseball friends.

To the public, Puckett sported an All-American image and marriage. He and his wife, Tonya, had adopted two children, a son, Kirby Jr., and a daughter, Catherine. Yet the couple divorced in 2002, shortly after Puckett was inducted into the National Baseball Hall of Fame in Cooperstown, New York. Tonya Puckett recounted what she said was a history of domestic violence, including a phone call in which the superstar threatened to kill her. "I feel Kirby went out and played ball and made a living," she told local writer Bob Sansevere. "My job was raising my children and being a wife and doing everything to build him up in the community and make it happen."

After that bombshell, Laura Nygren stepped forward. She claimed that she had been Puckett's mistress for eighteen years. "Kirby is not the person everyone thinks he is," Nygren told the (St. Paul) *Pioneer Press*.

Then, in October 2002, Puckett was charged with false imprisonment, criminal sexual misconduct, and assault after an incident at a restaurant in Eden Prairie, Minnesota. A woman accused him of pulling her into the men's room and groping her. The case went to trial, and although Puckett was found not guilty, his reputation would be forever tarnished. *Sports Illustrated* soon ran a story with the headline, "The Rise and Fall of Kirby Puckett."

Looking back on things, Brian Harper wished that Puckett had stayed closer to the game after being forced to abruptly go to the sidelines because of his vision problems. The catcher remembered being "emotionally done" when he hung up his uniform in 1995. "But Kirby's situation was different from any of the rest of us," Harper said. "He woke up one day, and his playing career was over. Just like that, it was over. He sure would have had more good years before the glaucoma. That had to be hard for him.

"I think he would have eventually gone into coaching. Obviously, he was struggling with a lot of things. Still, I had heard he was going to get with a nutritionist for his weight. He was ready to turn things around."

Chili Davis wasn't sure coaching—somehow staying in the game— would have helped. "That's tough to say," he said. "The only thing I wish for him is that he was peaceful when he went. As far as hanging in the game? He brought so much to the game already. I mean the man did enough.

"I'm glad he's in the Hall. He belongs in the Hall. He went through a couple of ordeals in Minnesota after his playing days ended. He had moved to Arizona to try and start his life over again."

Ron Gardenhire added, "Puck would have been great as a roving instructor. He would have enjoyed going to other cities, talking to everybody, from the outfielders on how to play the ball to talking to base runners about what to look for. The way he was I don't know if he could have tempered himself to coaching every day with the same outfit. He was so full of life and always going, always trying to see what was next. The grind of a full-time coaching for him? That would have been too hard for him, I'm afraid."

In March 2006 Puckett suffered a stroke and died soon afterward at St. Joseph's Hospital and Medical Center in Phoenix. He was forty-five years old.

Several of his closest friends in baseball—Davis, Dan Gladden, Ken Griffey Jr. among them—gathered at the hospital and said their good-byes, even though Puckett was on a respirator by that point.

"By then he couldn't hear us anymore," Gladden recalled. "Everything was working, except the mind was gone. But we were able to say good-bye—each of us in our own special way."

Davis added, "The only thing I wish is that I'd had the opportunity to spend more time with him after he moved down from Minnesota, before he passed. I talked him to him right around the Super Bowl that year. Dan Gladden was in town, and we called him up, and we were going to go by and see him, but he said he was busy. . . . It never happened, and the next thing I know Gladden is calling me, telling me that Puck had had the stroke."

A public memorial service for Puckett drew fifteen thousand to the Metrodome, the site of his biggest moment in baseball. At first Torii Hunter was scheduled to speak, along with Kent Hrbek, Tom Kelly, Al Newman, Harmon Killebrew, Cal Ripken, and Andy MacPhail. But in the end Hunter had to beg off. "What do they want me to do?" Hunter said. "Cry?"

Garth Brooks, a huge Puckett fan, couldn't even bring himself to attend. The country music star wasn't sure he could make it through the event without breaking down as well.

Only a few years before, Major League Baseball had wanted to eliminate the Twins as a major-league franchise through contraction. The former superstar had visited the state legislature, urging support for a new downtown ballpark. With Puckett's death, efforts for a new stadium soon gained momentum.

"Over the last week I've found myself closing my eyes and replaying all the times I spent with Kirby," Ripken said, "whether it was on the field [or] off the field. I found myself replaying the emotions over and over again. You know what happened? I started to feel better."

When it was Tom Kelly's turn to speak, he asked all of his former players in attendance to stand with him during his remarks. Their ranks included Jack Morris, who was seated next to Rod Carew.

Certainly there were tears, but there was laughter too. MacPhail urged that the crowd consider the memorial service as a celebration too. In that spirit, video clips were shown on the Jumbotron, including Puckett's 1997 appearance on the *Late Show with David Letterman*, in which he read the show's nightly Top Ten. On that evening it listed the ways his name was mispronounced. Among those were Englepuck Kirbydink, The Puckett Formerly Known as Kirby, Turkey Bucket, and even Kent Hrbek.

The real Kent Hrbek couldn't help but smile at this. "The people of Minnesota are losing an icon," Hrbek later said. "Paul Bunyan was big. Puck's as big as Paul Bunyan around here. He's still right alongside him."

Outside of the Twin Cities the baseball world briefly came to a stop that day. The White Sox's Ozzie Guillen watched the ceremony on television and wept. "I think Dave Winfield said the right thing," Guillen said. "[Puckett] was the only player in the history of baseball everybody loved."

Years later Hrbek joked about how so many cats and dogs and kids in this part of the world were named Kirby. Hrbek may have been a native son, a guy who went on to stardom in his hometown, but he played second fiddle to Puckett.

"And I loved every minute of it," he said.

———

All of it—the promise, the catch, the triple—would be remembered as prologue to Kirby Puckett's at-bat against Charlie Leibrandt in the bottom of the eleventh inning.

When that changeup rose up in the zone, Puckett did just enough to drive it over the fence. Near second base, as he circled the diamond, Puckett pumped his right arm several times, yelling "Yeah, yeah!" His home run trot became instantly as memorable as Carlton Fisk's sixteen years earlier in another Game Six.

"I figured it was out because I always watch the outfielders," said Ron Gardenhire, who was the Twins' third-base coach on this evening. "They were following it, but they weren't catching up to it. Then you start looking at the fans standing up, raising their eyes, and I was just kind of backing down the line after Puck hit it.

"The more I watched, the more I started to get myself in fist-pump mode. I was getting myself in line to shake his hand."

Chili Davis waited with the rest of teammates at home plate, watching Puckett round the bases, almost in disbelief by what had transpired.

"I don't care what people may say about Kirby Puckett these days, but I will always have a place in my heart for him," Davis said decades later. "He's my favorite player, my favorite teammate—ever. No ifs, ands, or buts. The guy was very giving. He livened up the locker room every day he was there. You'd never really see him have a bad day. If I said, 'Puck, I need something.' He'd say, 'Dog, it's in my locker. Get it. Take what you need.'"

Rounding third base, the Metrodome now complete bedlam, Puckett saw Gardenhire, who had both hands raised in the air. Puckett slapped them and continued on. "We were about as happy and as pumped up as you can be," Gardenhire recalled.

The Twins players poured out of the dugout, forming a half-circle at home plate. Backup catcher Junior Ortiz was there to greet Puckett, with Dan Gladden and Kent Hrbek right behind him, and Davis ready to hug his friend. When the slugger touched home plate the Twins gathered around him, forming a pile of humanity that briefly concealed their star player from view. When Puckett broke away from the crowd, walking toward the dugout, he raised his fist again in the air. After slapping hands again with Ortiz, he greeted hitting coach Terry Crowley and then hugged manager Tom Kelly.

Game Six remains a testament to Puckett's ability to rise to the occasion as a ballplayer. His triple back in the first inning drove in Chuck Knoblauch with the game's first run, followed by his leaping catch up against the Plexiglas, robbing Ron Gant of extra bases only a few feet away from where he would later put his game-winner. With that home run Puckett joined Carlton Fisk, Dusty Rhodes, Tommy Henrich, Eddie Mathews, Kirk Gibson, and Bill Mazeroski as hitters who won a World Series game with one swing of the bat. In addition, he became the first player to collect a sacrifice fly, a triple, and a home run in a World Series game.

"I never hit a game-winning home run," Puckett told a group of reporters on the field after the game. "Not that I can remember. Other guys have done it all around here—Dan Gladden, Herbie. I couldn't believe it. I finally did something I said I was going to do."

After midnight, deep in the bowels of the Metrodome, Braves manager Bobby Cox was questioned about using starting pitcher Charlie Leibrandt in relief. "Why not Charlie?" Cox replied. "He's faced Puckett before. He keeps the ball down. He's a fifteen-game winner. Charlie just got a ball up and Puckett hit it hard."

Braves catcher Greg Olson remembered hoping that when the ball left Puckett's bat it would glance off the fence and somehow stay in play. "But I had a feeling as soon as he hit it there was going to be a Game Seven."

Puckett finally made it up the long stairwell from the field to the Twins' clubhouse. Once he was there he sat down in front of his locker, shaking his head. "Man, oh, man," he said. "I don't believe it."

Gene Larkin remembered Jack Morris, who was scheduled to be Minnesota's starting pitcher in Game Seven, saying, "Now it's my turn to do my job. Kirby did his job."

In fact, Morris had already set the stage for Game Seven by telling the media, "In the immortal words of the late, great Marvin Gaye, 'Let's get it on.'"

"After Game Six, when we went back in the clubhouse, we were at ease," Gladden recalled, "because we looked over and there was Jack Morris, and you could tell that he was already getting his game face on. You just knew he was going to pitch us a great ballgame the next night."

Well past midnight, after the television cameras had thinned out in the home clubhouse, CBS's Pat O'Brien drifted by Puckett's locker. Reaching into his pocket, he pulled out a roll of greenbacks and jokingly held them out for the Twins' star.

"There's more where that came from," O'Brien said.

"Well, give it here," Puckett said, playing along with the gag.

With a smile, O'Brien slid the cash back into his pocket. On this evening it became the only play Puckett let slip away.

For the first time since 1987, when the Twins defeated the St. Louis Cardinals, the World Series was going seven games. For those watching at home on television, many of them could close their eyes and still picture Kirby Puckett swinging for the fences against Charlie Leibrandt and then running hard out of the batter's box, hustling as he rounded the first-base bag. Only when the Twins' star saw the ball somehow fall into stands did he raise his arms toward the heavens in celebration.

Fans would long remember what had happened this evening. How one individual, arguably the best-known ballplayer on either team, had risen to the occasion. And the best part? This Series still had one more game to play. As announcer Jack Buck told the national television audience, "And we will see you tomorrow night."

———

**FINAL SCORE: TWINS 4, BRAVES 3**

|     | 1 | 2 | 3 | 4 | 5 | 6 | 7 | 8 | 9 | 10 | 11 | R | H | E |
|-----|---|---|---|---|---|---|---|---|---|----|----|---|---|---|
| ATL | 0 | 0 | 0 | 0 | 2 | 0 | 1 | 0 | 0 | 0  | 0  | 3 | 9 | 1 |
| MIN | 2 | 0 | 0 | 0 | 1 | 0 | 0 | 0 | 0 | 0  | 1  | 4 | 9 | 0 |

ATTENDANCE: **55,155**    LENGTH OF GAME: **3 HOURS, 46 MINUTES**

# Game Seven

SUNDAY, OCTOBER 27, 1991
AT HUBERT H. HUMPHREY METRODOME
MINNEAPOLIS, MINNESOTA

The Braves' Mark Lemke best summed up the mood of both teams before the decisive Game Seven. "It seems every game we've played since the last week of the season was the seventh game of the World Series," he said. "Might as well play in the seventh game of the World Series."

As Jack Morris warmed up, Marvin Gaye's "Let's Get It On" appropriately played over the Metrodome sound system, and when stadium announcer Bob Casey warned the sellout crowd that there was no smoking inside the facility, Kent Hrbek one last time pantomimed smoking a cigarette and then shaking his index finger disapprovingly. As the fans roared, he then pretended to slug back a beer, following that recommendation with a big thumbs-up.

In the six previous games the Twins usually scored in the early innings, and the longest wait for the first run to go up on the scoreboard occurred in Game Five in Atlanta, when the Braves struck for four the fourth inning. And of course, that contest eventually became a 14–5 laugher. Yet early in Game Seven both teams realized that the respective pitchers were in control. Right-hander Jack Morris had been the Twins' Opening Day starter, the starting pitcher in the 1991 All-Star Game, against the Braves' Tom Glavine. Morris had pitched the first game of American League Championship Series and the first game of this World Series. On this evening, with a 6–1 record already in postseason play, his split-finger fastball displayed a lot of life.

Morris loved to throw the pitch, which darted down at the last moment, when he got ahead in the count. As a result, the Braves' hitters told themselves to be patient: try to stay out of two-strike situations because Morris would often then go with the split, which soon appeared unhittable this evening.

Atlanta did mount a threat in the second inning, when David Justice singled to center field. Running on the pitch, he went to second on Sid Bream's groundout. With one out, the Braves had a runner in scoring position, and they almost brought him around, and then some when Brian Hunter hit a line drive down the left-field line that just hooked foul. After that close call Morris struck him out with a high fastball and then induced Greg Olson to pop out to second baseman Chuck Knoblauch.

"From then on you could tell that Jack had it going," Twins shortstop Greg Gagne recalled. "All of his pitches had great movement in Game Seven. Especially that split of his."

The split-finger fastball was a modification of the forkball, which was used to great success by Bullet Joe Bush in the 1920s and Elroy Face three decades later. The forkball was held more in the palm of the hand, while the split-finger was often wedged between the index and middle fingers. It was thrown with the same motion and arm position as the fastball. In the 1980s not only Morris but also Roger Clemens, Dave Stewart, Mike Scott, Donnie Moore, Bruce Sutter, and nearly everybody on the San Francisco Giants pitching staff threw the split or modified forkball with relative degrees of success. If the slider had been the pitch of the sixties, the split-finger soon became known as the pitch of the eighties.

*Sports Illustrated* called it the "newest of the substitute spitters," following in the contrails of the curveball (allegedly originated by Candy Cummings in the 1860s), the screwball (perfected by Christy Mathewson and then executed so well by Carl Hubbell and, later, Fernando Valenzuela), the spitball itself (outlawed in 1920), and then the knuckleball, the slider, and even the circle changeup. Basically, all of these pitches, when thrown effectively, complement the fastball. A batter cannot be ready for a little high heat and some kind of breaking ball at the same time. Even a difference of six miles per hour between offerings can be enough to keep a hitter off balance and make a pitcher a winner.

The split-finger proved to be easy to learn and, back in the day, came with its own stirring advocate, Roger Craig. Standing six-foot-four, with an upbeat folksy manner, Craig believed only in God, country, and his longtime wife, Carolyn, more than the beloved split-finger. A right-hander, he had pitched for a dozen years in the big leagues, winning titles with the Brooklyn Dodgers, Los Angeles Dodgers, and St. Louis Cardinals. Still, Craig didn't discover the split-finger fastball in time to save himself as he lost a league-high twenty-four games and twenty-two games in consecutive seasons with the New York Mets before they were ever Amazin'. It wasn't until after his playing days were over that Craig stumbled upon the pitch that would change his life and the career of so many others as well.

In the winter of 1980 Craig was teaching at the San Diego School of Baseball. Most of his students were teenagers, and he wanted to come up with a breaking ball they could quickly use in games. That's when Craig tried the variation on the forkball, shifting the ball slightly away from the palm and throwing it with a fastball pitch motion that many of students could duplicate. The rest, they say, is history. Not only did Craig's kids soon gain mastery of the pitch, but when he joined the Detroit Tigers as Sparky Anderson's pitching coach the next season, he brought the inspiration along with him.

In the Motor City Craig's first disciples of the split were Milt Wilcox and Jack Morris. The Tigers won the World Series in 1984 and led the league in team ERA. Morris had two complete-game victories in that Fall Classic and later said that the split-finger fastball "turned me into a strikeout pitcher."

Despite widespread success, many in baseball soon became concerned about the pitch. Anderson maintained that if a pitcher threw the split too much, his fastball could lose velocity. "In the beginning it was so wonderful because it was a freak thing for the hitters," the Tigers' manager said. "But once you throw it, throw it, throw it, the hitters sit there and watch, and it's no longer the same pitch."

Craig strongly disagreed with his old friend. After leaving Detroit, Craig became manager of the San Francisco Giants in 1985. I met him the following season when I first began covering baseball for the *San Francisco Examiner* in the Bay Area, and I never found a more delightful person to talk baseball with. By that point Craig had become such an evangelist for the split-finger that he received a half-dozen or more calls weekly from across the country about throwing the pitch. The ballclub put together a question-and-answer form letter, ROGER CRAIG TALKS ABOUT THE SPLIT-FINGERED FASTBALL, which was sent to pitchers at all levels, including the major leagues.

In time Anderson and other critics of the split pretty much carried the day. Almost a quarter-century after the "Worst to First" World Series between the Twins and the Braves, the number of major-league pitchers throwing the split-finger fastball had dropped markedly, with Roy Halladay, Dan Haren, Jonathan Papelbon, and Koji Uehara among the star hurlers still using it on a regular basis. Such ballclubs as the Reds, Padres, Rays, Twins, and even Craig's old ballclub, the Giants, advised their younger pitchers to try another secondary or breaking pitch. Tampa Bay manager Joe Maddon said the pitch "put a lot of pressure on the elbow."

Pitcher Mark Grant on the Atlanta bench, sidelined for the 1991 season with a shoulder injury, watched Morris in Game Seven and thought about what could have been. Drafted in the first round, tenth pick overall, by the San Francisco Giants in 1981, this right-hander also fell under the tutelage of Roger Craig, but Grant hadn't been able to fully master the split-finger fastball. In addition, Grant saw how his elbow often tightened up after he threw the pitch. That's what made Morris's performance in Game Seven so amazing to Grant—he knew how painful and how difficult the split could be to throw, especially for strikes.

"Jack Morris's split was the probably the best ever," Grant remembered. "[Hall of Famer] Bruce Sutter's was right there with it. . . . It can be a devastating pitch."

This is also true sometimes for the catcher as much as the batter, because a split invariably results in pitches in the dirt. In Game Seven Morris wanted Braves hitters to chase that wicked breaking ball that dropped like a stone as it neared home plate. So it wasn't surprising when a passed ball by Twins catcher Brian Harper in the top of the third inning moved the Braves' Rafael Belliard to second base with one out. After walking Lonnie Smith, Morris again bore down, getting Terry Pendleton to fly out to left field and then inducing Ronnie Gant to chase another split, which he grounded weakly to Gagne at shortstop.

"Jack was locked in, able to get out of trouble, and when a pitcher is on like that, you get excited playing behind him," Gagne said. "You tell yourself to just do your job. He's on—just back him up and make the plays that come your way. You may be playing in Game Seven of the World Series, with the whole world watching, but it's not like you have to do things out of the ordinary. You just need to remember to do your job."

Cantankerous, outspoken, a bear to be around, especially on the days that he pitched, Morris rarely suffered fools gladly. Most players have their jersey number scribbled on the inside of their caps, usually on the bill. That assured everyone got the right lid when heading back out to take their positions. Instead of number forty-seven, however,

Morris's cap sometimes was inscribed with "A" for derriere. Still, the team became his refuge during the 1991 season. The right-hander was going through a divorce and spending time away from his two sons. "The clubhouse was my family," he said years later. "It was my peace of mind. It was my serenity. It was everything to me."

By 1991 Morris had earned a reputation as big-game hurler who regularly pitched to the situation at hand. Born in St. Paul, Minnesota, he began his career in Detroit in 1977, helping the Tigers to that championship in 1984 and going 198–150 in fourteen seasons in the Motor City before signing with Minnesota as a free agent. In the 1980s Morris won 162 games, the most by any pitcher in the big leagues, and in another time this would have resulted in a big payday for the right-hander. Although he expected a bidding war for his services following the 1986 season, instead everything dissolved into a series of non-committal meetings. At one point the pitcher expected to sign with his hometown Twins within a week. When Andy MacPhail begged off, telling the local newspapers he needed "to do some homework" and perhaps compare Morris with eventual Hall of Fame pitcher Bert Blyleven, it appeared that Morris would then sign with the New York Yankees. In the end, though, no contracts ever materialized. What Morris didn't know at the time was that baseball ownership had conspired to not sign other team's free agents. In other words, it was a classic case of collusion.

Morris, Roger Clemens, Tim Raines, Doyle Alexander, and Ron Guidry were among the stars who returned to their old ballclubs that offseason for a relative pittance as the average major league salary actually declined before the 1987 season. The Major League Baseball Players Association filed a grievance, and arbitrator Thomas Roberts eventually ruled that the owners had violated the basic agreement with the owners.

Morris would be forced to stay in Detroit for another four seasons before signing an incentive-laden contract with Minnesota before the 1991 season. But he wouldn't forget about missing out on a major contract, and some of his teammates believed that became a defining moment for him. Starting, finishing, and winning the game were the only things Morris believed in. In essence, they became his personal bottom line and perhaps the only thing he could control in the game after the collusion cases of the mid-1980s.

"I've been in many games with him where he'd give up a four- or five- or six-spot in the first two innings and refuse to come out of the game," said Kirk Gibson, who was Morris's teammate in Detroit and another victim of collusion. "He'd walk in the dugout and say, 'I've never lost with ten.' We'd win, 9–8.

"Or if he's out there and it's the eleventh inning and we're up by six runs and he has to give up four to win, he's certainly not coming out of the game."

Such an approach didn't lead to the best of numbers at times. Morris finished his career with 254 victories but a 3.90 ERA, leading to debate whether he deserved to be in the Hall of Fame. Still, within the game Morris was regarded as one of the best of his era.

"The pitcher who best fits the description of a workhorse today is Jack Morris, Detroit's ace for so long," Nolan Ryan wrote in his book *Kings of the Hill*, which came out shortly after the 1991 World Series. "The standard is going to be 250 innings, and Morris has been good for that nearly every season. He got to finish a lot of games with the Tigers because Sparky Anderson trusted him even more than he did his bullpen. That's remarkable when you consider that Willie Hernandez, the Cy Young Award winner and Most Valuable Player in 1984, was their stopper."

Twins bullpen coach Rick Stelmaszek remembered when Morris was going through that bitter divorce in 1991, "and by August, I was siding with his wife. But he was a competitor to the max. He was the pitcher of the eighties. If he had good stuff, he'd just laugh at you, and if he didn't, he'd battle you and figure out a way to beat you."

Ron Gardenhire's locker was located near Morris's for the worst-to-first season in the Metrodome. "So I got a first-hand look, day after day, about how he went about his business," the third-base coach remembered. "Nobody loved the big game, with it all on the line, more than Jack.

"If a start didn't go his way, he'd be growling about it for days afterward. He wasn't fun to be around then. But he'd find a way to eventually laugh it off and move on, and then he'd start getting focused on the next start, and nobody was better at that part of the process.

"He'd concentrate, do his homework, know the tendencies and weaknesses of every hitter he would face. He was a pretty serious guy and the most intense guy I ever came across in the game. Game Seven, with it all on the line? That was a perfect situation for him."

Heading into Game Seven, Morris had pitched 273 innings—246 2/3 in the regular season and 26 1/3 in the postseason. The workload left his manager, Tom Kelly, wondering how much he had left—how many more innings could he pitch at such a high level?

For his part, Morris felt no trepidation about fatigue or being on the mound in the biggest game in years. "It's going to sound wrong, but I knew everybody was watching, and how much fun is that?" he told Bob Costas decades later. "I mean, I pitched games in Cleveland when there were 250 people in the stands—and 200 of them related to somebody on the field and the rest were only there for the beer. So I remember those games, and to be on a stage when the whole world is watching, if you don't relish that, you're in the wrong business."

———

In the fall of 1991 John Smoltz's best pitch was the fastball, which he complemented adeptly with a slider, changeup, and curveball. No sign of a split at that point in his career. That Smoltz was about to go against his boyhood idol must have bordered upon the surreal for him and his family. Growing up, he was raised to be a polka player, not a big-league ballplayer. By the age of four he regularly played accordion in his father's band, the Sorrentos. His mother gave lessons, his uncle owned a music store, and young John competed in contests, playing in recitals and in the family band throughout southern Michigan. As the oldest child, he remembered being "the anointed leader of the next generation of proud accordionists."

Within a few years, though, Smoltz announced that his dream was to be a professional baseball player and that he needed to stop playing music. "I don't know if I can adequately explain how big a deal it was for my parents to let me quit the accordion," he wrote in his autobiography, *Starting and Closing*. "This was like the oldest son shunning the family business, and not because he wasn't capable, but because he wasn't interested. It was clear I had inherited the same musical gene that my parents were blessed with, and to my family it was a tough pill to swallow. My mom says to this day that she really thought her uncle was going to disown her and our entire family for allowing me to quit."

On the surface Smoltz's decision didn't make much sense. Unlike his accordion playing, Smoltz was entirely self-taught when it came to sports. He didn't attend camps or have expert instruction. Instead, he watched games on television, usually his favorite team, the Detroit Tigers, and threw a rubber ball against a brick wall at the family home in Lansing, Michigan. There, he had sketched out a strike zone with tape. About the only advice he received came when one of his deliveries missed its mark and hit the aluminum screen door. Only then would his mother yell at him to throw strikes.

If music was the common thread in the Smoltz household, baseball came a close second, though. Smoltz's grandfather worked at the old Tiger Stadium for more than thirty years, first on the grounds crew and then in the pressroom. As a boy Smoltz listened to the Tigers games on the radio and made several trips to Detroit every summer to see his heroes in person. Throwing a rubber ball against the brick wall, Smoltz often imagined himself pitching in the big leagues, and it was always the postseason, usually the deciding game of the World Series that he held in his mind. So as Smoltz began his warm-ups on this evening in the Metrodome, he felt a sense of déjà vu. Not only was he in the Fall Classic for real, but he was also going up against his boyhood hero, longtime Tiger Jack Morris.

Any butterflies disappeared as Smoltz stood with the rest of the sellout crowd, listening to seven-year-old Jacqueline Jaquez belt out the national anthem. Years later Smoltz said something clicked after he heard the rendition. In his mind he was back at the brick wall back home in Michigan, ready to live out his dream.

"No one could catch me," he recalled. "I took a rubber ball and I imagined it. So when I was getting ready to go out there and do it, I was right where I wanted to be."

That Smoltz was here, starting Game Seven, had as much to do with the power of the mind as anything else. He had gotten off to a terrible start in 1991, going 2–11. Time after time things would unravel in a hurry on him, to the point that once runners reached base, he began to expect them to score. He wasn't injured or suffering from any mechanical flaw; his delivery remained fundamentally sound. What he was dealing with, he later recalled, was "a complete collapse of confidence."

Braves manager Bobby Cox and general manager John Schuerholz suggested that Smoltz see a sports psychologist, and the pitcher began to meet with Dr. Jack Llewellyn during the 1991 All-Star break. Their sessions had nothing to do with a shrink's couch and baring one's soul; instead, they usually met at Llewellyn's house, often shooting pool and just talking. Soon the psychologist suggested that the videotape personnel from the team assemble a highlight reel for the pitcher. The final result ended up being about two minutes of the right-hander at his best on the mound, and after it was assembled, Smoltz began to watch it repeatedly.

"The very next game after the tape was made I faced that same moment on the mound that had owned me all season," Smoltz later wrote. "Runners were in scoring position and things were on the verge of getting ugly. But this time I thought about the tape: I saw myself overcoming adversity in the past, and I didn't let myself think I couldn't do it. I stood there on the mound and dug in deep.

"I made the adjustment in my mind, and I faced adversity in front of me. And not only did I face it my first time out, but I nailed it my first time out, pitching my way out of a jam and keeping runs off the scoreboard for the first time in what seemed like all year."

Soon Smoltz didn't need the VHS tape anymore. He could picture his personal highlight tape in his mind and go to it whenever he needed. As a result, Smoltz turned his season around, going 12–2 in the second half of the regular season and picking up two victories against Pittsburgh in the National League Championship Series.

Mental imaging and mind games have long been an integral part of sports, even though few athletes like to talk about it publicly. In the days leading up to the coming Sunday's game quarterback Fran Tarkenton would visualize the game plan until he was "running whole blocks of plays in my head." Gold-medal decathlete Bruce Jenner said he used to dream of running the fifteen hundred meters, his sport's final event, and he always crossed the finish line winning the overall competition. Golfer Jack Nicklaus claimed he "never hit a shot, not even in practice, without having a very sharp, in-focus picture of it in my head. It's like a color movie."

Life coach Jim Fannin once explained that "Visualization works because your subconscious mind does not know the difference between fantasy and reality"—hence, the philosophy that to do anything of merit and consequence, you first have to imagine it.

But not that long ago such mind games were kept strictly hush-hush. In 1991 sports shrinks and plumbing the mental side remained downright radical to many players, coaches, and, certainly, fans. Smoltz became one of the first pro athletes to go public with how a psychologist helped him raise his game. Cameras began to be trained on Llewellyn in the stands for Smoltz's starts. Some were convinced that the shrink was somehow flashing secret signs to the pitcher. None of it was true, of course, and Smoltz admittedly waited too long, well into the following season, before setting the record straight. Still, the power of the mind was on display in Game Seven as both starting pitchers settled in.

In the bottom of the second inning the Twins put two men on with two out, and Smoltz got Mike Pagliarulo to ground out. An inning later Dan Gladden doubled and then moved to third. Smoltz ended the threat by striking out Game Six hero Kirby Puckett.

On this night, going against his boyhood idol, Smoltz found that he could match Morris pitch for pitch. Both proved adept at wriggling out of jams, and soon a series of zeroes began to stretch across the scoreboard inside the Metrodome.

———

While Smoltz had his personal highlight reel going on, Morris at times embraced being both a native son and a hired gun on this evening in Minneapolis.

In the top of the fifth inning Mark Lemke singled to right field—his tenth hit of the series. As expected, Rafael Belliard followed with a high-hopper sacrifice bunt, and just like that, the Braves were back in business, with a man on second and one out.

Lead-off hitter Lonnie Smith, always one for surprises, decided to bunt too. After taking a wild hack for strike one, Smith laid one down along the third-base line. Twins third baseman Mike Pagliarulo was playing deep, and his throw pulled Hrbek off the bag, as Smith slid into first base for some reason. When the dust cleared the Braves had men on first and third base, with one out.

Terry Pendleton, who was 4-for-9, with runners on base to this point in the series, stepped in to face Morris. Even though the Metrodome had grown so loud by this point that Morris could understand his teammates only by reading their lips, he later said he never felt more at peace, more determined about what he had to do. Morris had grown up in the Twin Cities, as disappointed as everyone else in town when the Vikings lost four Super Bowls during the 1970s. He was tired of his hometown teams losing the big game, so he told himself that a

Minnesota team wasn't about to drop one this time, not with him on the mound. Decades later, he said, "I never had so much will to win a game as I did that day."

On the mound Morris's mannerisms became more deliberate, forcing Pendleton to briefly call timeout. After Pendleton stepped back in, Morris placed a split-finger fastball on the outside corner. Pendleton popped it up, not deep enough to score Lemke.

With two away, Ron Gant came to the plate. Although the Braves' outfielder was struggling at the plate, Morris knew nobody outside of Justice could "ruin his day" faster than Gant. In the regular season the Braves' slugger had hit 32 home runs and driven in 105 runs. The inscription inside his cap had nothing to do with "A"; instead, Gant's message read, "I Will. I Can. I Am."

Working carefully, Morris bounced a 1–2 pitch in the dirt, and Harper wasn't able to field in cleanly. The ball bounced well in front of the plate toward Morris, who couldn't resist throwing to third base in an attempt to pick off Lemke. Pagliarulo snared the ball, with Lemke getting back to the base safely. As Kelly shook his head in the Twins' dugout, Morris decided to throw over to first base in attempt to get Smith. In the end both base runners were safe, and the Twins somehow kept the ball in the infield.

Gant worked the count to 3–2. Throughout the game both starting pitchers voiced their displeasure at times with home plate umpire Don Denkinger. His strike zone wasn't exactly generous on this evening. But when Morris hit Harper's glove on the outside corner, Denkinger raised his arm in the air. Gant had struck out for the final out, and Morris celebrated by windmilling his arm around as the hometown crowd roared. Of all the innings Morris pitched in 1991, he was never better than in this one.

In early innings Morris had gotten by with a good fastball and slider. He remembered his changeup and split not being all that sharp early on. But the split-finger, his best pitch, "came back around in the sixth [inning], and it was a very effective pitch in the late innings," he said.

That proved to be pivotal because the Braves were about to come at him again. In the top of the eighth inning, with the heart of the Atlanta order due up, Lonnie Smith led off with a single to right field. In the Twins' bullpen, relievers Steve Bedrosian and Mark Guthrie began to warm up.

Concerned that Smith would try to steal second, Morris threw over to first base several times with Pendleton back at the plate. Although Morris admitted he never had much of a pick-off move, he had worked hard to develop a slide step in 1991, allowing him to hold runners slightly closer that season.

With the count 1–2, Morris and the Twins believed they had struck out Pendleton on a pitch down in the dirt. But third-base umpire Terry Tata ruled that the National League MVP had fouled the pitch off. Replays later showed the call was incorrect. Pendleton had missed the pitch entirely; although the Braves' hitter should have been ruled out, there he stood, still in the batter's box, ready to drive in the first run of the game.

"The biggest turning point in the game, where an umpire could have made the right call and didn't," Morris later told the (St. Paul) *Pioneer Press.* "So now Lonnie becomes the goat for all Braves fans."

On Morris's next offering, his hundredth pitch of the evening, Pendleton lashed a liner toward left-center field. So much of baseball can be waiting, considering all the possibilities, making the necessary adjustments until the game bursts open again at the seams. That's when so many things can be in play that keeping up with it all becomes next to impossible. After climbing and climbing the incline at the roller coaster, we're suddenly plummeting downhill, and everything dissolves into a glorious train wreck. Now it began anew, here in the top of the eighth inning at the Metrodome.

Pendleton's drive split the Twins outfielders—Dan Gladden in left field and Kirby Puckett in center field. Running on the pitch, Smith had good speed and could have scored easily. But he hesitated, coming to a brief yet full stop around second base. Only after he saw that the ball had dropped in for a hit did he begin to run again, ending up at third base as Pendleton pulled into second with a double.

As with any big play, everyone soon had an opinion about what had happened. On the television replay CBS analyst Tim McCarver maintained that a fake double play, pulled off in high style by second baseman Chuck Knoblauch and shortstop Greg Gagne, was the reason Smith stopped dead in his tracks. Indeed, the Minnesota duo may have pulled off the best-looking double play ever without a ball.

At the crack of Pendleton's bat Gagne began to run toward the outfield. After all, he knew where the ball was going and he needed to be ready as the relay man for a throw from Gladden or Puckett. That's when Knoblauch barked at him, and the Twins' shortstop turned back toward second base. Instead, Gagne was ready to play along, as the second baseman pantomimed fielding the ball. Gagne fielded the fake throw and came toward the bag as though he were going to throw on to Kent Hrbek at first base.

"To this day I have no real clue about everything that happened on that play," Gagne said. "In fact, I've never studied a replay of it. I don't want to. That play exists in some sweet spot in my memory. I don't want to overanalyze it too much.

"What I do remember is that when the ball was hit, my first reaction was to get out to the outfield. I was the relay man on that side. But then Knoblauch yelled, 'Gags,' and I knew immediately what he was up to.

"We had been talking about deking their base runners—see if we could slow them down a bit. We practiced it too. It was just something we messed around with during infield practice. That's something I don't believe teams do enough about today—take infield. That gets you ready for the game, and it allows you to go over stuff together like this.

"So Knob yells, 'Gags,' and I peeled around toward second base, like we were going to do a double play. He made the fake throw, and I even made a kind of a fake throw on to Hrbek at first. Knoblauch sold it so well that I felt I had to do the same. Lonnie Smith froze for a few steps, but I didn't know if our fake play had much to do with it, honestly. As soon as it was over, I was on my horse, running back into short left field for the throw. That was the first and foremost thing in my mind—the relay throw I knew I had to make, not necessarily fooling Lonnie Smith."

The fake double play soon became part of baseball folklore. A perfect combination of chutzpa and guile that left poor Lonnie Smith stopped in his tracks. Admittedly, Smith had his share of misadventures on the basepaths. "Nobody ever realized I was naturally clumsy," said the player nicknamed "Skates." "You can ask my mother. . . . I was always knocking over things—falling. Earlier in my career I was known more for falling and tumbling than anything else."

Base runners are told to ignore the infielders—trust only where the ball is hit. Find it and then proceed accordingly. Years later Smith maintained that was exactly what he was trying to do. He insisted that he wasn't fooled by any fake double play from Knoblauch and Gagne. "No way I was faked out," he said dismissively.

Smith maintained that if he thought it had been the makings of a double play, he would have slid into second base, and many on the field that evening ultimately agree with him.

"If I'd taken the time to take one look, that could have been the difference," Smith added. "If I saw the ball off the bat, there's a good chance I could have scored. But I didn't see it. I didn't take that look in. That's my mistake."

Except for a glance in Knoblauch's direction, Smith's attention remained on the outfield. He had lost sight of the ball off Pendleton's bat, another victim of the sightlines and the Teflon-colored roof at the Metrodome. In that moment he briefly became concerned that Gladden or Puckett could perhaps snare Pendleton's line drive.

"I just didn't pick up the ball and didn't pick up Jimy," he later told the *Sporting News*, referring to Braves third base coach Jimy Williams. "People want to blame me, that's okay. The media's version that Knoblauch fooled me is not true. I just didn't see the ball. The only part the media got right was that I didn't score on the play."

Tom Kelly agreed that Smith didn't go for any fake, no matter how well planned or elaborate. "He just didn't know where the ball was," the Twins' manager said.

From his vantage point behind home plate, Minnesota catcher Brian Harper saw it all play out in front of him. Years later he believed Smith has gotten a bum rap. "Sure, it's easy to say he should have scored," Harper said. "But people forget that Gladden faked like he was going to catch it too. You actually had two fakes on that play.

"The ball hit off the wall. In the Metrodome, especially when you're the visiting player, it was really hard to pick up the ball. . . . Lonnie looked for the ball and he couldn't see it. And then he saw Gladden raise his glove for an instant, like he was going to catch it. And so he stopped, which is probably what he should have done. With no outs, you can't just keep running if you don't know where the ball is. The ball hit the wall, and Gladden played it perfectly and got it in quickly.

"I don't believe the criticism was justified. It was a tough play, it's tough to pick up the ball, and you had three guys in Gladden, Gagne, and Knoblauch trying to fool him."

Gagne added, "We caused enough confusion for him not to score on the play. That's all I know."

Pendleton, who had hit the double that should have scored the game's first run and perhaps the only one needed this evening, remembered pulling into second base and looking over at third base coach Williams. "I was ready to give him a pump of the fist or something. I mean we finally were on the board, and that's when I realized that Lonnie was standing there right next to him," Pendleton said. "I couldn't believe it, but it wasn't any panic or anything like that. We had second and third with nobody out. It was no big deal. We've been here before. Frankly, I still expected us to score a couple of runs that inning. Break it open against Jack Morris."

Even without Smith crossing the plate on the play, the Twins were in a heap of trouble.

"Some want to say that the shortstop and second baseman faked Lonnie," Pendleton continued. "Well, I beg to differ. On the play he's looking all over the place, and that's because he couldn't find the ball off the bat. So Jimy Williams finally waves him over to third. I mean this isn't the end of the world for us.

"We have second and third with nobody out. To this day everybody wants to blame Lonnie Smith for not scoring, but it isn't like that at all. We had second and third with nobody out. You listening to what I'm saying? Second and third with nobody out."

Years later Harper agreed with Pendleton. "If [Smith] was in the eighth hole and it's the pitcher coming up next, maybe you're a little more aggressive on the basepaths. Maybe you try to score even if you're not sure where the ball is. But it was three-four-five—Ron Gant, David Justice, and Sid Bream—coming up for Atlanta after that. Maybe the blame should be more on those guys."

All Gant needed was a fly ball, deep enough to score a run. Three innings before, Morris froze Gant with a fastball, and home plate umpire Don Denkinger had called the Braves' slugger out. This time Gant wanted to be ready for anything near the plate. In doing so, Gant perhaps swung at a ball he should have let pass, grounding it up the first-base line. Hrbek easily caught it, held the runners, and tagged Gant for the unassisted out. That made Gant 0-for-4 in the ballgame.

Moments after Hrbek got the first out of the inning Kelly came out of the dugout for a conference with Morris. The manager's strategy was to walk David Justice and pitch to Sid Bream, with the bases loaded. Years later Morris said he agreed with Kelly's decision. Harper, the Twins' catcher who was there, remembered things differently.

"Kelly comes out to the mound, and we're meeting there, and he tells Jack to walk Justice," Harper said. "And Jack keeps saying, 'No, I can get him out. I can get him out. I don't want to walk him.'

"Finally Kelly says, 'Jack, we're going to walk him.'

"Jack replied, 'All right. I don't like it, but I'll walk him.' So we walked Justice to load the bases."

Walking back behind the plate, Harper suddenly thought about the worst-scenario for him as the catcher. Why this of all things flashed through his mind at this particular moment he will never know, even years later when he thinks about Game Seven. But it came at him in a rush—a personal nightmare that momentarily rocked his world.

"That's when I envisioned a come-backer to Jack, he throws it to me at home plate, and I then airmail one past Hrbek and down into right field. We lose the World Series, and I'm the goat of all time. I would be the next Bill Buckner. I literally thought this right after we walked David Justice.

"So then I'm thinking, *Okay, get that thought out of your head. Lord, please help me to relax here and let me do my job.* I had to really push that negative thought out of my mind. I had to do it right then and there. Pro athletes have negative thoughts all the time, and sometimes it's all you can do to rid your mind of such things."

In a stunning turn of events Bream swung at the fourth offering, a Morris split that didn't have much bite, and Harper's nightmare began to play out for real. The only difference was that the grounder went to Hrbek at first base rather than back to Morris on the mound. Hrbek fielded it and threw home to Harper at the plate. The ball arrived well ahead of Smith, who came down the line from third base, and all the Twins' catcher had to do was throw the ball back to Hrbek, who moved over to first base. That's all he had to do and Minnesota would somehow get out of the inning without Atlanta scoring.

"You're never really looking for a 3–2–3 double play because that is so rare," Harper remembered. "But here it comes, rolling out for real. Herbie threw it to me, and all I have to do is throw it back to him, nice and easy. Bream was the slowest guy on the Braves, so I have plenty of time. Maybe too much time. So now I get to thinking about it, remembering what flashed through my head seconds before.

"But somehow I did it. Just nice and easy back to Herbie, and we've survived this jam. In that game there was so much pressure—a passed ball, a wild pitch—one thing like that could lose you the game, and everybody knew it."

———

F. Scott Fitzgerald, who was born in St. Paul, Minnesota, believed that we are never more alive than when we are doing something we love. At such times we do appear to be put on this earth for a purpose. For a moment or two we can move to the dance of mindfulness that the Buddha talked about, and time can stop for a beat or two as the rest of world gathers around. It's as though the gods themselves cannot believe what they are bearing witness to.

Fitzgerald hinted that such moments can fortify us for a short time against the tides of fate and even buffer us against death itself. Unfortunately, that notion didn't play out as well as he would have liked, as the novelist died from a heart attack while writing *The Last Tycoon*, a story that could have been even better than *The Great Gatsby*. The unfinished novel ends with a hodgepodge of scenes and notes—where Fitzgerald happened to be in the writing when he died. So perhaps it's somehow appropriate that the last line in *The Last Tycoon* reads simply, in all caps, ACTION IS CHARACTER.

For that can be the final determination of so much. People can talk about what they plan to do or even what they have done, but it's how they act to the day-to-day beat of another morning that ultimately determines how they will be remembered.

———

After catching Harper's careful throw for the third out, Hrbek pumped his fist and then celebrated by spiking the baseball into the Astroturf. Morris waited for Hrbek outside the dugout to slap gloves with him. Somewhat shaken, Harper walked slowly to the home dugout.

Thanks to a base-running miscue for all time and some real bad luck, the game remained scoreless heading into the bottom of the eighth.

"Jack Morris was never afraid about pitching in big games," Pendleton said, "and that's not good if you're on the team that's facing him in one of them. When we didn't score in that situation, you knew it was going to be tough. Because this was Jack Morris. Somehow we hadn't dented him."

In the bottom of the frame Twins pinch-hitter Randy Bush singled to center. Al Newman replaced him as a pinch-runner. Then Dan Gladden popped out to center after he failed to bunt the runner over. When Knoblauch singled to right, on a beautiful inside-out swing, Smoltz's night came to an end. Game Six hero Kirby Puckett was due up next, and Smoltz wouldn't best his boyhood hero on this night. After going seven and a third innings, allowing only six hits and striking out four, the Braves' starter was lifted for reliever Mike Stanton.

When Cox came out to the mound Smoltz was adamant that he could get Puckett. What he didn't realize was that the Braves' manager was a step or two ahead of him strategy-wise. "Bobby was going to intentionally walk Puckett and have Stanton pitch to Hrbek," Smoltz said.

Years later, in 2002, when the Braves returned to Minnesota for an interleague series, Smoltz and Morris would meet again. The first words out of Smoltz's mouth? "I'm still mad about that game," he told Morris.

Back in 1991 Smoltz could only watch as Stanton did walk Puckett intentionally to load the bases with one out. Ironically, the Braves now found themselves in the same jam that the Twins had somehow escaped in the top of the same inning. And, perhaps, the baseball gods do have a sense of humor. For next up was Hrbek, who had started the stunning double play only minutes before.

The Twins' first baseman had struck out three times in the series against Stanton. Bearing down, Hrbek put good wood on the ball this time, only to line it sharply toward second baseman Mark Lemke. Now it was Knoblauch's turn to make a base-running mistake. Taking off with the pitch, he was easily doubled off when Lemke, his counterpart on the Braves, snared Hrbek's liner and scampered to second base for the unassisted double play. If the Braves had gone ahead, would Knoblauch's gaffe be remembered as much as Smith's today? Who knows, but the Braves had somehow one-upped the Twins when it came to getting out of bases-loaded jams.

———

Through nine innings Morris had thrown 118 pitches. Thankfully for the Twins and their fans, his manager didn't put much credence in pitch counts. Instead, Tom Kelly kept tabs on how much time his starting pitcher actually spent on the mound. In a game without a clock, Kelly grew increasingly concerned when his starting pitcher went past the two-hour mark. For him, that's when performance could go downhill in a hurry, and Morris was pushing up against that time barrier now in Game Seven.

After Morris set Atlanta down in order in the top of the ninth inning closer Rick Aguilera began to warm up, ready to come in for the tenth inning. In the Twins' dugout Kelly told Morris, "That's all. Can't ask you to do any more than that."

Some of what followed has suffered from revisionist history too. Predictably, Morris didn't want to come out of the game. He claimed he had plenty left, and years later Kelly said that he was simply testing his staff ace. A quick one-two-three inning had convinced the skipper that Morris had more in the tank.

Looking back on things, Morris said that Kelly was giving him a chance to come out of the game. An invitation that the player and manager, both of whom could be among the most hard-headed guys in the game, knew wouldn't be accepted.

"Jack was such a competitor that when he pitched, you never really talked to him. For lack of a better term, he was grouchy," Harper recalled. "He's a great guy, but he was so focused when he pitched. Now obviously he was locked in that night. In the ninth inning we had Aguilera warming up. Kelly goes to Jack and says, 'Awesome job. Now we'll bring Aggie in.'

"Jack looked at him and said, 'I'm not coming out of this game.'"

Harper remembered Kelly reminding Morris that he had already thrown more than one hundred pitches and that he was pitching on three days' rest.

Morris told him Kelly again, "I'm not coming out of the game. There's no way I'm coming out of this game."

Harper sat back, watching all this unfold, and thought to himself, 'This is going to be interesting.' Kelly briefly huddled with pitching coach Dick Such and then walked back Morris.

Those eavesdropping recalled their skipper saying, "Okay, big guy, go get 'em."

Then Kelly turned and muttered, "Oh hell. It's only a game."

In essence, Kelly went totally against the book. The strategy then—and now—would be to go to the bullpen. Managers want the odds in their favor. They love to study the matchups—better to have a right-handed pitcher throw to a right-handed batter, for example. And, of course, pitch counts have become paramount. More so today than at any time in baseball's history, a manager cannot be faulted if he lifts his starting pitcher late in a game. After all, a quality start has been defined as six innings and allowing no more than three earned runs, and as a result, many pitchers aren't expected to finish what they started.

"That may be one of the biggest changes, probably not for the better, since the day when I pitched," Nolan Ryan said. "Back then a starting pitcher took responsibility. He wanted to and was expected to begin and end a game, no matter what it took. That's something we've lost over the years."

Former big-league pitcher Jim Kaat, who was a sideline reporter for CBS Sports in the 1991 Series, said Morris "just talked or even bullied his way into staying in that game. He simply declared, 'This is my game,' and nobody could take it from him.

"In looking back on it that's something that's often misunderstood when it comes to today's game. Some pitchers have this surge of adrenaline—they can really smell the finish line, and it doesn't matter how many pitches they've thrown. In times like that pitch counts don't mean anything. You've got to let them try and finish things off. That said, I'm pretty sure Jack Morris was the only one Tom Kelly would have broken the rules for. He wouldn't have let Kevin Tapani or Scott Erickson talk him into something like that."

In looking back at this moment in Game Seven Morris said, "[Kelly] put his ass on the line by leaving me in there, and you don't realize it at the time. You start reflecting back on the reality of the situation, and even me, if I was managing I'd say to myself, 'Man, I've got Rick Aguilera, who's done a pretty damn good job. What do you do here?' And he did something 99 percent of the baseball world wouldn't do."

For the first time in World Series history three games had gone into extra innings, and Morris was still very much a part of this one. If anything, the veteran right-hander appeared to be getting stronger as the game went into extra innings, as he became the first starting pitcher since Tom Seaver in 1969 to continue past the ninth inning in the World Series. Morris set the Braves down in order in the top of the tenth on only eight pitches, and Kelly had already decided his staff ace would go out for the eleventh—if things went that far.

"A lot of times you attend a sporting event . . . and not realize at the time how sensational it is," Jack Buck told his national television audience. "You look back and say, 'I'm glad I was there. That was something.' Tonight, it's so apparent that this is one of the most remarkable baseball games ever played."

The longtime voice of the St. Louis Cardinals, Buck had called just about everything in baseball and also was the radio voice for *Monday Night Football*. This would be his last World Series for television.

Soon Buck's voice rose in excitement as Dan Gladden led off the bottom of the tenth inning with a broken-bat drive to the outfield. When the ball hit high in front of Brian Hunter, Gladden kept going, sliding into second base with a double.

"The bat broke on the handle, about six inches above my hands," Gladden remembered. "It was a little flare in front of Hunter and Gant, and I was digging right out of the batter's box.

"I was going for second as soon as I realized that the bat had broken. I know I surprised some people, even some in my own dugout, but I had played in that ballpark long enough to know where the ball was going and what would probably happen next on that turf. I knew I was good unless it was somehow caught, and I really didn't see that happening. By that point, frankly, I was tired of playing too. I had to get to second base somehow—just try to end things."

Puckett later said, "That was Dan Gladden—all or nothing."

Chuck Knoblauch, who was next up, was told to bunt Gladden over. When the rookie let the first pitch, a fastball from Atlanta reliever Alejandro Peña that split the heart of the plate, go by for strike one, Kelly muttered, "Bunt the damn ball."

On the third pitch Knoblauch did his job, laying down a bunt to the third base side that Pendleton had no choice but to throw on to first for the inning's first out. With the winning run standing on third base, Braves manager Bobby Cox decided to intentionally walk Puckett and then Hrbek, making for a force play at every base. Once again a team found itself with the bases loaded and praying for some kind of miracle to keep the game going.

"I knew they would walk Puckett, and I wasn't surprised when they walked Hrbek too," said Gladden, who now stood at third base, only ninety feet away from ending the series for good. "There was no other way to play it really. So here we were again. Bases loaded, and we'd see if one of these teams could finally score a run."

Jarvis Brown, who had come into the game as a pinch-runner in the ninth inning, was the next Twins hitter due up. Brown had appeared in only thirty-eight games that season, hitting .216. Kelly decided he could do better and once again went for a more experienced hand.

Gene Larkin had been swinging a bat, warming up for what seemed to be hours in the runway leading back to the hometown clubhouse. The only problem was that Larkin's left knee was so swollen that he could barely run. If he hit one on the ground, he could have been slower than the Braves' Sid Bream heading down to first—setting up a sure double play.

"The tendinitis was really bad," Larkin recalled. "By that point of that season I couldn't play defense or run the bases hardly at all. If anything, I felt fortunate to be in uniform frankly. I could have easily been left off the [World Series] roster."

The knee flared up during the American League Championship Series with Toronto, and the Twins' brass seriously considered leaving Larkin on the sidelines. Yet manager Tom Kelly liked Larkin's grit, how he methodically approached each and every at-bat, even if his knee was killing him. At first glance Kelly and Larkin appeared to have little in common. The Twins' manager was a baseball lifer, and his pinch-hitter had once been a big man on campus. Before breaking in with the Twins in 1987, Larkin played at Columbia University. A diehard Yankee fan, he reminded some Gotham fans of Lou Gehrig, who had also once played on the Upper West Side. The son of a retired New York City police officer, Larkin broke through his senior year, breaking or tying thirteen school batting records, including Gehrig's for most home runs. The major leagues, as is often the case, proved to be a more difficult scenario for a collegiate star. Larkin became a role player, and even though he hit a career-best .286 in 1991, he appeared in only ninety-eight games that season. And now, after all that, he had a chance to win it all for Minnesota.

"When they did walk Hrbek, I knew I was getting the call," Larkin remembered. "It was nothing extraordinary in how it happened. TK just called my name, and I went up there. But I'll tell ya in the on-deck circle my knees were shaking, and when I'm walking to the batter's box I'm still shaking. You cannot tell when you see it on replay, but I was as nervous as an athlete can be right then.

"But the funny thing was, once I stepped into the batter's box, a sense of calm came over me. It wasn't like I hadn't been in a situation like that before. Certainly not as big as that—seventh game of the World Series. But I took a deep breath, and mentally I was telling myself that I had to hit the first pitch fastball that Peña gave me. I didn't want to get into a situation where it was two strikes and the umpire could come into it. I didn't want to leave it to the umpire to make a tough call on an outside or inside pitch."

For his part home-plate umpire Don Denkinger did try to encourage Larkin, at least a little bit, by telling him that the Braves were moving their outfielders in and the Twins' pinch-hitter had a good chance to drive one over their heads. Larkin was too nervous, too dry in the mouth, to reply.

"Peña's history was that he liked to get ahead of the hitter," Larkin said decades later. "With the bases loaded, he doesn't want to walk me. His best pitch was a fastball. And fortunately for me he threw a fastball up and out over the plate, which is the perfect pitch to put a fly ball into play. It would have been a routine fly ball if the outfield was at normal depth."

Of course, the Braves' outfield had to play in, ready to throw to the plate and cut off the lead runner and the winning run.

"Once I put the bat on the ball, I knew it would be far enough out into left field to drive Danny from third base," Larkin remembered. "It was going to carry over Hunter's head, and I didn't have to worry any more about running. Right then and there I knew we were going to win the game and be World Series champions. There's no greater feeling than when you know that's about to happen to you, to your team."

As soon as Gladden saw the ball leave Larkin's bat, he raised a fist in the air, and when the ball bounced off the Astroturf, past Hunter in left field, he headed for home. There he stomped on the plate with both feet and the first one to greet him was Morris, the Twins' starting pitcher, who still held his glove and hat in his hand.

"Somebody had to go home a loser," Morris said years later, "but nobody was a loser in my mind."

John Smoltz said that the "bottom line was who was going to run out of nine lives first."

Gladden added, "What was great about Game Seven when you look back on it is that pretty much everybody in both lineups had a chance to be the hero and drive in a run on a night when only one run was needed. Everybody who stepped into the batter's box had the opportunity—top to bottom in both batting orders for both teams. We played and played and finally somebody did it, somebody finally came through."

In finally deciding this series for the ages, the hero ended up being Gene Larkin, a guy who many in the Metrodome and those watching on television least expected. A guy who could barely run down the line to first base drove in the winning run in the perhaps best World Series ever played.

"When I look back on it, I think I was swinging the bat for every average or even below-average player who ever played this game," Larkin said. "I just got the chance to come through."

The players themselves were reluctant to clear the field after Gladden crossed home plate as the Braves' Terry Pendleton hugged Shane Mack and Kirby Puckett while Tom Kelly talked with Ron Gant. A scene that was as close to hockey's shaking of hands before the Stanley Cup is awarded briefly unfolded. In the Twins' clubhouse Commissioner Fay Vincent declared this "was probably the greatest World Series ever played," and the Twins soon afterward broke into an impromptu rendition of Queen's "We Are the Champions." Players on both teams talked about how the World Series trophy could have been, perhaps should have been split in half—that's how close and well played these handful of games, almost each one with its own particular hero or two, had been. In the end, of course, the hardware stayed in the Twin Cities, and with winter coming on hard, everyone involved was left with memories of the last fine time in baseball.

———

**FINAL SCORE: TWINS 1, BRAVES 0**

|      | 1 | 2 | 3 | 4 | 5 | 6 | 7 | 8 | 9 | 10 | R | H | E |
|------|---|---|---|---|---|---|---|---|---|----|---|----|---|
| ATL  | 0 | 0 | 0 | 0 | 0 | 0 | 0 | 0 | 0 | 0  | 0 | 7  | 0 |
| MIN  | 0 | 0 | 0 | 0 | 0 | 0 | 0 | 0 | 0 | 1  | 1 | 10 | 0 |

ATTENDANCE: **55,118**   LENGTH OF GAME: **3 HOURS, 23 MINUTES**

# Epilogue

After the 1991 World Series both cities held downtown parades for their respective ballclubs. Nearly 750,000 attended the event in Atlanta, and fans there had to remind themselves that their beloved Braves had actually lost. In reality the two teams were at the crossroads, with one destined to fade to the ranks of also-rans to the point of almost ceasing operation, whereas the other would soon be regarded as a perennial contender.

The Twins finished second to the Oakland Athletics in 1992, and Tom Kelly would manage through the 2001 season. As baseball began to divide into two distinct categories of teams—the haves and have-nots—the Twins finished about .500 only twice during the new era in baseball.

A decade after the Twins won the World Series the baseball owners voted twenty-eight to two to downsize the number of teams at the big-league level. Two teams—the Minnesota Twins and Montreal Expos—were slated to cease operations before the 2002 season. The decision reversed nearly a half-century of expansion and would have been the first time since 1899 that teams had been disbanded at the major-league level.

But the Major League Baseball Players Association pushed back, calling the decision "most imprudent and unfortunate" in a statement.

Dan Gladden, who had scored the winning run in the 1991 World Series, predicted the Twins would still be playing in Minneapolis for years to come. He remained convinced even though Twins ownership wanted Commissioner Bud Selig to eliminate the ballclub in exchange for a contraction payment.

In the end the Expos moved from Montreal, where they were averaging fewer than eight thousand fans a game in the deteriorating Stade Olympique, to Washington, DC, and became the Washington Nationals. The Twins stayed in Minnesota, where the construction of a new outdoor ballpark, Target Field, bolstered their attendance.

In the meantime the Braves made it to the World Series again in 1992, defeating the Pittsburgh Pirates in another classic postseason championship series. This time the Braves lost the championship to the Toronto Blue Jays in six games. Before the 1993 season free-agent pitcher Greg Maddux, the defending Cy Young winner, joined the Atlanta staff. The five-year, $28 million deal was the kind of signing that was now beyond the Twins' reach. Even with Maddux on board, the Braves would lose to the Philadelphia Phillies in the National League Championship Series.

After realignment shifted Atlanta to the NL East, the Braves finished second to the Montreal Expos in 1994, as the long-simmering labor acrimony between the owners and players boiled over, canceling the World Series. The following season the Braves again reached the World Series and downed the Cleveland Indians to capture Atlanta's first title. With Bobby Cox at the helm the Braves reached the playoffs in fourteen consecutive seasons.

"I always wondered what would have happened had we won [in 1991]," Mark Lemke said. "Would we have gotten fat and happy, soft?

It left the hunger there. You think about it. I don't believe Minnesota did anything after that. It kept going on for us.

"I know we'd like to have won more World Series, but boy, that certainly started one heck of a run that I don't think will ever be duplicated."

In 1997 the Braves moved into a new stadium, which was originally built for the 1996 Summer Olympics. The facility was named after owner Ted Turner. (By late 2013 plans were afoot for the Braves to move into a new stadium in neighboring Cobb County.) Meanwhile the Twins relocated to Target Field in 2010. The outdoor facility was constructed in downtown Minneapolis, within blocks of a light-rail network, and was hailed as perhaps the best of the new retro ballparks, which began with the opening of Camden Yards in Baltimore.

Decades later Pendleton, Lemke, and other members of the 1991 Braves couldn't help but think that the better team had somehow lost. While Smith's base-running blunder became the play many remembered, others pointed to Cox's loyalty to Charlie Leibrandt, in which the Atlanta manager started him in Game One and brought him out of the bullpen to try to close out the Series in Game Six. The Braves also had starter Scott Erickson on the ropes in Game Six but roughed him up for only three runs. Then there were the improbable home runs by the Twins' Greg Gagne in Game One and Scott Leius in Game Two. Big flies hit by individuals who were afterthoughts on most scouting reports were reminders that pretty much everyone in the Braves' batting order struggled except for Lemke at .417, Rafael Belliard at .375, and Pendleton at .367. In comparison, Ron Gant and David Justice, the two players on the front of the 1991 Braves media guide, combined to hit .263 and only two home runs, both by Justice.

To this day Pendleton, who in any other Series could have driven the deciding run, won't admit that the Twins were the better team that season. "There was no better team than us in baseball in 1991," he said.

Lemke won't go that far. "It's hard to say if we should have won, but we sure had our chances," he said. "We needed to take a road game, and we just couldn't do it. Time after time it looked like we were about to break through against them."

So what helped tipped the balance? As Pendleton feared, the last guy Atlanta wanted to face in a winner-take-all Game Seven was Jack Morris. And then there was the setting. Professional athletes aren't supposed to be influenced by any home-field advantage. Yet in 1991 where the games were played had a profound impact. Not only did both teams rise to the occasion in front of their hometown fans, but the difference in the stadiums—one indoor, the other outside—also became the background noise and major concern for whoever was the visiting team.

"[The Metrodome] had to be the toughest home-field edge I've ever encountered," Lemke added. "It wasn't just the noise and those hankies, but that roof sure could wreck havoc with the best of ballplayers and teams."

Jim Kaat, who played in two World Series, 1965 and 1982, and covered another half-dozen more, including the 1991 World Series for CBS, said he never witnessed a more "significant home-field advantage" than the Metrodome.

"I don't know if the Twins win . . . without playing four games there," he said. "Being there reminded me of when we'd used to go into the Astrodome. The place was so different that by the time you adjusted, you were leaving after losing a few.

"I don't know if the Braves were the better team, but I could see how they felt they were. That Atlanta team had everything except a quality closer. If you put somebody like Mariano Rivera on that club, they would have been unbeatable. That's not to be critical of the guys they had. A pitcher like Charlie Leibrandt was a real veteran, but he wasn't your prototypical closer.

"When you look back on those great Braves teams, that's what they were lacking. An automatic, lockdown guy coming out of the bullpen."

When the dust settled, Atlanta general manager John Schuerholz declared that the Twins were the champions of the games played indoors in 1991, and his Braves were the champs of the games held outdoors.

————

The summer after the Twins-Braves Series I went to Cuba for the first time, and even fans there were asking whether this was the best World Series ever. My assignment was an exhibition series between the United States and Cuban Olympic baseball teams before the 1992 Summer Games. Back then I thought I knew everything there was to know about baseball—after all, I had just covered my first World Series, and an epic one at that. But nothing could really prepare me for that first game in Cuba.

The exhibition series was held in Holguin, on the eastern end of the island, and by noon the Soviet-style stadium was filled to overflowing for a 7:30 p.m. first pitch. The US roster was young but loaded with players who would soon reach the major leagues—Nomar Garciaparra, Phil Nevin, Darren Dreifort, Charles Johnson, and Jeffrey Hammonds.

As dusk settled over the land, the foul poles glowed neon pink in the tropical twilight—the better to determine fair from foul—and the crowd grew more rambunctious thanks to the salsa band and the incessant ringing of cowbells. I walked into the stadium alongside Hammonds. As we gazed out upon the site, he nodded at the outfield fence. "What does that mean?" he asked about the *Socialism o Muerte* slogan, which was splashed in red lettering. I told him that I believed it meant "socialism or death."

There was no real press box, so members of the US press—all six of us—sat in the stands. During the early innings I gazed out at Hammonds, who was playing in center field, only a few feet away from the *Socialism o Muerte* proclamation. That's when an old man, a Cuban, sat down next to me. I was at the end of the row, and he sat in the aisle to my right.

"You're an American?" he asked.

I nodded.

"Please tell me about the Minnesota Twins," he said in broken English.

I began to tell him how the Twins had just won one of the best World Series ever played. That said, it would be difficult for them to repeat, as they didn't have the deep pockets to hold on to all their stars and their best players were only getting older.

"I know all that," the Cuban gentleman interrupted.

"Then what do you want to know?" I answered.

"What do they look like?"

What do they look like? That remains one of the most curious questions I've ever been asked. With that single query, the old Cuban made me realize how star-crossed his nation is and how memorable the Twins-Braves Series remains.

In my tourist Spanish, with help of my good friend Milton Jamail, I went about the diamond, describing the 1991 world champions. Of course, I put Kent Hrbek at first base (*grande pero con elegante*), Brian Harper behind the plate (*hombre resuelto*) and Jack Morris (*lanzador bigote*) on the mound. I finished with Kirby Puckett in center field, a guy who is difficult to describe in English, let alone a second language. How do you tell somebody about a bowling ball of a man who always seemed to smile and had such a flair for the dramatic?

As I spoke I turned to Milton to my left and also gazed out toward the field, trying to come up with the best words. When I finished I turned back to the old man. His eyes had swelled with tears and he stood up, clasping me on the shoulder.

"Thank you," he said. "Now I know."

Then he disappeared down the row toward home plate and into the crowd. Even today, when I think about that memorable Series and the Twins and the Braves, two teams that always seemed ready to rise to the occasion, I see the old man's face. That odd mix of happiness and sadness, determination and relief, still sums up those times the best for me.

# APPENDIX I
## AFTERMATH

## *The Twins*

**KIRBY PUCKETT** Puckett spent his entire twelve-year career in Minnesota, where he hit .318, won six Gold Gloves and appeared in ten All-Star games.

During spring training in 1996, Puckett awoke with blindness in his right eye. The diagnosis was glaucoma, and it forced him to retire before his time. A decade later, he suffered a fatal stroke and became the second-youngest person to die who had already been enshrined in the National Baseball Hall of Fame in Cooperstown, New York. Lou Gehrig, at thirty-seven, was the only Hall of Famer younger than Puckett.

"A seven- or eight-year-old kid watching the game would pick him out, and he just looked different," sportscaster Bob Costas once said of the Twins' star. "He had an affection for the game, and there was a kind of energy about it that was fun.

"I'm sure he took it seriously. You have to take it seriously in order to be a great player, but there was nothing grim about the way he went about it."

Puckett was cremated after his death but left no written instructions about what should become of his remains. Jodi Olson, his fiancée, claimed that Puckett had told her he wanted his ashes spread across an inner-city ballfield. In addition, she said she would like some of his ashes to wear in locket around her neck. But Puckett's children were the primary beneficiaries in his 2003 will. The battle over his ashes and his estate went to court, where five of Puckett's siblings agreed in court papers that Catherine and Kirby Jr., then sixteen and fourteen years old, respectively, should have the ashes, and the remains should not be divided in any way. Judge Benjamin E. Vatz in the Maricopa County (Arizona) Superior Court agreed in his ruling in October 2006. He wrote that if Puckett had wanted his remains to go to Olson "then he would have taken care to express that wish in writing."

A statute to Puckett stands outside the Twins' new home at Target Field in Minneapolis. Unveiled before the home opener in 2010, it joined statues to such Twins greats as Harmon Killebrew and Rod Carew. Local artist Bill Mack portrayed Puckett in the moments after his Game Six home run, as he rounded second base, his arm raised overhead in a fist.

**JACK MORRIS** Soon after Game Seven, Morris exercised his option for free agency and signed with Toronto, briefly becoming the game's highest-paid pitcher. Perhaps the World Series MVP understood better than others that the national pastime was first and foremost a business, and often a cruel enterprise at that. After losing out as a free agent in 1986, Morris wasn't about to let it happen again. He said that leaving the Twin Cities became strictly "a business decision."

"The majority of people in the world today have played Little League baseball or some form of baseball," he told *USA Today*'s Hal Bodley in the spring of 1992. "It's easy for them to say, 'I could have done that.' Everybody relates to baseball, so it's difficult for them to comprehend what's going on today with salaries. They ask, 'How much is enough?' I guarantee you, in their right mind, if they are thinking clearly, they would have done the same thing."

Even though Toronto's offer was about $2 million higher than Minnesota's proposal, some in the Twin Cities derided Morris for leaving after one season, saying he had shed crocodile tears upon becoming misty-eyed at his Twins signing. "But I think he was sincere when he returned to town to play for the Twins," official scorer Stew Thornley said, "and I think he was sincere when he left, too."

As the new member of the Blue Jays' rotation, Morris won a league-high twenty-one games and found himself back in the World Series on another winner. Yet in the '92 postseason, Morris went winless on the big stage and Lonnie Smith, of all people, hit him up for a grand slam in Game Five of that year's World Series.

As part of his free-agent windfall, Morris bought a seventy-five-hundred-acre farm near Great Falls, Montana. By 1994, he was in Cleveland, and at age thirty-nine he was expected to be elder statesman on the Indians' young staff. When two of his farmhands back in Montana quit, Morris began to split time between the ball club and his farm. In August 1994, the Indians gave the five-time All-Star his unconditional release. "You can be benevolent to a point, but there comes a time when you've got to do something," Indians general manager John Hart said. Two pitchers from Triple-A, Chad Ogea and Julian Tavarez, competed for Morris's spot in the rotation.

An incredibly durable athlete, Morris left the game having made fourteen Opening Day starts and at one point going 515 consecutive starts without missing a turn in the rotation. In his eighteen-year career, he was on the disabled list only twice.

Despite a rocky relationship with the media, many felt he deserved to be in the National Baseball Hall of Fame. From 1979 through 1992, according to ESPN's Jayson Stark, Morris won 233 games compared to Nolan Ryan's 168. As of this date, though, Ryan was enshrined in Cooperstown, and Morris remained on the outside looking in.

"He's arrogant, sure," Detroit manager Sparky Anderson once said. "He knows he's good. He's like a great thoroughbred who'll bite you if you try to get near him."

Morris went on to a second career in broadcasting, first with the Twins and then with the Blue Jays, and maintained that compliments he received from strangers about his performance in Game Seven, what he termed as "warm fuzzies," took the sting out of the Hall of Fame slights.

**KENT HRBEK** The first baseman played fourteen seasons in the major leagues, all with his hometown team. Stars like Hrbek, George Brett (Kansas City Royals) and Tony Gwynn (San Diego Padres) played with one team for their entire major league careers and now appear to be icons from a forgotten time. Hrbek left the game before he was ready, a victim of the baseball owners voting to curtail the end of the regular season and cancel the World Series in 1994. Even a larger-than-life star like Hrbek couldn't rise above the looming labor war. After retiring, Hrbek took the lead in raising money and awareness in the fight against amyotrophic lateral sclerosis (ALS), which had killed his father, Ed. "When we get a cure for this thing, I'm going to rent out the Metrodome for a party," Hrbek told *Sports Illustrated*, "and everyone's invited." A restaurant/bar at Target Field, the Twins' new ballpark, was named for him and has memorabilia from his playing days. A series of photographs there show him once again pantomiming the no smoking pregame warning from the old Metrodome and giving the thumbs-up to another beverage.

**GREG GAGNE** The shortstop played only one more year with the Twins before moving on to the Kansas City Royals and then finishing his big-league career with the Los Angeles Dodgers. Afterward, he returned home to Somerset, Massachusetts, where he coached high school baseball.

**CHUCK KNOBLAUCH** Gagne's double-play partner (with or without a ball in his hand) played in the Twin Cities for seven seasons, leading the league in doubles in 1994 and in triples in 1996. Before the

1998 season, he was traded to the New York Yankees for four players, including left-hander Eric Milton and shortstop Cristian Guzmán. With the Yankees, Knoblauch made key defensive plays to help preserve the perfect games by David Wells and David Cone, and was on three more World Series championship teams. Toward the end of his twelve-year career, Knoblauch began to have difficulty making accurate throws. The mental block became as debilitating as it would be for Steve Blass, Mackey Sasser, Dave Engle, Steve Sax, and the Braves' Mark Wohlers. In 2001, the *New York Times* chronicled him making seven wild throws in three days and he retired after the 2002 season.

**DAN GLADDEN** After scoring the winning and only run in Game Seven, Gladden signed with the Detroit Tigers for the 1992 season. After two years in the Motor City, he played a season in Japan, helping the Yomiuri Giants win the championship in that country. His aggressive play sparked the first on-field brawl in that country in fourteen seasons. After his playing days ended, he found himself in the broadcast booth as a color commentator for the Twins Radio Network. A Harley-Davidson enthusiast, he attends motorcycle rallies when his schedule allows.

He loves to tell the story about how in the wee hours after he scored the winning run in Game Seven, he and some buddies returned to the Metrodome and found his broken bat in a garbage can. He brought it home, where it now hangs on his wall.

**RICK AGUILERA** The right-hander saved 318 games in his sixteen-year career, becoming one of the top closers of his era. His time with the Twins seemed to be over in 1995 when he was traded midseason to the Boston Red Sox as a cost-cutting measure. The Red Sox were in Minneapolis at the time, which meant Aguilera said his goodbyes in the home clubhouse and then walked down the hallway to the visitors' dressing room. It was a far cry from his arrival to the Twins when Kirby Puckett personally greeted him. But Aguilera returned to play with the Twins from 1996 to 1999. He finished his career with Chicago Cubs in 2000, saving twenty-nine games, and now lives in southern California.

**BRIAN HARPER** The Twins declined to pick up the $2.5 million option on the catcher's contract before the strike-shortened 1994 season, leaving Harper to wonder how much his religion had come into play. "As a Christian, when I do something wrong, I ask God to forgive me," he told the *(Minneapolis) Star Tribune.* "So when some-body does something wrong to me, I'm obligated, according to the Bible, to forgive them. I felt that there have been some wrongs done, but I'm obligated to forgive." After his playing days ended he became a minor-league manager for the Angels, Giants, and Cubs. Playing for the '91 Twins remained the highlight of his sixteen-year playing career with seven different teams. "We were a loose bunch, joking around, laughing, enjoying our work," he said. "We just loved coming to the ballpark."

**GENE LARKIN** He was one of seven Twins to be a part of the 1987 and 1991 World Series teams. (The others were Kirby Puckett, Kent Hrbek, Randy Bush, Greg Gagne, Al Newman, and Dan Gladden.) Larkin retired after the 1993 season and still makes his home in the Minneapolis area, where he works as a financial planner. His son, Geno, followed in his father's footsteps, becoming a switch-hitter who can play first base or the outfield. Occasionally, the two of them watch footage of the 1991 World Series together.

**SCOTT LEIUS** In his first full season in the majors, Leius played in all seven games of the '91 series. After four more seasons in Minnesota, he played a season in Cleveland, was out of the majors in 1997, before returning to play two more seasons in Kansas City. He served as a youth coach in the Minneapolis area.

**KEVIN TAPANI** Traded to the Los Angeles Dodgers, Tapani played briefly for the White Sox before moving across town for five seasons with the Cubs. After retiring, he returned to the Twin Cities, where he still makes his home.

**SCOTT ERICKSON** A twenty-game winner in 1991, Erickson lost a league-high nineteen games two seasons later. He went on to a fifteen-year career in the majors, but the closest he came to the twenty-victory plateau again came in consecutive seasons in 1997 and '98 with the Baltimore Orioles. After his pitching days were over, Erickson returned to the West Coast, where he had grown up, and went into television and film production and was a minor-league pitching coach. In 2004, he married Lisa Guerrero, a former sideline reporter with *Monday Night Football*.

**CHILI DAVIS** He finished his nineteen-year playing career with the New York Yankees in 1999, the only other team that he said was as close knit as the '91 Twins. After two seasons in Minnesota, Davis returned to the West Coast. As the designated hitter with the California Angels, he set a major league record for most RBI in a season (112) without the benefit of a sacrifice fly.

"A big part of what allowed me to set that record was how Kirby Puckett and I just talked about hitting, your approach at the plate, about hitting with runners in scoring position," Davis remembered. "Puck would say, 'Don't let them steal your at-bat. Pick out your pitch, and drive him in with a hit, drive him in with a knock.'"

That remained his philosophy after his playing days were over and he became a hitting coach, most recently with the Oakland Athletics.

**TOM KELLY** He managed for sixteen years in the majors, compiling a 1,140–1,240 record, which included two pennants and two World Series titles.

# The Braves

**MARK LEMKE** After eleven years in the majors, Lemke tried to make it as a coach, but his arm couldn't take throwing batting practice day after day. He moved to the broadcasting booth, hosting the pre- and postgame shows for the Braves Radio Network. When Skip Caray died, Lemke was the choice to be color analyst, joining Pete Van Wieren. Years after being the best Braves player in the World Series, Lemke remains close to the team and a fan favorite in Atlanta.

"Even though we didn't win that year, I'd say for most of us we never were a part of something with more excitement and just general passion than those games," he said. "And then to see the city where you play go berserk over baseball, that's something you never forget. We wouldn't win it all until '95, but nobody on either team will forget that Series in '91."

Lemke hit .286 in four World Series and .282 in five NLCS. In comparison, he hit only .246 during the regular season in his career. "He was a postseason phenomenon about every year," Andy Van Slyke said. "I always used to kid him. I'd say, 'Mark, if you were in the playoffs for the whole year, you might make some real good money.' There always seem to be that guy in postseason—the guy who comes out of nowhere."

**RON GANT** He would play sixteen years in the majors, including seven with Atlanta. During his career, Gant hit thirty or more home runs in four seasons. In 2005, he began as a color commentator for TBS in Atlanta and seven years later debuted as a news anchor for WAGA-TV, cohosting the morning show *Good Day Atlanta*.

**STEVE AVERY** The future looked bright for the left-handed phenom in 1991 as he went 18–8 and became the youngest pitcher to win a playoff game. But Avery would reach that victory total only once more in his eleven-year career, going 18–6 in 1993. Eventually, he was dropped from the best rotation on baseball, which included Tom Glavine, John

Smoltz, and Greg Maddux. By the 1996 World Series, he was relegated to mop-up duty and he went on to pitch for Boston and then Cincinnati before returning to the game for a brief stint with his hometown Detroit Tigers in 2003 in which he went 2–0 and batted 1.000 (1 for 1).

Yet Avery will tell you that the biggest miracle in his life is his son, Evan. Born in 1994, three months premature, Evan Avery wasn't expected to survive. Years after his father was out of baseball, Evan graduated from high school, where he played football and baseball.

**TERRY PENDLETON** A key figure in the Braves' '91 run, Pendleton led the league with a .319 batting average, along with twenty-two home runs and eighty-six RBI in 1991. He tied for the league lead with 303 total bases, helping him earn the National League MVP Award, as well as Comeback Player of the Year honors. He retired in 1998 after fifteen years in the majors, which saw him average .270 and capture three Gold Gloves (in 1987 and '89 with St. Louis and in '92 with Atlanta) as the best defensive player at his position.

In 2002, Pendleton joined the Braves' staff as the hitting coach and he had a major hand in helping such young hitters as Andruw Jones. The Braves collected three hundred doubles in a season nine times in franchise history, including each of the last eight seasons (2003–2010) in which Pendleton served as the hitting coach. In 2011, he became the team's first base coach.

**TOM GLAVINE** After winning the National League Cy Young in 1991, the left-hander went on to capture the award again seven years later. Glavine would lead the league in victories five times in his twenty-two-year career. He would finish with a 305–203 record in the majors and be elected to the Hall of Fame in 2014.

**JOHN SMOLTZ** An eight-time All-Star, Smoltz won the Cy Young Award in 1996. After starting much of his career, he became a reliever in 2001 after Tommy John surgery. A year later, he became only the second pitcher in history to enjoy both a 20-win season and a 50-save season (the other being Dennis Eckersley). Smoltz is the only pitcher in major league history to top both 200 victories and 150 saves in his career.

Smoltz, who once organized the golf outings by the Braves' pitchers, continued to excel at the game after his baseball days were over. Tiger Woods said Smoltz, who had a plus-4 handicap, is the best golfer outside of the PGA Tour that he has seen. Smoltz became a broadcaster, doing games for TBS and the MLB Network.

**DEION SANDERS** Despite potential on the diamond, playing for the Braves, New York Yankees, Cincinnati Reds, and San Francisco Giants, "Neon Deion" proved to be even better on the gridiron. He played in the National Football League with the Atlanta Falcons, San Francisco 49ers, Dallas Cowboys, Washington Redskins, and Baltimore Ravens. He was on Super Bowl champion teams in San Francisco and Dallas. Besides bringing the Tomahawk Chop to Atlanta, he's also credited with making the do-rag bandana a sports fashion statement.

An outstanding cornerback and kick returner during his fourteen-year football career, he was inducted into the Pro Football Hall of Fame in 2011. He was an analyst with CBS and then the *NFL Network*.

**ALEJANDRO PEÑA** The right-handed reliever stayed in Atlanta for another season before moving on to pitch for Pittsburgh, Boston, and Florida, with a brief return to Atlanta. He retired after the 1996 season and became a pitching coach for the Los Angeles Dodgers in the Dominican Republic.

**GREG OLSON** In 1992, Olson was behind the plate when a collision late in the season, this time with the Houston Astros' Ken Caminiti, broke his right ankle. After one more season in Atlanta, Olson was released to make room for catching prospect Javy Lopez. He still lives in the Twin Cities area.

**MARK GRANT** A leader of the rally caps, Grant never recovered from the shoulder injury that sidelined him for all of the '91 season. After pitching only forty-three more games at the big-league level he joined the San Diego Padres' television broadcasts, teaming up with Mel Proctor, Matt Vasgersian, and, most recently, Dick Enberg.

**OTIS NIXON** The leadoff hitter and top base stealer returned atop the Braves' lineup after serving his sixty-day drug suspension. He hit .294 with forty-one stolen bases during the 1992 regular season and added another eight bases in the postseason. In a curious twist, he made the final out of the 1992 World Series when he attempted to bunt for a base hit with a runner on third base with two out.

From 1994 to '97, Nixon played in the American League, with Boston, Texas, and Toronto, before returning to the National League with Los Angeles. He finished his seventeen-year career fittingly back in Atlanta. In the 1999 National League Championship Series against the New York Mets, Nixon made one of the key plays. After the Braves had given up 5–0 and then 7–3 leads in Game Six, he stole second base in the eighth inning and went to third when the throw sailed into the outfield. Nixon would score and the Braves won the game in extra innings.

After his playing days were over, Nixon stayed in the Atlanta area, beginning On-Track Ministries. Unfortunately, in May 2013, Nixon was arrested for cocaine possession.

**LONNIE SMITH** While he was with the Braves when they returned to the World Series in 1992, by the following season he was on to Pittsburgh before finishing his seventeen-year career with Baltimore. Smith played for three different World Series–winning teams (St. Louis, Philadelphia, and Kansas City). After retirement, he still lives in the Atlanta area and in 2002 he returned to the Braves' home ballpark and signed autographs.

"I've known how it is to struggle," he said. "I've had the struggles with my drug problems, struggles with a divorce, struggles of having great years and coming back with poor years. Something like [1991] isn't going to affect me."

**BOBBY COX** He won fifteen division titles (one with Toronto), five pennants, and a World Series in 1995. In addition, Cox was manager of the year four times in three different decades (1985, 1991, 2004–2005) and did it in both leagues. He finished with a 2,504–2,001 record.

He lives outside of Atlanta, where he has a farm and is a director at a bank in Adairsville, Georgia. Cox makes regular trips to the ballpark to chat with his successor, Fredi Gonzalez.

In 2013, Cox, Joe Torre, and Tony La Russa were elected to the Hall of Fame.

## *Other notables from the 1991 season*

**RICKEY HENDERSON** After breaking Lou Brock's all-time steals record, Henderson won a second World Series ring in 1993 with the Toronto Blue Jays. He retired, at least at the big-league level, in 2003 after twenty-five years in the majors.

"He's the greatest leadoff hitter of all time," Oakland general manager Billy Beane said, "and I'm not sure there's a close second."

In the end, Henderson said the only thing that left him perplexed was how others misunderstood "the type of person I really am and what I accomplished. People who played against me called me cocky, but my teammates didn't."

**DENNIS ECKERSLEY** Before Trevor Hoffman and Mariano Rivera, there was "the Eck." The right-hander with pinpoint control would go on to save 390 games in his twenty-four-year career and put together several of the best seasons a relief pitcher has ever enjoyed. In 1992, he led the American League with fifty-one saves and became only the ninth pitcher to capture the MVP and Cy Young Awards in the same year.

"He taught me something about fear," Oakland manager Tony La Russa said. "Eck tells me he spends the whole game being afraid. Fear makes some guys call in sick or be tentative. He uses fear to get him ready for every stinking time he pitches."

**BRIEN TAYLOR** Two years after the New York Yankees made him the first overall pick in the 1991 amateur draft, Taylor was involved in a bar fight, injuring his pitching shoulder. The left-hander was never the same pitcher and by 1999 he had been released. According to *Baseball-Reference.com*, he and catcher Steve Chilcott were the only top picks never to play at the major-league level. In 2012, Taylor was arrested on multiple drug charges and sentenced to thirty-eight months in prison.

**JIM LEFEBVRE** After being fired by the Seattle Mariners in 1991, Jim Lefebvre took the helm of the Chicago Cubs the following season. Even though he led the Cubs to a winning record, going 84–78 in 1993, he was let go again. After a brief stint with the Milwaukee Brewers, Lefebvre became the coach of the Chinese Olympic team in the 2008 Summer Games. Along with former major-league pitcher Bruce Hurst, Lefebvre tried to raise the bar on one of baseball's last frontiers.

"At the international level, baseball is still very young in China," Lefebvre said, "but in time, I really think it could become the number-one team sport in the country. And someday, China will be a world power in baseball."

Returning home, Lefebvre tried his best to make sure baseball remained popular with American kids. He worried that showcase tournaments and travel teams were taking the fun out of the national pastime. "The average retirement age of the average baseball player in the U.S. is twelve years old," he warned youth coaches. "Twelve years old."

**SCOTT BORAS** A year after he brokered Taylor's record $1.55 million contract with New York, Boras negotiated the five-year, $28 million deal that saw Greg Maddux move to Atlanta. The deal reportedly eclipsed the second-best offer by $9 million. Since then Boras has represented a number of baseball superstars, including Alex Rodriguez, Matt Holliday and Prince Fielder.

**JANET MARIE SMITH** After being a driving force in the construction of Camden Yards in Baltimore, the architect/urban planner helped with the building of Atlanta's Turner Field and renovations at Fenway Park in Boston and Dodgers Stadium in Los Angeles.

**CANDICE WIGGINS** On November 7, 1991, only a week after the World Series concluded, basketball star Earvin "Magic" Johnson announced that he was retiring immediately because he had the HIV virus. While the sports world mourned Johnson's sudden exit, a young Candice Wiggins had a much different reaction.

"Magic Johnson announcing that he was HIV positive probably had a bigger impact on me at the time than my dad dying," she said decades later. "That's because Magic may have been HIV positive, but he wasn't dead. It wasn't like life was over. There was some hope. Maybe it's not the end after all.

"From then on, I really followed Magic Johnson and what he's done with his fight against this, against the perception of AIDS. It changed from judging people about this issue to how we can help people who suffer from this."

Wiggins began to play basketball competitively in large part because of Magic Johnson. She remembered that Pepsi-Cola had a "We Believe in Magic" advertising campaign centered on the NBA star.

"That was a great indication of what his impact was with all of this," she said. "That it was OK to believe in magic, miracles, just life. It was something that was so desperately needed in my life. As a four-, five-year-old, I was desperately trying to make sense of all this—AIDS, my father's death. But I could understand that Magic Johnson was alive and maybe things could work out."

Candice Wiggins went on to become a four-time basketball All-American at Stanford University. After college, she played professional in the Women's National Basketball Association, with the Minnesota Lynx and the Tulsa Shock, and she became an advocate for AIDS research and understanding.

In 2011, Wiggins threw out the first pitch at a Minnesota Twins home game and ended up staying for the afternoon at Target Field.

"Until that point, you have to remember, baseball wasn't something my family loved anymore," she said. "It was something that took a person from us. But in 2011, I stayed and I watched the whole game. I got to feel the energy and people told me how it was played and what to look for and I saw that this was my dad's game. What he loved and was good at. This is what his life was and it was so crazy that it took me years to find it."

**PETE ROSE** How the crime, or at least the perception of it, can change over the years. By the end of the 2013 season, in the wake of the Biogenesis steroids scandal, support grew for Rose to be enshrined in the National Baseball Hall of Fame in Cooperstown, New York.

After decades of denial, Rose acknowledged that he had gambled on baseball. "I made mistakes. I can't whine about it. . . . They haven't given too many gamblers second chances in the world of baseball."

Then Rose added that if baseball's powers that be gave him "a second chance, I won't need a third chance."

Former Commissioner Fay Vincent said that Rose's statement was "the first time I've heard him recognize the reality of the situation. If he had done this twenty-five years ago, or was better advised, it might be different for him. But he handled it as badly as a person can handle it. He kept talking about how we mistreated him and how his rights were violated."

**USA TODAY BASEBALL WEEKLY** Despite a drop in circulation, blamed in large part upon baseball's labor dispute in 1994, the publication continued to exist. The name was changed to *Sports Weekly* and it began to cover other sports—football, stock-car racing, basketball and hockey.

Paul White, the first editor, is the only one from the original staff still employed by *USA Today* Sports.

# APPENDIX II
## GREAT WORLD SERIES MOMENTS

With five games decided by a run, four games coming down to the final at-bat, and three extending into extra innings, the 1991 World Series will be remembered as one of the best played. But was it the best ever? ESPN thought so decades later, and commissioner Fay Vincent agreed soon after the fact. But fans of particular teams can latch on to other memorable Fall Classics.

In Pittsburgh, they will forever cherish the 1960 triumph over the New York Yankees and against Baltimore in 1979. In Cincinnati, there will always be 1975 and the victory against Boston Red Sox, another series that saw five games decided by one run. In New York, there's the Yankees' many championships and the Mets' triumphs in 1969 and '86.

When you have a dog in the fight, things can become downright personal. I can already hear those in Oakland saying I forgot about the Athletics defeating Cincinnati in 1972 (a World Series with six games decided by one run) or those in Washington remembering when the Senators rallied past the Giants in 1924, with Games One and Seven both going twelve innings and Walter Johnson being the hero.

Perhaps it's best to focus on particular moments of true greatness in the World Series. "Give me a scene or two the viewer cannot forget," a Hollywood producer once told me. "The setup, the payoff—all the rest I can finesse. But that big scene? I always need help with that."

So, with that in mind let's focus on the unforgettable moments. The '91 World Series offered two all-time classics, maybe more. Kirby Puckett hit that clutch home run to win Game Six and an evening later Jack Morris pitched into the night and nobody, not even his manager, dared stand in his way. We also had amazing plays at the plate involving David Justice and Mark Lemke. So, how do they stack up against some of the best World Series plays ever?

**CHRISTY MATHEWSON'S SHUTOUTS (1905):** Against the Philadelphia Athletics, Mathewson won Game One for John McGraw's New York Giants with a four-hit shutout. Three days later, he pitched another four-hit shutout and on one days' rest he put up a five-hit shutout. His line for the Series? Three victories, twenty-seven innings pitched, eighteen strikeouts and one walk.

**JOHNNY PODRES' CLINCHER (1955):** In Game Seven, the Brooklyn left-hander shut out the Yankees, and the Dodgers were bums no more. In the sixth inning, left fielder Sandy Amoros made a running catch, which started a crucial double play.

**DON LARSEN'S PERFECT GAME (1956):** Larsen didn't know he was pitching on October 8, 1956, until he arrived at the ballpark. That was Yankees' manager Casey Stengal's way of keeping his pitchers on their toes. Despite a lackluster outing in Game Two against the Dodgers, Larsen made the most of his opportunity by delivering a perfect game. He threw ninety-seven pitches—seventy-one of them for strikes.

**BILL MAZEROSKI'S HOME RUN (1960):** Despite being outscored 46–17 in the first six games, the Pirates found themselves in a deciding Game Seven against the powerful New York Yankees. Bill Mazeroski made sure they didn't miss a chance at the remarkable upset when he hit a walk-off homer. No matter that the light-hitting second baseman had only forty-eight home runs in his five-year career. Mazeroski hit one of the biggest ever as the Pirates celebrated their first championship in thirty-five years.

**BOB GIBSON'S RECORD SEVENTEEN STRIKEOUTS (1968):** When the Cardinals' staff ace struck out the Tigers' Al Kaline to tie Sandy Koufax's World Series record of fifteen K's, St. Louis catcher Tim McCarver went out to the mound. McCarver wanted to tell Gibson what he had just accomplished, but the Cardinals' pitcher just told him, "Give me the damn ball." After briefly acknowledging the cheers from the hometown crowd, Gibson got back to business, fanning Norm Cash and then Willie Horton to win Game One of this memorable World Series.

"That day Bob Gibson was the toughest pitcher I ever faced in any particular game . . . ," Horton later said.

**CARLTON FISK'S REPLAY FOR THE AGES (1975):** Game Six had already been one to remember before the Red Sox catcher led off the bottom of the twelfth inning with the score tied at six-all. Bernie Carbo's three-run homer had tied it with Cincinnati seemingly poised to capture the World Series. Boston's Dwight Evans' great catch at the wall made sure it stayed tied, setting up Fisk's dramatic shot. His long fly down the left-field line struck the foul pole as Fisk waved it fair, becoming one of the most replayed home runs in baseball history.

**REGGIE JACKSON'S THREE HOME RUNS (1977):** Some shy away from the spotlight, while others embrace it, and nobody reveled in the attention more than "The Straw That Stirred the Drink." With the New York Yankees on the verge of defeating the Los Angeles Dodgers for the championship, Jackson made sure the title belonged to Gotham. In the fourth inning, the New York slugger homered off Burt Hooton. In the fifth, he did likewise to Elias Sosa and then Jackson drove the ball an estimated 450 feet off knuckleballer Charlie Hough in the eighth. In the end, it was a performance that even had Dodgers first baseman Steve Garvey applauding.

**KIRK GIBSON'S IMPROBABLE BLAST (1988):** If Gene Larkin was having a difficult time getting around in the '91 World Series, the Dodgers' star could barely walk, thanks to an injured right knee and left hamstring. Still, that didn't stop Gibson from stepping in against Oakland closer Dennis Eckersley in Game One. What's often forgotten is that Mike Davis, who hit only .196 that season, walked before Gibson came up. It was only Eckersley's fourteenth walk issued in 1988.

After getting two strikes on Gibson with fastballs, Eckersley tried to end the game with a backdoor slider. But Gibson was ready and jerked the offering down the right-field line to win the game. The next evening, NBC inter-spliced shots of Gibson limping around the bases with shots of Robert Redford from the movie *The Natural*.

**JOE CARTER'S WALK-OFF (1993):** The Blue Jays were looking to repeat as World Series champions and Carter made sure they did so. The Blue Jays' star had often pictured himself hitting the game-winning home run to win the Fall Classic. In this Game Six, against the Philadelphia Phillies, he transformed such dreams into reality. The table was set in the bottom of the ninth when Rickey Henderson walked and then Paul Molitor singled against Phillies closer Mitch Williams. With the count 2-and-2, Carter tagged a lackluster slider, lining it barely over the left-field fence at SkyDome. Carter rounded the bases, running and jumping, as the celebration was on once again in Toronto.

**EDGAR RENTERIA'S ONE FOR THE RECORD BOOKS (1997):** The Florida Marlins rallied to tie Game Seven against the Cleveland Indians in the bottom of the ninth inning. They won it in the bottom of the eleventh when Renteria's single to center field brought around Craig

Counsell. In doing so, the Marlins became the first wild-card team to win the Fall Classic.

**LUIS GONZALEZ'S BLOOPER (2001):** After witnessing the New York Yankees rally to take Games Four and Five, the Arizona Diamondbacks came from behind against closer Mariano Rivera. The deciding blow occurred on Gonzalez's single over a drawn-in infield, which plated the Series-winning run.

**DAVID FREESE'S HEROICS (2011):** In a Game Six where the St. Louis Cardinals were twice down to their last strike, Freese did his best impersonation of Kirby Puckett. Freese's home run in the bottom of the eleventh inning forced a Game Seven, which St. Louis won.

# ACKNOWLEDGMENTS

Any book can come down to a series of moments when you're searching for any sign that things will work out. If anything, you feel as if you're on thin ice, perhaps a long ways from shore and the ice is beginning to crack. At such moments the next conversation, the next piece of advice can make all the difference.

Robert Pigeon, my editor at Da Capo, was there at such times, always with good counsel and great enthusiasm. So was Chris Park, my agent extraordinaire at Foundry Literary+Media. Thanks to both of them, as their suggestions often made all the difference.

For many of my recent books—this one, *High Heat,* and *Summer of '68*—I've begun at the National Baseball Hall of Fame and Museum in Cooperstown, New York. Any trip there is both eye opening and reassuring. Not only is so much material about the national pastime gathered in one place, but I love to walk those floors, take in the exhibits and check in with my friends Erik Strohl, Jim Gates, John Odell, Tom Shieber, Brad Horn, Lenny DiFranza, Mary Quinn, Tim Wiles, Scot Mondore, Gabriel Schechter, and Jeff Idelson. Special thanks to Pat Kelly, who went out of her way to track down several hard-to-find photographs at the eleventh hour. In addition, the Hall's Bill Francis remains one of the best researchers and baseball experts around. Good to have him in my corner.

Lori Hobkirk at the Book Factory and copy editor Josephine Mariea made sure this came together on the actual page. A tip of the hat to Lissa Warren and Justin Lovell at Da Capo, who always keep me on track.

Several years ago, acclaimed photographer Jose Luis Villegas and I worked together on a book for National Geographic entitled *Far From Home: Latino Baseball Players in America*. In the late innings of this project, Jose Luis once again stepped up and delivered many of the images in this new book. Thank you, Jose Luis.

Few major-league ballclubs employ team historians, but after visiting Minneapolis and spending time with Clyde Doepner, the oracle of all things about the Minnesota Twins, I cannot fathom why more teams don't have a full-time person in that position, too. Clyde not only took the time to show me around Target Field but also made sure I understood the ramifications of that epic 1991 World Series. Thanks to John Rosengren for making sure Clyde and I connected. In the Twins' press box, I found another expert in Stew Thornley, the team's official scorer. Thanks to those gentlemen for taking the time to walk me through a golden era in that franchise's history.

Adrienne Midgley came through for me when it came to the Atlanta Braves. In addition, I was fortunate to fall in with the Magnolia Chapter of Georgia of the Society of Baseball Research there. In fact, chapter president Mil Fisher brought me down for visit in 2009, which I realize became one of the starting points for this book. Thanks to him, as well as Leslie Heaphy, Lyle Spatz, Larry Taylor, and Terry Sloope.

Dave Raglin and Mark Pattison continue to be a treasure trove of information. In fact, when Dave bequeathed me a stack of *Baseball Americas* from this amazing season, I knew I was on to something.

Sometimes conversations with one person will lead you to another and then another. Over the years, I've often turned to my good friend and esteemed author Paul Dickson for advice. He introduced me to Frank Ceresi, who has become another good friend, and to Thomas Mann, the master of time and space at the Library of Congress. It was

Frank who introduced me to Jeffrey Martin, who may rival Clyde Doepner when it comes to all things Twins.

The good folks at the Minnesota Historical Society—Adam Scher, Dan Cagley, and Brian Horrigan—were insightful about directions I could take with this project.

Closer to home, my good friend Sam Moore continues to be the baseball man I can always count on.

I'm grateful for interviews and conversations through the years with the following people: Hank Aaron, Rick Aguilera, Michael Allen, Sparky Anderson, Fred Anklam, Bud Anzalone, Tony Attanasio, Ann Bauleke, Budd Bailey, Johnny Bench, Peter Bhatia, Steve Blass, Scott Boras, Erik Brady, Gary Brozek, Shaun Burke, Randy Bush, José Canseco, Rod Carew, Joe Carter, Jeanie Chung, Tom Coffey, Pat Coleman, Bob Costas, Bobby Cox, Roger Craig, Jonathan Crowe, Terry Crowley, Steve Dalkowski, Chili Davis, Ken DeCell, Frank Deford, Tom DiPace, Bryan Donaldson, John Dowd, Lizz Downey, Dave Duncan, Dennis Eckersley, Eric Enders, Greg Frazier, Greg Gagne, Ron Gant, Ron Gardenhire, Tim Gay, Barbara Jean Germano, Dan Gladden, Tom Glavine, Kirk Gibson, Pat Gillick, Jay Goldberg, Don Gooselaw, the Reverend Billy Graham, Mark Grant, Brian Harper, John Hart, Dana Heiss, Rickey Henderson, Whitey Herzog, Steve Hirdt, Kent Hrbek, Reggie Jackson, Milton Jamail, David Justice, Stan Kasten, Jim Kaat, Joe Kelly, Tom Kelly, Orv Kelly, Mike Kennedy, Steve Kettmann, Gary Kicinski, Andrea Kirby, Tony La Russa, Rick Lawes, Gene Larkin, Jane Leavy, Scott Leius, Jim Lefebvre, Ryan Lefebvre, Mark Lemke, Drew Lindsay, Larry Lucchino, Andy MacPhail, Howard Mansfield, Buck Martinez, Leo Mazzone, Jack McKeon, Tim McQuay, Paul Molitor, Joe Morgan, Jack Morris, Dustin Morse, Charles Nagy, Jim Naughton, Bob Nightengale, Dave Parker, Terry Pendleton, John Pietrunti, Phil Pote, Scott Price, Kirby Puckett, Rob Rains, Tom Reich, Alvin Reid, Bobby Richardson, Cal Ripken, Frank Robinson, Ted Robinson, John Rosengren, Nolan Ryan, Tom Sakell, Norm Sherry, John Schuerholz, Glenn Schwarz, Janet Marie Smith, Lonnie Smith, Ozzie Smith, John

Smoltz, Deron Snyder, Jim Souhan, Tom Stanton, Terry Steinbach, Dave Stewart, Dick Such, Bruce Sutter, Don Sutton, John Thorn, Joe Torre, Andy Van Slyke, Ron Washington, Earl Weaver, Paul White, Candice Wiggins, Jerry Willard, Pete Williams, Dave Winfield, Lisa Winston, and Andrew Zimbalist.

Special thanks to Charles Eisendrath and the Knight-Wallace Fellowship folks at the University of Michigan.

The Writing Department at Johns Hopkins University continues to be my professional home and where I've done much of my best work. Thanks to David Everett, my students, and fellow faculty members.

Thanks to my parents, Jane and Peter Wendel, and my siblings, Amy, Bryan, Chris, and Susan. We've been through a lot over the years, and we are still able to talk and share a smile about it all.

And my last pitch goes out to Jacqueline Salmon, Sarah Wendel, and Christopher Wendel. They remain the heart of my order.

# NOTES

## PROLOGUE

ix   "an arena that looked as if": "Warts, Love and Dreams in Buffalo," *Sports Illustrated*, Jan 20, 1969.

ix   "last fine time: Verlyn Klinekenborg, *The Last Fine Time*, 3–7.

## GAME ONE

1   as loud as they had been in 1987: Greg Gagne, author's interview, Feb 21, 2013.

1   despite a bad knee: Gene Larkin, author's interview, May 7, 2013.

2   "What people target is that both of them": Ibid.

2   thinking nearly the same thing: Brian Harper, author's interview, Feb 14, 2013.

3   Such postseason classics can be counted: Discussions with the researchers at the National Baseball Hall of Fame in Cooperstown, New York.

4   "Every pitch, every strike": Terry Pendleton, author's interview, May 21, 2013.

4   "My father told me": "Jack Morris and Tom Kelly Relive Game Seven," *(St. Paul) Pioneer Press*, Aug 5, 2011. Kelly said

something similar in the victorious clubhouse after the final game in 1991.

4   "great for our industry": "Last-to-1st Duel Would be Sweet," *Chicago Tribune*, Oct 14, 1991.

4   marked only the third time in last sixty-one World Series games: "World Series notes," *USAT Today Baseball Weekly*, Oct 18–24, 1991.

5   had risen quickly: "Rookie settles in," *USAT Today Baseball Weekly*, Oct 18–24.

6   "Chuck's development": Andy MacPhail, author's interview, Sept 19, 1991.

6   "He's stepped in": Terry Crowley, author's interview, Sept 19, 1991.

7   "It was a glamour team": "At last, Atlanta," *Sporting News*, Oct 14, 1991.

8   "Just kidding": author's observation.

8   "It's the feel": Frank Robinson, author's interview, July 9, 1995.

10   "be ready for the fastball": Gagne interview.

10   "that's what he got": Tom Kelly, press conference, Oct 19, 1991.

11   "I wasn't close to any of them": Gagne interview.

12   "He struck out Kirby Puckett twice": Greg Olson, author's interview, Oct 19, 1991.

12   In short order: Paul White, author's interview, June 9, 2013.

14   "Damn right I was worried": Tom Kelly, press conference, Oct 14, 1991.

14   "Sure, you wonder": Joe Carter, author's interview, August 1, 1993.

15   "we knew he could play": Kirby Puckett, postgame, Oct 19, 1991.

15   "We had a very patient ownership group": Pat Gillick interview, Hall of Fame, accessed at http://article.wn.com/view/2011/07/24/Pat_Gillick_built_teams_with_a_personal_touch/#/related_news.

16   "Thanks for that phone call": author's observation.

17   "it wasn't a popular thing to say": MacPhail interview.

17   "She was more embarrassed than anything": Fay Vincent, post-game comments, Oct 19, 1991.

18   "the most human baseball player": "The Crazy & The Wacky," *ESPN The Magazine*, May 2004.

18   "if he wasn't in baseball": Joe Kelly, author's interview, Aug 16, 1991.

18   "If I wasn't managing baseball": Tom Kelly, author's interview, Aug 17, 1991.

19   "It gave me an understanding": "The Twins' Silent Partner," *New York Times*, July 13, 1992.

19   "You ain't doing diddly": Ibid.

21   "such a competitor": Harper interview.

21   "We didn't invent the rally caps": Mark Grant, author's interview, April 13, 2013.

22   "doing deep-breathing exercises": Footage of the Braves after the National League Championship Series, http://www.youtube.com/watch?v=gzQbp5r0RVI.

23   "They got us to the seventh game of the World Series": "Pitching Potential," *USA Today Sports Weekly*, June 18, 2003.

23   "the best pitching in baseball": Andy Van Slyke, author's interview, June 11, 2013.

### GAME TWO

27   Metrodome events: Gary Gillette and Eric Enders, *Big League Ballparks: The Complete Illustrated History*, 364–367.

28   "nuke this place": "Pave paradise, put up a Metrodome," *Baltimore Sun*, Oct 19, 1991.

28   "good uses for nuclear weapons": "Jim Caple's Worst Ballparks," ESPN.com, http://espn.go.com/mlb/photos/gallery/_/id/8073928/image/6/the-metrodome-jim-caple-worst-ballparks.

28 "the rain pelting": "The Metrodome has its moments," ESPN.com, page 2.

28 "problem with the roof": "NL champ to enter house of horror," *USA Today Baseball Weekly,* Oct 19–25, 1991.

28 "You cannot do that in the Metrodome": Harper interview.

29 "Lemke has much better range": Pregame press conference, Oct 20, 1991.

29 Team payrolls: *USA Today,* accessed at http://content.usatoday.com/sportsdata/baseball/mlb/salaries/team/1991. It's amazing to change the year from 1991 toward future dates on this Web site. You literally see the separation between the haves and the have-nots in baseball. The Oakland Athletics go from being the team with the biggest payroll in the game to the team of *Moneyball* before your eyes.

30 "I'm not stupid": Chili Davis, author's interview, May 18, 2013.

30 "He helped everybody": "Words flow easily—but infrequently—from Chili Davis," *(Minneapolis) Star Tribune,* Oct 6, 1991.

30 "the guys won about 75 percent": Davis, Pregame comments, Oct 20, 1991.

31 "it's synonymous with my name": "Ex-umpire Don Denkinger feels for umpire Jim Joyce," *Associated Press,* June 4, 2010.

31 "Had I got that play right": "Study shows 1 in 5 close calls wrong," ESPN.com, Aug 16, 2010.

31 "My back and my arm were killing me": Harper interview.

31 "We try to stay away from circuses": Tom Kelly and Ted Robinson, *Season of Dreams: The Minnesota Twins' Drive to the 1991 World Championship,* 255.

32 "double my size": Ron Gant, postgame comments, Oct 20, 1991.

32 tale of the tape: *The Baseball Encyclopedia: The Complete and Definitive Record of Major League Baseball,* Macmillan, 1993.

32 "The officiating has got to be better": Gant, postgame comments, Oct 20, 1991.

32  "He came into the base": Kent Hrbek, postgame comments, Oct 20, 1991.

32  "His momentum": Drew Coble, postgame comments, pool reporter, Oct 20, 1991.

33  "There is no appeal": Don Denkinger, postgame comments, pool reporter, Oct 20, 1991.

33  "You don't like to cry": Bobby Cox, postgame comments, Oct 20, 1991.

33  "Ron Gant forgot to slide": Dan Gladden, author's interview, May 28, 2013.

33  "Andy was asking me the usual questions": Harper interview.

33  "Umpires don't like to be embarrassed": Cox, postgame comments, Oct 20, 1991.

34  "gave our approval": "Twins bobblehead on Aug. 5 to immortalize Hrbek/Gant tango," *(Minneapolis) Star Tribune*, March 7, 2011.

34  "still cursed": Gladden interview. This is another reason why I'll tune in the Twins' broadcasts. Gladden will do the goofiest stunts.

34  reminded pitching coach Leo Mazzone of Whitey Ford: "Glavine is the Whitey Ford of his era," *USA Today*, July 22, 2002.

34  "stoic figure": Ibid.

35  signature pitch: "A Gripping Tale," *Sports Illustrated*, July 13, 1992.

35  "dial up on that heater": Major League Baseball Network, July 20, 2009.

35  "made all the difference to me:" *Sports Illustrated*, "A Gripping Tale, July 13, 1992.

35  "changeup after changeup": John Schuerholz with Larry Guest, *Build to Win: Inside Stories and Leadership Strategies From Baseball's Winningest GM*, 50.

36  Montana, for example pitched no-hitters: "When smiles leave the game," *USA Today*, Aug 22, 2005.

36    McGwire quit baseball temporarily: Ibid.

37    "just one black crayon?": "The Specialists," *USA Weekend*, Aug 27, 2000.

37    "lottery ticket": Ibid.

37    "old basketball move": "When smiles leave the game," *USA Today*, Aug 22, 2005.

38    "Everyone dreams": "Whoopee for the Kid from U.P.!" *Sporting News*, Aug 6, 1990.

39    "my pitches are hittable": Kevin Tapani, author's interview, Sept 9, 1991.

39    "always could command his fastball": Harper interview.

40    "But who's up next?": Ibid.

40    "In looking back:" Kevin Tapani, author's interview, Aug 2, 2001.

40    Back home after 9/11: "Kevin Tapani, in his own words, MLB. com," Sept 16, 2001.

41    "sweet spot in time": Steve Hirdt, author's interview, Jan 30, 2013.

42    "There's no question": "Baseball union observes anniversary," *(Bend) Bulletin*, July 2, 1991.

42    "to turn back the clock": Tom Reich, author's interview, July 16, 1991.

42    "hated the feeling": "The Two Sides of Tom Glavine," *Sporting News*, May 1, 1995.

43    "Fans were ticked off": "Glavine has vintage Ford look," *USA Today*, July 23, 2002.

43    "big fan of Mike's": Scott Leius, author's interview, Feb 22, 2013.

44    "I didn't know if I was really ready or not": Ibid.

44    "were both happy": "Leius matches hero with dramatic homer," *USA Today Baseball Weekly*, Oct 25–31, 1991.

44    "a great coach": Leius interview.

45    "Glavine had all his pitches going": Ibid.

45  "Every night it's somebody different": "Leius matches hero with dramatic homer," *USA Today Baseball Weekly*, Oct 25–31, 1991.

45  "kind of that team we were": Ibid.

45  "didn't know what to do": Leius interview.

46  Early save numbers: National Baseball Hall of Fame.

47  Dalkowski's rise and fall: Steve Dalkowski remains one of my favorite characters in baseball. For more about this phenom fireballer who didn't make it, check out my book *High Heat: The Secret History of the Fastball and the Improbable Search for the Fastest Pitcher of All Time*.

48  The current template for relief pitching and closers: The 1986–1987 Oakland Athletics were one of the first teams I ever covered on a daily basis, which I touch on several times here. They were a colorful group, and nobody was more of a showman than Dennis Eckersley, the pitcher that manager Tony La Russa and pitching coach Dave Duncan made into the prototypical closer.

48  "Eck always threw strikes": "One Eck of a Guy," *Sports Illustrated*, Dec 12, 1988.

50  "used like Jeff Reardon": "Aguilera has last Minny ha-ha," *(New York) Daily News*, July 15, 1990.

51  "Off the field": Harper interview.

### GAME THREE

54  "That series": "Series becomes a classic one run at a time," *USA Today Baseball Weekly*, Oct 19–24, 1991.

54  "so sweet": Ibid.

55  "His concentration level is so great": "Avery: New Steve Carlton?" *Sporting News*, April 30, 1990.

55  grew up a Tigers fan: "NL Beat," *USA Today Baseball Weekly*, Aug 21–28, 1991. It does boggle the mind what could have been for the Detroit Tigers if they had somehow signed Avery and

hung on to John Smoltz. The ballclub in the early 1990s had Cecil Fielder and the double-play combination of Lou Whitaker and Alan Trammell, but after staff ace Jack Morris left to sign with the Twins the starting rotation was Frank Tanana and not much else.

56  "Makes you wonder:" Tom Kelly, pregame comments, Oct 22, 1991.

56  Postseason pitching comparisons: "At 21, Avery owns October," *(New York) Daily News,* Oct 18, 1991.

56  "It's just a style I prefer": "Who Is This Guy?" *Baseball America,* Aug 9, 1991.

56  "It's not his stirrups, shoes, or glove": "Armed and Dangerous," *Los Angeles Times,* July 15, 1991.

56  "another day of death": "The Prince of Darkness," *USA Today Baseball Weekly,* Aug 15–21, 1991.

56  "Rockhead": "Tense and intense," *(Minneapolis) Star Tribune,* Aug 4, 1991.

56  "snake in the grass": Ibid.

56  *Top Gun* at least one hundred times: "Night owl, future accountant, movie buff is multifaceted guy," *(Minneapolis) Star Tribune,* "July 25, 1991.

57  "Ted Ortiz": Ted Robinson, author's interview, Feb 25, 2013.

58  attendance in Wisconsin dropped: "The Franchise Transfer that Fostered a Broadcasting Revolution," *The National Pastime: Baseball in the Peach State,* Aug 2010.

59  Georgia-born all-star team: "The All-Time Atlanta Braves All-Star Team," *The National Pastime.* While he may have grown up a St. Louis Cardinals fan, Terry Sloope certainly embraced the Braves after moving to the Atlanta area. Not only did he compile this All-Star team, but he's one of the key members of the Magnolia Chapter of the Society of American Baseball Research in Atlanta. I see now that one of this book's beginnings came in 2009 when chapter president and author Mil

Fisher brought me down to speak to the Magnolia Chapter about my book *High Heat,* in which I went in search of the fastest pitcher of all time. It was a great evening as Mil, Terry, and other chapter members talked baseball into the night and stayed in touch ever since.

59  the Black Crackers: "The Atlanta Crackers," *The National Pastime.* Leslie Heaphy wrote this piece and few know more about the game's beginnings in this part of the country than him.

60  "I'll never forget meeting him": the Rev. Billy Graham, author's interview, May 27, 1994.

60  Salvation Army gospel group: Mike Sowell, *July 2, 1903: The Mysterious Death of Hall-of-Famer Big Ed Delahanty,* 55.

60  Baseball and girls: Graham interview.

61  "He's from North Carolina": Bobby Richardson, author's interview, May 15, 1994.

62  "baseball is good as our national pastime": Graham interview.

62  1978 San Francisco Giants: "The Gospel and Game: The Growing Number of Born-Again Christians in Baseball Tests Clubhouse Chemistry," *USA Today Baseball Weekly,* June 14, 1994.

62  "we always have guys hitting extra": Kirby Puckett, author's interview, May 1, 1994.

63  "completely different breed": Ibid.

63  "That's where I drew the line": Kent Hrbek, author's interview, April 29, 1994.

63  "death in the family": Ibid.

64  "It had nothing to do with one's religion": Andy MacPhail, author's interview, May 3, 1994.

64  by design: Greg Cylkowski, author's interview, May 2, 1994.

64  Gaetti option: Dennis Bracken and Patrick Reusse, *Minnesota Twins: The Complete Illustrated History,* 124–125.

65  one of baseball's real innovators: "The Franchise Transfer that Fostered a Broadcasting Revolution," *The National Pastime: Baseball in the Peach State,* Aug 2010.

65    "You're looking at a genius": "Ted Turner, Hank Aaron influenced each other as well as Georgia," *Savannah Morning News*, February 14, 2010; Hank Aaron, author's interview, Oct 4, 1998.

66    to call his own: "The Franchise Transfer that Fostered a Broadcasting Revolution," *The National Pastime*, Aug 2010.

66    "It would be Bobby Cox": "What a beautiful ride: The Life and Times of Bobby Cox's MLB managerial career," Yahoo Sports, Nov 9, 2010.

66    "Where's Dave?" "Ted Turner managed to shake up baseball in '77," *Washington Times*, May 9, 2005.

67    "take some credit for this": Ibid.

67    Turner's flair: Van Slyke interview.

67    "very, very marginal": "Vincent tells Nixon to sit," *USA Today*, Sept 17, 1991.

68    "We coped": "Nixon's Caught," *Philadelphia Inquirer*, Sept 17, 1991.

68    "pieces that were necessary to compete": Pendleton interview.

69    Wiggins had wheels: National Baseball Hall of Fame research department.

70    "became our catalyst": Jack McKeon, author's interview, May 3, 2000.

70    "one of the best sparkplugs": "Alan Wiggins, AIDS and the San Diego Padres," *Misc. Baseball*, Jan 4, 2011.

70    "I wouldn't be telling the truth": "Dick Freeman interview," *San Diego Magazine*, April 2004.

70    "Line of Death": Tony Attanasio, author's interview, June 3, 2013.

71    shared needles: Attanasio interview; Candice Wiggins, author's interview, May 7, 2013.

71    "It shocks you": Pendleton interview.

72    "The only thing I know": "Nixon's Caught," *Philadelphia Inquirer*, Sept 17, 1991.

73  "Go ahead and do it": Ibid.

73  "spread like wildfire": Van Slyke interview.

73  "Rickey on 'roids?" "Rickey Henderson," *The New Yorker*, Sept 12, 2005.

76  "We had other superstars": "Reminiscing with Lemke about 1991World Series," *Atlanta Journal-Constitution* blog, Oct 24, 2012.

77  "I ain't missing it": Davis interview.

77  "It's not a good feeling": Pendleton interview.

78  "We want Ted Turner to meet with us": "Indian protests are loud, but peaceful," *(Baltimore) Sun*, Oct 20, 1991.

79  "I feel betrayed": "Indians' Protest Began Long Before the Chop," *Los Angeles Times*, Oct 20, 1991.

79  "only one pitcher embarrassed": Kelly, postgame comments.

81  "I felt pretty comfortable": Rick Aguilera, author's interview, April 1, 2013.

81  "I surprised a few people": Aguilera interview.

82  "open range": Pendleton interview.

82  "too many balls tailing away": Mark Lemke, author's interview, Aug 10, 2013.

83  "roller coaster ride": Greg Olson, postgame comments.

83  "storybook ending": Randy Bush, postgame comments.

83  "weirdest thing": Kevin Tapani, postgame comments.

**GAME FOUR**

85  "most underpaid pitcher out there": "Series becoming classic," *USA Today Baseball Weekly*, Oct 25–31, 1991.

86  "the chanting makes it special": Ibid.

86  "That's the way": Leius interview.

87  "I thought": "Braves knock homers, heads," *USA Today Baseball Weekly*, Oct 25–31, 1991.

87  "I think back now": Harper interview.

87  "Maybe it's the adrenaline": Ibid.

87    Buck Martinez breaks ankle: In my opinion, this is one of the wackiest, most courageous plays ever. Several years ago, I was a guest on Sirius/XM Radio morning baseball show and Martinez was one of the cohosts. I told him that this was one of my favorite plays and he replied that sometimes baseball can be a strange game. He had no explanation why this happened to him. Here's the YouTube footage, *www.youtube.com/watch?v=IGksb1YOFC8*.

88    "Sometimes playing catcher": Buck Martinez, author's interview, May 15, 2009.

88    "We hit straight on" Harper interview.

89    "He lost a lot of his career": Bill James, *The New Bill James Historical Baseball Abstract*, 428.

89    nothing on the gridiron: Harper interview.

90    "A catcher must want to catch": Baseball Hall of Fame research department.

90    "I was satisfied if I could just be a backup catcher": Harper interview.

90    "I knew that Brian was strong": "Harper crashes into World Series history," *USA Today Baseball Weekly*, Oct 25-31, 1991.

90    "I knew I was hurt": "Rose's hit, claims still hurt Fosse," Fox Sports, July 5, 2012.

91    John Dowd: "Why Rose can't enter the Hall," *USA Today Baseball Weekly*, Jan 7, 1998. Much of this section comes from a cover story I did for *Baseball Weekly*. John Dowd remains one of the most passionate and most honest people I've ever met in baseball. You always know where you stay with the guy. He has nothing to hide and no matter how much you may love Pete Rose and how hard he played, it's difficult to defend the guy after hearing Dowd out.

96    "allow him to be on the ballot": "Pete Rose's image boosted by PED scandal," *USA Today*, Aug 12, 2013.

96    Pete Rose baseball card: Mark Lemke, author's interview, Feb 15, 2000.

96    "I wanted to play this game": Ibid.

97    "It was a lot of fun": "Hot Bat is Lemke's Reward for Patience," *New York Times*, Oct 26, 1991.

98    "It doesn't shock anyone": "Sacrifice was worth it for Willard, Braves," *USA Today Baseball Weekly*, Oct 25–31, 1991.

98    "waited all season": "Hard-Hitting Braves Run the Twins Out of Town," *New York Times*, Oct 25, 1991.

99    Curtis Strong trial: "Outfielder fights back from drug problems," *(Cleveland) Plain Dealer*, May 10, 1989; "Royals' Smith blasts baseball's drug program," The Associated Press, July 29, 1987; "Lonnie Smith not shy in discussing his past drug problems," *Kansas City Star*, May 19, 1985.

99    Wanting to shoot Schuerholz: "Lonnie Smith still battles demons from his playing career," McClatchy Newspapers, Nov 9, 2006; "Lonnie Smith is safe at home," *Atlanta Journal-Constitution*, July 12, 2003; "Lonnie Smith wanted to shoot John Schuerholz," Deadspin.com, http://deadspin.com/212899/lonnie-smith-wanted-to-shoot-john-schuerholz.

99    "was a special player": "Baseball Renaissance," *Sporting News*, Aug 7, 1989.

100    Smith-Schuerholz hug: "Lonnie Smith is safe at home," *Atlanta Journal-Constitution*, July 12, 2003.

100    "Mark Lemke": Gene Larkin, author's interview, May 17, 2013.

101    Jim Lefebvre call: I cannot tell you how rare it is to have a big-league manager call you at the office to air a gripe. That's how Lefebvre is. He doesn't believe in letting things fester.

101    *Gilligan's Island:* "Bat Boy to Batman That's Jim Lefebvre," *Houston Chronicle*, March 19, 1969.

101    Pursuing his love: "Frenchy Lefebvre: He Found Romance in Hotel Coffee Shop," *Los Angeles Times*, March 21, 1969.

102     Fistfight with Lasorda: "Lefebvre reveals his side of story," *(Cleveland) Plain Dealer,* March 13, 1980; "After fight, Lasorda black and (Dodger) Blue," Associated Press, Feb 18, 1980.

103     "there's no guarantee": "Money Madness Goes Back to '58," *Baseball America,* June 25, 1991.

103     "out for my scalp": "Big Money Takes No Prisoners," *Baseball America,* Dec 10, 1991.

103     "tire companies": Ibid.

103     Don Zimmer-Ryne Sandberg: "How Do You Really Feel, Zim?" *Baseball America,* July 25, 1991.

104     "end of payroll balance": Ted Robinson interview.

105     "die with your boots on": "It's the Young-Boy Network for Baseball Management," *New York Times,* Oct 23, 1991.

105     "But I got fired": Ibid.

106     "I was in the card game" Tom Kelly, author's interview, August 15, 1991.

106     "I came to Seattle": "Lefebvre Joins List of Fired," *Los Angeles Times,* Oct 11, 1991.

106     "been with several clubs": "Sacrifice was worth it for Willard, Braves," *USA today Baseball Weekly,* Oct 25–31, 1991.

107     "looked for Mack": Ibid.

107     "Thank God": Ibid.

108     "helluva call": "Harper crashes into World Series history," *USA Today Baseball Weekly,* Oct 25–31, 1991.

108     "I made contact": Ibid.

108     "you're out most of the time": Ibid.

108     "TK screwed up": "The Ultimate Gamer," *Sports Illustrated,* March 31, 2003.

**GAME FIVE**

109     told to put away his glove: Discussions with Chili Davis and Andy MacPhail, then and now, underscored that the onetime

outfielder was considered a full-time designated hitter by the 1991 season.

110 "I knew the National League parks": Davis interview.

110 "defensive liability": Tom Kelly comments during the American League Championship Series, author's notes.

110 "You're talking to Puck, right?" Davis interview.

110 "got sick and tired": "Trip to Atlanta a total washout for Twins," *USA Today Baseball Weekly*, Nov 1–7, 1991.

110 "there's nothing left:" Davis interview.

110 "This guy": Ibid. Over the years, Twins manager Tom Kelly has justifiably gained the reputation for methodically handling a ballclub. But team announcer Ted Robinson says that putting Davis in the field underscored how desperate the Twins were to win a game in Atlanta. Robinson and Davis agreed that the two close losses in Games Three and Four led to this roll of the dice.

111 "I was playing him shallow": Davis interview.

112 The son of a dairy farmer: Love him or hate him, there's no more intriguing person in baseball than super agent Scott Boras. I've had several conversations with him over the years, but a good starting point is BloombergTV, "Risk Takers," Aug 10, 2013, http://www.bloomberg.com/video/73780580-scott-boras-profiled-bloomberg-risk-takers.html.

113 "Ask anyone": "Boras' Clients Break the Bank," *Baseball America*, Oct 10, 1991.

113 "enough is enough": Ibid.

114 "he was the man for us": "Taylor, Yankees Reach an Impasse," *Baseball America*, July 25, 1991. "Acrimony Surrounds Taylor Deal," *Baseball America*, Sept 25, 1991.

114 "should be shot": *Baseball America*, "Steinbrenner Ruins Amateur Draft," Oct 10, 1991.

115 "then pay for it": Scott Boras, author's interview, May 20, 1993.

This remains a basic principle of Boras' working philosophy and a statement that he has made many times.

115 "Tommy threw the ball great": "Braves Rout Twins, 14–5, Take World Series Lead," *Washington Post*, Oct 25, 1991.

116 Mazzone's fears: Leo Mazzone, author's interview, July 26, 1998.

116 "wish I knew": "Wildly Out of Control," *New York Times*, Aug 23, 1998.

116 "mark of a quality pitcher": Nolan Ryan, author's interview, June 10, 2009.

117 "you ain't nobody": "This Day in Sports History," Total Sports, Aug 22, 2010.

117 "there's no luck": Bill Rigney, author's interview, April 21, 1992.

117 "No contest": "Ageless Wonder," *New York Times*, May 1, 1991.

118 "we've only got nine or so guys": Norm Sherry, author's interview, June 1, 2009.

118 string test: Ibid.

119 "Just ask Nolan or Sandy": Jeff Torborg, author's interview, June 28, 2009.

119 "compatible with warehouse": Gillette and Enders, 402.

120 Metrodome interior: Ibid, 364.

121 "By the time": Ibid, 355.

122 "That was it": Michael Allen, author's interview, May 15, 1992.

122 "retractable fences": "Raising the Roof," *Sports Illustrated*, June 12, 1989.

123 "eighth wonder of the world": Ibid.

123 "Stonehenge of America": Baseball Almanac, http://www.baseball-almanac.com/stadium/baseball_field_construction.shtml.

123 "stars were aligned": Janet Marie Smith, author's interview, April 10, 2013.

124 nod to the past: Ibid.

124   "It was fitting": "Camden Yards turns 20," ESPN.com, April 6, 2012.

125   "It was very exciting": Ibid.

125   "downtown setting": Smith interview.

125   Lonnie Smith accomplishments: National Baseball Hall of Fame research department. Smith was an accomplished performer in the postseason. Unfortunately, he will always be remembered for the base-running blunder in Game Seven. But to be with Lou Gehrig, Johnny Mize, Hank Bauer, and Reggie Jackson? That's fine company.

126   "My two favorites": Larry Taylor, author's interview, March 6, 2013.

126   "you were lucky": Brian Doyle, author's interview, Feb 1, 2013.

126   "There's a phenomenon": Fay Vincent, pregame comments, Oct 24, 1991.

127   "a thousand knife marks": "Justice triumphs in the end," *USA Today Baseball Weekly*, Nov 1–7, 1991.

127   "all about home-field advantage": "Braves Give Plot a Twist," *Washington Post*, Oct 26, 1991.

127   "I remember": Terry Slope, author's interview, March 1, 2013.

128   Bobby Cox backstory: "What About Bob?" *Coach and Athletic Director*, Nov 2006; "Power Socker Cox Joins Yank Third-Base Tussle," *New York Times*, Dec 23, 1967; "Cox of Yankees Called a Dedicated Player," *New York Times*, June 9, 1968.

129   "It wasn't only the X's and O's": Grant interview.

129   "the patience of grandma": Pendleton interview.

130   "There's no place like it": "Hard-Hitting Braves Run the Twins Out of Town," *New York Times*, Oct 25, 1991.

133   "We've hidden all the razor blades": "Game Five notes," *USA Today Baseball Weekly*," Nov 1–7, 1991.

133   "Like what?": "Braves Give Plot a Twist," *Washington Post*, Oct 26, 1991.

133 "been in this situation before": "Trip to Atlanta a total wash-out for Twins," *USA Today Baseball Weekly*," Nov 1–7, 1991.

133 "didn't create anxiety": Aguilera interview.

134 "We're off track": "Trip to Atlanta a total washout for Twins," *USA Today Baseball Weekly*," Nov 1–7, 1991.

134 "can't blame TK": Ibid.

134 "We'll be fine once we get home": Ibid.

135 "affected his family": Ibid.

135 Hrbek's mother: "Hrbek's mother would like to forget the whole thing," *Atlanta Journal-Constitution*, Oct 24, 1991; "For Twins, Powers That Be Aren't," *New York Times*, Oct 23, 1991.

135 Deciding on baseball, Hrbek interview.

135 "seventeenth-round pick": Scout says Hrbek his top find," *USA Today*, May 5, 1993.

136 "a high point and low point for me": Catching Up With . . . ," *Sports Illustrated*, May 17, 1999.

136 "hometown guy": Gagne interview.

136 "just tried to enjoy every minute": Larkin interview.

137 "a lot of flashbulbs": "Trip to Atlanta a total washout for Twins," *USA Today Baseball Weekly*," Nov 1–7, 1991.

137 "All I have to do": Ibid.

## GAME SIX

139 "You listening, Dog?": Any writer is thankful to anyone who will talk to him when he's trying to pull together scenes for a book, especially when it concerns events that happened decades ago. But any writer will also tell you that not all inter-views are equal. Some can crystallize a project—help one see all the angles and ramifications. When I was writing *High Heat*, I remember a discussion with Nolan Ryan when he got up from behind his desk at the Rangers Ballpark in Arlington, Texas, and began to demonstrate pitching mechanics and how a small adjust or two made all the difference in his delivery.

With *Summer of '68*, one of the first people I spoke with was Jon Warden, who was a rookie pitcher in that season. A guy from nowhere who found himself in downtown Detroit when a curfew had been issued, wondering if the city was about to go up in flames again. With this book, my chat with Chili Davis proved to be crucial. Game Six remains one of the classics, but only the Twins' DH knew how close it came to be a different game plan and likely a different outcome.

142  "If he hadn't made that catch": Larkin interview.

142  "Jump on board": Comments were reported by a number of media outlets, including the newspapers in the Twin Cities and *USA Today*.

142  "in a bad way": Larkin interview.

142  "Everybody has a price": "A few questions, lots of laughs," *(Minneapolis) Star Tribune*, Aug 3, 2001.

143  Puckett biography and background: Kirby Puckett, *I Love This Game!: My Life in Baseball*; "Kirby Puckett," BioProject by Society of American Baseball Research.

144  cab to Anaheim: This account has been retold in several publications, but I'm going with the account by longtime Twins reporter Stew Thornley.

144  Averages and personal dimensions: *Baseball Encyclopedia*.

145  "People loved to watch him": Gagne interview.

145  "unbelievable hitter": Harper interview.

145  "you'd have to smile": Hrbek interview.

148  "no cabs or subway": Robinson interview.

148  "always kept up a wall": "CP Flashback," *City Pages*, March 7, 2006.

148  "I was standing there": Aguilera interview.

149  "how not to handle fame": "Little Steven's Underground Garage," Sirius/XM radio, July 8, 2013.

149  Trip to Fargo: Near the end of the 1998 season, with Mark McGwire and Sammy Sosa, about to break the single-season

home-run record I went to North Dakota. Many people there still maintain that Roger Maris, their hometown hero, is still the true record holder and as the years go by you cannot help by agree with them.

150 "I was told": "Roger Maris: Hometown Fargo Tells Tale of Home Run Record Holder," *USA Today Baseball Weekly*, Aug 19–25, 1998.

151 "God, he loved to hit": Ibid.

152 "The only peace I had": Ibid.

154 "This was the last game of the year for me": "Erickson game it his all," *USA Today Baseball Weekly*, Nov 1–7, 1991.

154 "didn't have his good stuff": Ibid.

154 "It went farther than I thought": Ibid.

156 "how much he was bleeding": "Bloody beanball ends Puckett's season early," *New York Post*, Sept 29, 1995.

156 "never took the game for granted": "Eye Forces Puckett to Retire," *Washington Post*, July 13, 1996.

156 "Considering what's happened": "Twins' Puckett Sees Signs to Retire," *Los Angeles Times*, July 13, 1996.

156 "It was a tough day": Leius interview.

156 "It was a very scary time": Wiggins interview.

157 "The good ones you know right away": "Coast to coast: Baseball is a blast in '98," *USA Today Baseball Weekly*, Oct 14–20, 1998. During the 1998 World Series, I briefly jumped off the media bus and visited with several baseball notables, including a trip to the Twin Cities to talk with Kirby Puckett. This was our last conversation.

157 Metrodome's home-field advantage: *Big League Ballparks*, 366.

158 "I was running hard": "Coast to coast: Baseball is a blast in '98," *USA Today Baseball Weekly*, Oct 14–20, 1998.

158 "I wasn't a home-run hitter": "When the ball meets bat," *USA Today Baseball Weekly*, Nov 4–11, 1998.

158    "I'm happy as an ex-player": "Coast to coast: Baseball is a blast in '98," *USA Today Baseball Weekly,* Oct 14–20, 1998.

159    "Do you ever shut up?" Ibid.

160    "made a living": "The secret life of Kirby Puckett," *Knight Ridder/Tribune News Service,* Dec 18, 2002.

160    "not the person": "Kirby Puckett's Tarnished Image," *(Minneapolis) Star Tribune,* April 7, 2002; "After the game: The Kirby Puckett we never knew," *(Minneapolis) Star Tribune,* Oct 29, 2006; "The Rise and Fall of Kirby Puckett," *Sports Illustrated,* March 17, 2003.

161    "situation was different": Harper interview.

161    "tough to say": Davis interview.

161    "would have been great": Gardenhire interview.

162    "couldn't hear us anymore": Gladden interview.

162    "The only thing": Davis interview.

162    "What do they want me to do?" "Hunter says he won't be able to speak at Puckett service," *(Minneapolis) Star Tribune,* March 10, 2006.

162    "Over the last week": "Cheers and tears for Kirby," *(Minneapolis) Star Tribune,* March 12, 2006.

163    "losing an icon": Ibid.

163    "I figured it was out": Gardenhire interview.

163    "said the right thing": Ozzie Guillen, author's interview, May 1, 2006.

164    "I will always have a place in my heart for him": Davis interview.

164    "We were about as happy": Gardenhire interview.

165    "I never hit": "Puckett's heroics end tense struggle," *USA Today Baseball Weekly,* Nov 1–7, 1991.

165    "Why not Charlie?" Ibid.

165    "I don't believe it": Ibid.

165    "Now it's my turn": Larkin interview.

165    "we were at ease": Gladden interview.

165   Pat O'Brien anecdote: "Puckett's heroics end tense struggle," *USA Today Baseball Weekly*, Nov 1–7, 1991.

## GAME SEVEN

167   "Might as well play": "The Best Series Ever," *USA Today Baseball Weekly*," Nov 1–7, 1991.

167   Pregame atmosphere: Ibid.

168   be patient: Pendleton interview.

168   "Jack had it going": Gagne interview.

169   "newest of the substitute spitters": "The Pitch of The '80s," *Sports Illustrated*, June 9, 1986.

169   league-high twenty-four games: *Baseball Encyclopedia*.

170   first disciples: "The Pitch of The '80s," *Sports Illustrated*, June 9, 1986; Baseball Hall of Fame research department.

170   "once you throw it": Ibid.

170   "a lot of pressure": "Split-Finger Fastball, Once Popular, Is Falling Away," The Associated Press, Oct 1, 2011.

171   "probably the best ever": Grant interview.

171   "Jack was locked in": Gagne interview.

172   "The clubhouse was my family," Morris interview.

173   "I've been in many games with him": "The clutch gene exists, and Morris is proof of it," *MLB.com*, Jan 22, 2013.

173   "The pitcher who best fits": Nolan Ryan, with Mickey Herkowitz, *Kings of the Hill: An Irreverent Look at Men on the Mound*, 99.

173   "siding with his wife": "Morris reaches the end," *(Minneapolis) Star Tribune*, April 19, 1995.

173   "first-hand look": Gardenhire interview.

174   "It's going to sound wrong": "Interview with Bob Costas," MLB Network, July 12, 2010.

175   "how big a deal it was": John Smoltz, Don Yeager, *Starting and Closing: Perseverance, Faith, and One More Year*, 28–29.

176   "No one could catch me": Ibid.

176 "The very next game": Ibid, 238–240.

177 "running whole blocks of plays": Michael Murphy and Rhea A. White, *In the Zone: Transcendent Experience in Sports*, 155.

177 always crossed the finish line: Ibid, 159.

177 "never hit a shot": Ibid, 154.

177 "fantasy and reality": "Jim Fannin: "What I've Learned," *Esquire.com*, May 2013.

179 "I never had so much will": Morris interview.

179 "ruin his day": "Jack Morris and Tom Kelly relieve Game 7 of the 1991 World Series," TwinCities.com, Aug 5, 2011.

180 "The biggest turning point": Ibid.

181 "I have no real clue": Gagne interview.

182 "naturally clumsy": "Lonnie Smith interview," Talking Baseball with Ed Randall, May 15, 2007.

182 "my mistake": "After agonizing loss, team has Brave face," *USA Today Baseball Weekly*, Nov 1–7, 1991.

182 "The media's version": "Lonnie takes the blame," *Sporting News*, March 16, 1992.

183 "He just didn't know": "Jack Morris and Tom Kelly relieve Game 7 of the 1991 World Series," *TwinCities.com*, Aug 5, 2011.

183 "You actually had two fakes on that play": Harper interview.

183 "We caused enough confusion": Gagne interview.

183 "a pump of the fist": Pendleton interview.

184 "Well, I beg to differ" Ibid.

184 "you're a little more aggressive": Harper interview.

184 "Kelly comes out": Ibid.

185 "a come-backer to Jack": Ibid.

185 "that is so rare": Ibid.

186 ACTION IS CHARACTER: F. Scott Fitzgerald, *The Last Tycoon*, 190.

187 "never afraid": Pendleton interview.

187 "I'm still mad": "The Ultimate Gamer," *Sports Illustrated*, March 31, 2003.

188   game without a clock: "The Twins' Silent Partner," *New York Times*, July 13, 1992.

188   "Jack was such a competitor": Harper interview.

189   "one of the biggest changes": Ryan interview.

190   "talked or even bullied his way": Jim Kaat, author's interview, Aug 13, 2013.

190   "and not realize at the time": "Jack Morris and Tom Kelly relieve Game 7 of the 1991 World Series," TwinCities.com, Aug 5, 2011.

191   "The bat broke on the handle": Gladden interview.

191   "That was Dan Gladden": Puckett interview.

191   "I knew they would walk Puckett": Gladden interview.

192   "The tendinitis was really bad": Larkin interview.

192   "I knew I was getting the call": Ibid.

193   Denkinger did try to encourage: Ibid; "The Ultimate Gamer," *Sports Illustrated*, March 31, 2003.

193   "Peña's history": Larkin interview.

193   "Once I put the bat on the ball": Ibid.

194   "Somebody had to go home a loser": Morris interview.

194   "What was great": Gladden interview.

194   "When I look back": Larkin interview.

### EPILOGUE

197   only twice: http://www.baseball-reference.com/managers/kellyto01.shtml.

198   "most imprudent and unfortunate": "Owners vote to drop two clubs, but don't identify them," SI.com, Nov 7, 2001.

198   Gladden's stance: Ibid.

198   Braves finished second to Expos in 1994: accessed at http://espn.go.com/mlb/history/season/_/year/1994. The Expos had the best record in baseball—74–40—when the sport closed down due to the labor disagreement, eventually forcing the cancellation of the World Series.

198     "fat and happy, soft?": "Reminiscing with Lemke about 1991 World Series," *Atlanta Journal-Constitution* blog, Oct 24, 2012.

### APPENDIX I: AFTERMATH

203     second-youngest person: http://sports.espn.go.com/mlb/news/story?id=2357158.

203     "affection for the game": http://www.milb.com/news/article .jsp?ymd=20060307&content_id=45760&vkey=news_t516& fext=.jsp&sid=t516.

204     battle over Puckett's ashes: "Puckett's fiancée: He wanted ashes spread on ball field," *(Minneapolis) Star Tribune*, May 9, 2006; "Puckett's ashes awarded to his children," *(Minneapolis) Star Tribune*, Oct 25, 2006.

204     "The majority of people": "Home is where the money is for Morris," *USA Today*, March 2, 1991.

205     "You can be benevolent to a point": "Indians cut farm owner Morris, look to farmhands to fill void," *USA Today Baseball Weekly*, Aug 10, 1994.

205     Jayson Stark assessment: http://sports.espn.go.com/mlb/hof07/columns/story?columnist=stark_jayson&id=2724111.

205     "great thoroughbred": "Comin' at ya," *(Minneapolis) Star Tribune*, Feb 6, 1991.

206     "warm fuzzies": Morris interview.

206     "everyone's invited": "Catching Up With . . . ," *Sports Illustrated*, May 17, 1999.

207     seven wild throws: "The Knoblauch Numbers: 3 Days, 7 Wild Throws," *New York Times*, March 13, 2001.

207     broken bat: Gladden interview.

208     "I'm obligated": "Ex-Twin Harper can forgive," *(Minneapolis) Star Tribune*, April 29, 1994.

208     "loose bunch": Harper interview.

208     watch footage: Larkin interview.

209     married Lisa Guerrero: http://lisaguerrero.com/biography/.

209 "drive him in with a knock": Davis interview.

210 "I always used to kid him": Van Slyke interview.

211 biggest miracle: "Cabrini's Evan Avery overcomes odds as dad Steve's miracle," *Detroit Free Press*, June 1, 2012.

212 Tiger Woods: "Tiger vouches for John Smoltz's golf game," *Orlando Sentinel*, March 23, 2011.

214 "I've know how it is to struggle": Smith to Ed Randall.

214 "greatest leadoff hitter of all time": http://baseballhall.org/hof/henderson-rickey.

214 "my teammates didn't": Henderson interview.

215 "He taught me something about fear": http://baseballhall.org/hof/eckersley-dennis.

215 Brien Taylor and Steve Chilcott: http://www.baseball-reference.com/bullpen/Brien_Taylor.

215 "At the international level": "Teaching Baseball as Second Language in China," *New York Times*, July 5, 2008; http://www.baseball-reference.com/bullpen/Jim_Lefebvre.

215 "Twelve years old": *www.baseballcoaches.org/lefebvrearticle.pdf.*

216 Earvin "Magic" Johnson announcement: http://www.history .com/this-day-in-history/magic-johnson-announces-he- is-hiv-positive; http://sports.espn.go.com/espn/espn25/story?page=moments/7.

216 bigger impact: Wiggins interview.

217 "I made mistakes": "Pete Rose says he picked wrong vice," Yahoo Sports, Aug 12, 2013.

217 "It's the first time": "New light shining on Rose," *USA Today*, Aug 13, 2013.

# SELECTED BIBLIOGRAPHY

**BOOKS**

Bracken, Dennis and Patrick Reusse. *Minnesota Twins: The Complete History*, MVP Books, 2010.

Canseco, José. *Juiced: Wild Times, Rampant 'Roids, Smash Hits, and How Baseball Got Big*, It Books, 2006.

Dewan, John. *The Scouting Report: 1991*, HarperPerennial, 1991.

Dickson, Paul. *The New Dickson Baseball Dictionary, Third Edition*, W. W. Norton, 2009.

Enders, Eric. *Baseball's Greatest Games*, MLB Insiders Club, 2008.

Fainaru-Wada, Mark and Lance Williams. *Game of Shadows: Barry Bonds, BALCO, and the Steroids Scandal That Rocked Professional Sports*, Gotham Books, 2006.

Gillette, Gary and Eric Enders, with Stuart Shea and Matthew Silverman. *Big League Ballparks: The Complete Illustrated History*, Metro Books, 2009.

Glavine, Tom. *None but the Braves: A Pitcher, A Team, A Champion*, HarperCollins, 1996.

James, Bill. *The New Bill James Historical Baseball Abstract*, The Free Press, 2001.

James, Bill and Rob Neyer. *The Neyer/James Guide to Pitchers*, Fireside, 2004.

Kelly, Tom and Ted Robinson. *Season of Dreams: The Minnesota Twins' Drive to the 1991 World Championship*, Voyageur Press, 1992.

Kettmann, Steve. *One Day at Fenway Park*, Atria, 2005.

Leavy, Jane. *The Last Boy: Mickey Mantle and the End of America's Childhood*, HarperCollins Publishers, 2010.

Maraniss, David. *Into the Story*, Simon & Schuster, 2010.

Mazzone, Leo, with Scott Freeman. *Leo Mazzone's Tales From the Mound*, Sports Publishing, 2006.

Morris, Willie. *New York Days*, Little Brown, 1993.

Murphy, Michael and Rhea White. *In the Zone: Transcendent Experience in Sports*, Penguin, 1995.

Posnanski, Joe. *The Machine*, Harper, 2009.

Puckett, Kirby. *I Love This Game!: My Life and Baseball*, HarperCollins, 1993.

Ritter, Lawrence S. *The Glory of Their Times: The Story of the Early Days of Baseball Told by the Men Who Played It*, Vintage Books, 1985.

Ryan, Nolan and Mickey Herskowitz. *Kings of the Hill: An Irreverent Looks at Men on the Mound*, HarperCollins, 1992.

Schuerholz, John, with Larry Guest. *Built to Win: Inside Stories and Leadership Strategies From Baseball's Winningest GM*, Warner Books, 2006.

Smoltz, John with Don Yaeger. *Starting and Closing: Perseverance, Faith, and One More Year*, William Morrow, 2012.

Sowell, Mike. *July 2, 1903: The Mysterious Death of Hall-of-Famer Big Ed Delahanty*, Macmillan, 1992.

Thorn, John and John Holway. *The Pitcher: The Ultimate Compendium of Pitcher Lore: Featuring Flakes and Fruitcakes, Wildmen and Control Artists, Strategies, Delivers, Statistics and More*, Prentice Hall Press, 1987.

Ward, Geoffrey, and Ken Burns. *Baseball, An Illustrated History*, Alfred Knopf, 1994.

Wolff, Rick. *The Baseball Encyclopedia: The Complete and Definitive Record of Major League Baseball*, Macmillan, 1993.

Zimbalist, Andrew. *Baseball and Billions: A Probing Look Inside the Big Business of Our National Pastime*, Basic Books, 1994.

——. *The Bottom Line: Observations and Arguments on the Sports Business*, Temple University Press, 2006.

## FILM AND VIDEO

Major League Baseball Productions, 1991: *The Greatest World Series Ever*, 2011.

——. *Baseball's Greatest Games: 1991 World Series Game 7*, 2011.

——. *Magic in Minnesota*, 2011.

——. *Minnesota Twins*, 2006.

# INDEX